1. Christ In My Life

CHRIST in my LIFE

Practical Meditations

David J. de Burgh, S.D.B.

ST. PAUL EDITIONS

NIHIL OBSTAT:
Carlo De Ambrogio, S.D.B.,
Rome, Italy

IMPRIMI POTEST:
Dante Magni, S.D.B.
Provincial
Central Province, Rome, 1972

NIHIL OBSTAT:
Rev. John J. Manning, O.F.M.
Censor Librorum

IMPRIMATUR:
✠ Lawrence B. Casey
Bishop of Paterson

April 12, 1976

Acknowledgments

The Revised Standard Version Bible, Catholic Edition, copyrighted © 1965 and 1966.

The Jerusalem Bible, copyright © 1966 by Darton, Longman & Todd, Ltd. and Doubleday and Company, Inc. Used by permission of the publisher.

The Documents of Vatican II (Abbott)—with permission of America Press. All rights reserved. © 1966 by America Press, 106 W. 56 St., New York, N.Y. 10019.

Acts of Superior Council—Salesian Congregation.

M.B.: Memorie Biografiche: Don Bosco, S.E.I. Turin, Italy.

Antologia Biblica, G. Pace, S.D.B.
Salesian Publications.

Photo credits:
A. ACHILLI 44, 47, 177, 353 – G. ALVES 69 – N. CARROLL 154 – V. MANCUSI 88 – F. NAGNI 77 – SAHATA 140 – P. SCHELL 303

Library of Congress Cataloging in Publication Data

De Burgh, David J.
Christ in my life.

1. Jesus Christ—Biography—Meditations. I. Title.
BT306.4.D4 232.9'01 76-50558

Printed in U.S.A. by the Daughters of St. Paul
50 St. Paul's Ave., Boston, Ma. 02130

The Daughters of St. Paul are an international religious congregation serving the Church with the communications media.

DEDICATION

To
Father Patrick McQuaid, S.D.B.,
in perennial gratitude

PREFACE

Vatican Council II, in its *Decree on the Appropriate Renewal of the Religious Life (Perfectae Caritatis),* stressed emphatically that the life of all religious should be based essentially and practically on that of Jesus Christ. It said in fact:

> *The more ardently they unite themselves to Christ through a self-surrender involving their whole lives, the more vigorous becomes the life of the whole Church and the more abundantly her apostolate bears fruit.... Since the fundamental norm of the religious life is a following of Christ as proposed by the Gospels, such is to be regarded by all communities as their supreme law.... Let the religious follow Him as their one necessity. Let them listen to His words and be preoccupied with His work...strive to associate themselves with the work of redemption and to spread the kingdom of God....*

In order to encourage this knowledge, love and imitation of Jesus, the Council also urged all to read the Scriptures, especially the Gospels, with great attention and reverence. At times, however, it is easy to miss even the obvious; it is possible to read the Bible reverently and yet fail to apply anything to ourselves except rather vaguely. The Gospels need prayerful pondering, leading to realistic imitation of Christ. That is the purpose of this book of meditations based on the life of Jesus up to His Passion. Its aim is to point out possible workable applications to daily life and to suggest helpful forms of personal prayer: in other words—Consideration, Application, Prayer—essentially combined in a down-to-earth fashion. It has been easier to refer always to the masculine, but women will find this no obstacle to adaptation!

These simple meditations are obviously not intended for experts in theology or exegesis, but it is hoped that they will lead to a deeper study of the Bible. The longer first point may possibly fully satisfy for a whole period of meditation; the other two shorter points could then be omitted or used later.

A prayer for the author would be deeply appreciated. May God bless you and help you to know, love and imitate our Lord Jesus Christ daily more and more.

David J. de Burgh, S.D.B.
Rome, Italy

MEDITATION

To meditate on the life and sufferings of Jesus Christ I have called wisdom; in these I have placed the perfection of righteousness for me, the fullness of knowledge, the abundance of merits, the riches of salvation.... In a word, my philosophy is this, and it is the loftiest in the world, to know Jesus and Him crucified.

(St. Bernard)

The meditation of my heart shall be understanding.

(Ps. 49:3)

Seek in reading and you will find in meditation; knock in prayer and it shall be opened to you in contemplation.

(St. John of the Cross)

May my meditation be pleasing to Him, for I rejoice in the Lord.

(Ps. 104:34)

Let the words of my mouth and the meditation of my heart be acceptable in Thy sight, O Lord.

(Ps. 19:14)

CONTENTS

Annunciation

In the sixth month the angel Gabriel was sent from God to a city of Galilee named Nazareth, to a virgin betrothed to a man whose name was Joseph, of the house of David; and the virgin's name was Mary. And he came to her and said, "Hail, full of grace, the Lord is with you!" But she was greatly troubled at the saying, and considered in her mind what sort of greeting this might be. And the angel said to her, "Do not be afraid, Mary, for you have found favor with God" (Luke 1:26-30).

Sometimes people are amazed to hear that Mary was very young at the time of the Annunciation. However, it was the custom among the Hebrews for a girl to become engaged between the ages of thirteen and fourteen, a young man between eighteen and twenty-four. Mary was engaged to Joseph, she probably very young, he older but not the very old man portrayed by well-meaning artists of the past! We may well reflect here on the gift and graces of youth. Youth is a wonderful time of life, with such splendid opportunities for the development of a fine character: that certainly is the intention of God, but how often the opportunity is not even reverted to in this light or is flung away carelessly. So much depends on homelife and example, background and education. Mary was blessed with the finest advantages in this respect, having been hand-picked by God from all eternity. But I too have been chosen by God for a very definite aim and vocation in life. If I am still young, let me thank God now for the splendid gift of my youth; let me ask Mary to help me understand better the graces that are part and parcel of this very precious time of life; let me beg St. Joseph to help me imitate the strength of character that made him fit to become engaged to Mary. (If I am no longer young, let me now—without morbidity, but with a deep sense of humility—beg God's pardon for graces lost during my youth, knowingly or unintentionally.) Let me pray to Mary and Joseph, too, for the youth of today. Their lives are no longer so protected as in earlier times; temptations are stronger and more abundant; youth needs much help and sympathy. Perhaps God wants to use me to help today's youth in a very special manner by my tactful and kindly words and advice, by my own upright and sincere example of rectitude and sound principle, by my frequent prayers. Let me speak now quite simply to Mary and Joseph about this.

God sent a special spirit or angel to Mary. Gabriel means "the strong one of God," but notice his extreme courtesy throughout his visit. Strength of body or of character should never exclude courtesy in all its forms. Given such a vital and important message to bear, Gabriel could well have been imperious in his manner, but we find him tactful and courteous throughout. Mary was "greatly troubled at the saying." Gabriel reassures her gently: "Do not be afraid, Mary, for you have found favor with God." What a fine lesson for me in my dealings with others! True, I am no angel, but there can never be any excuse for a lack of Christian gentleness, and godlike courtesy. Can I honestly say that, thanks to God, I am even noted for these qualities in regard to: a) my own community? b) my charges? (Notice Gabriel's use of Mary's name: a fine point!); c) outsiders? d) laity? e) visitors? f) servants? g) others? Or am I courteous and kind only with certain categories? My charity should be universal, not snobbish or condescending. Let me pray now to Gabriel, "the strong one of God," to help me to act always, towards *all*, with gentle courtesy. Let me ask Mary to obtain for me the great and necessary grace of always appreciating the true human and divine dignity inherent in everyone with whom I come into contact, despite their appearance.

"Mary was troubled...." Mary understands trouble, therefore, she knows what it is to be worried and perplexed. Obviously, then, we have in Mary someone who appreciates our own state of mind in times of doubt and anxiety. The fact that she was "full of grace" and infinitely dear to God, because of her very special and exalted vocation as Mother of Jesus, did not exempt her from the trials,

troubles and perplexities of ordinary human life, and as the years went on her burden increased. We know, however, that she carried her heavy cross of worry and anxiety right to Calvary, and there, being formally made our Mother by her dying Son, she extended her own arms like His to embrace the sufferings of all mankind, her children. Mary's understanding then of our problems and doubts could not be wider or greater. Do I automatically have recourse to her when worries and anxieties beset me? If I do so with faith and trust, then she will surely give me the same gentle reassurance she herself received from Gabriel: "Do not be afraid." However, there is one important proviso: what applied to her should be true of me also: "...for you have found favor with God." If my conscience is right, then I need not linger in doubt and fear: God is with me and I am in His favor. Let me ask Mary now to help me ensure that this is always the case in my own life—with special regard to the day ahead.

How Can This Be?

"And behold you will conceive in your womb and bear a son, and you shall call his name Jesus. He will be great and will be called the Son of the Most High; and the Lord God will give to Him the throne of his father David, and He will reign over the house of Jacob for ever; and of his kingdom there will be no end." And Mary said to the angel, "How can this be, since I have no husband?" And the angel said to her, "The Holy Spirit will come upon you, and the power of the Most High will overshadow you; therefore the child to be born will be called holy, the Son of God" (Luke 1:31-35).

Surely anyone who loved God as much as Mary did would have been deeply thrilled at the astounding words announced to her so unexpectedly by the angel Gabriel, God's very special messenger to her. It is difficult indeed to realize the full impact of the words he uttered, for this was the very turning-point in the history of the world. Through Mary's consent to the invitation made to her, redemption was offered to humanity, salvation was made possible for all. Yet Mary remains eminently practical, with a maturity of mind marvelous in one so young. She does not rush in on the wave-crest of a justified emotion; she does not decide hastily. Full of the theological virtues of faith and hope and charity, she valued to a high degree the cardinal virtue of prudence. She was as yet only engaged; her marriage to Joseph had not taken place, and might not take place for some time, so how could she decently conceive a child? How much we can learn here from the prudence and practicality of the sensible young maiden of Nazareth! So often the young (and the not-so-young!) are tempted to think that they "know all the answers." With that proud spirit they "rush in where angels fear to tread." They make so many unfortunate mistakes, thus hampering God's wonderful plans for them. Does this not apply to me sometimes? In spite of Gabriel's assurance that she had found favor with God because she was "full of grace," Mary nevertheless wanted further reassurance against any possibility of delusion. Am I not perhaps over confident of myself and my so-called wisdom, possibly about my state of grace and virtue before God, rushing into decisions not based sufficiently on prayer and prudence? Let me now pray to Mary, Seat of Wisdom, to save me in the future—and especially today—from such immaturity.

Gently, Gabriel gave Mary the reassurance she needed. We may well say, therefore, that Jesus was born of the virtue of prudence, a virtue remarkably in evidence throughout His life. Through the sound and practical prudence of Mary, let me learn to cultivate this extremely necessary virtue. Without it, my life as a priest, a religious, a Christian, can be only a series of disasters. The cultivation of prudence is a vital part of Christian and human maturity—a process that must continue throughout life. Our Lord Himself tells us so. The psalmist David was highly praised by God for his prudence, but it was the gift of prayer: "Lead me in your truth and teach me, for you are the God of my salvation; for you I wait all the day long.... Set a guard over my mouth, O Lord; keep watch over the door of my lips." Can I truthfully say that I am a person of remarkable prudence? If I feel I can say that, then on what facts do I base this high opinion of myself? Am I really careful about all my words ("The mind of a wise man will know the time and the way"—Eccl. 8:5)? Are my actions always prudent? What about my thoughts?

Mary highly valued her virginity as a special gift to God and it is most probable that she desired to retain it even after her formal marriage—with the consent, of course, of Joseph himself. Nor was Mary trying to lay down any conditions before the word of God. Again it was her spirit of utter simplicity and prudence that made her speak and inquire as she did, making sure there was no question of delusion. There is scope here for ample and yet further meditation for me on these two virtues of simplicity and prudence so dear to God and to Mary. Coupled with them, too, in my own regard, I might well examine myself prayerfully concerning my vow of virginity. Do I hold my chastity as something most precious in the sight of God? Do I act sensibly and positively in preserving it, without living in suspense with negative fears, doubts and scruples? Am I prudent in all that concerns holy purity, without being morbid or overmodest? What sensible resolution can I now make? O Immaculate Virgin Mother, help me in this respect to be in every detail the kind of pure and sensible religious your Son wishes me to be.

With God Nothing Impossible

And the angel said to her, "The Holy Spirit will come upon you, and the power of the Most High will overshadow you; therefore the child to be born will be called holy, the Son of God. And behold, your kinswoman Elizabeth in her old age has also conceived a son; and this is the sixth month with her who was called barren. For with God nothing will be impossible." And Mary said, "Behold, I am the handmaid of the Lord; let it be done to me according to your word." And the angel departed from her (Luke 1:35-38).

In the Old Testament we read that a mysterious cloud lingered above the Ark of the Covenant in the Holy of Holies: "The cloud covered the tent of meeting and the glory of the Lord filled the tabernacle" (Ex. 40:34). Mary was to be the new Holy of Holies and now God's angelic messenger tells her at the Annunciation that the Holy Spirit will come upon her to produce the miracle of the Incarnation, God's human presence among us. This, then, was the answer to all Mary's natural queries. Now, perhaps for the first time, she realizes the full import of those earlier words: "Hail, full of grace." Her humility, so sound and genuine, made her worthy to hear those tremendous words. Only because she was full of grace could she be the recipient of the incredible favor of becoming the mother of the Son of God, with all the profound implications of that unique title. In Mary indeed were fulfilled these words of Scripture: "The greater you are, the more you must humble yourself; so you will find favor in the sight of the Lord. For great is the might of the Lord; he is glorified by the humble" (Eccl. 3:18-20). Let me now ponder my own standing in regard to this essential virtue. What efforts do I actually make to be humble—not just in outward appearances but in fact? Do I not sometimes try to give the impression of humility to others, regardless of the fact that is rests on no solid foundation? O humble maid of Nazareth, please help me to get my thoughts right first of all: my thoughts about myself. Help me, like you, to realize that I am only what I am in the all-seeing, all-knowing eyes of God, who reads me through and through.

> *And behold your kinswoman, Elizabeth, in her old age has also conceived a son; and this is the sixth month with her who was called barren. For with God nothing is impossible (Luke 1:36-37).*

Among the Hebrews it was humiliating for a woman not to be able to bear children, and for many long years Mary's cousin, Elizabeth, had endured this heavy trial with no human hope of ever being relieved of it. And now suddenly, by the signal grace of God, the immense burden is lifted from her: "For with God nothing is impossible." We can imagine the deep sympathy Mary had always had for her cousin, and now her tremendous joy at this news. It was to Mary the final proof, if such were needed, of the authenticity of the angel's message. Applied to myself, let me consider my own attitude toward those who are in distress or trouble. Am I always sympathetic? Is there no hardness or lack of understanding in my heart about even one particular person? Do I always try to be kind and helpful to those who are sad or upset? Let me ask Mary to help me to imitate her own exquisite sense of concern for others.

> *"For with God nothing is impossible." And Mary said, "Behold, I am the handmaid of the Lord; let it be done to me according to your word." And the angel departed from her (Luke 1:37-38).*

Now at length comes the greatest moment in human history after creation. The whole of creation had been, as it were, holding its breath in awe, awaiting the momentous reply of young Mary of Nazareth: "Behold, I am the handmaid of the Lord; let it be done to me according to your word." At that very instant the Holy Spirit did indeed come down upon Mary "and the Word became flesh and dwelt among us" (Jn. 1:14) because, again, "with God nothing is impossible." From that very moment the Son of God within her began to depend on Mary as His Mother. This gives me ample matter for meditating on Mary's humble submissiveness to the will of God, on the tremendous fact of the Incarnation and on the almighty power of God Himself. Let me not neglect, however, to make this meditation practical to my own life. Perhaps if I were more humble, less obstinate, then on so many occasions God would find me more willing to accept His holy will. If I possessed that truly docile heart mentioned in the Scriptures, then indeed the Holy Spirit could often come down and the power of the Most High would be able to give birth to something really marvelous in me, too—something planned not just for myself but also for many other souls. How often lack of docility impedes the plans of God! O Mary, my model of humility, help me to seek only the will of God, not my own, and then to accept it courageously in whatever form it comes. Help me on this day in particular to be ever on the lookout for God's will so that I may fulfill it humbly.

Visitation

In those days Mary arose and went with haste into the hill country, to a city of Judah, and she entered the house of Zechariah and greeted Elizabeth. And when Elizabeth heard the greeting of Mary, the babe leaped in her womb; and Elizabeth was filled with the Holy Spirit and she exclaimed with a loud cry, "Blessed are you among women, and blessed is the fruit of your womb! And why is this granted me, that the mother of my Lord should come to me? For behold, when the voice of your greeting came to my ears, the babe in my womb leaped for joy. And blessed is she who believed that there would be a fulfillment of what was spoken to her from the Lord" (Luke 1:39-45).

Possibly if anyone else but Mary had been told the astounding news that she was to be the Mother of the Son of God, she might well have spent the following hours, days, weeks and months in an understandable ecstasy of wonder, joy and thanksgiving. Yet with Mary, we find a complete lack of selfishness. St. Luke tells us that she "went with haste into the hill country" in order to be of service to her cousin, Elizabeth. According to ancient tradition, Zachary and Elizabeth lived at Ain Karim, and the journey on foot would take at least five days from Nazareth. Such an exquisite spirit of charity filled the heart of Mary that she felt the need of hastening straight away to help someone in need, even at a great distance. For her, the love of God and neighbor were not distinct; so wide was the range of the term "neighbor" for her that she made no count of distance but went with haste into that far off hill country with no thought of self. She was the humble handmaid of the Lord, anxious to seize every opportunity of serving Him in others, no matter how inconvenient. How does my spirit of practical charity measure up to that of Mary? Perhaps under certain conditions I am willing to be charitable and helpful—with an eye always on my own convenience: too many conditions, not enough generosity, not enough true love of God who is found under so many aspects in my neighbor! Is this a fair picture of my so-called charity? Mary, dear Mother, you put me to shame for my lukewarm love of God and neighbor. Please help me now to think out sensible ways and means of remedying this situation, starting this very day. Inspire me as I hasten forward into the hill country of charity, but let me not count the cost.

And when Elizabeth heard the greeting of Mary, the babe leaped in her womb; and Elizabeth was filled with the Holy Spirit and she exclaimed with a loud cry, "Blessed are you among women, and blessed is the fruit of your womb!" (Luke 1:41-42)

In the privacy of her humble room at Nazareth, Mary had heard astounding words of praise from God's own special messenger. Luke tells us that as she greets her dear cousin Elizabeth, she hears wonderful praise from her. In giving it, Elizabeth "was filled with the Holy Spirit" and gave forth her praise "with a loud cry." What special recognition do I give to Mary's place in the Church and in my life? Vatican Council II has stated: "Mary has by grace been exalted above all angels and men to a place second only to her Son, as the most holy Mother of God who was involved in the mysteries of Christ: she is rightly honored by a special cult in the Church" (*Lumen Gentium*, 66).

Perhaps I willingly concede her this high place of honor in theory, but how practical is my expression of devotion to God's holy Mother? Is it all just a question of *Ave's* uttered perhaps many times a day but without much thought—a beautiful prayer ruined through a thoughtless monotony of routine? What a pity if that is so! Do I turn to her prayerfully only in times of real stress? Am I like Elizabeth, loud in my praises of the holy Mother of God, who in so many kindly ways shows her motherly protection and help toward me? O Mary, my Mother, forgive my lukewarmness. Help me to be henceforth more aware of your loving presence in my life. O Jesus, Son of Mary, teach me to imitate Your own love and appreciation of a Mother so dear to both of us.

And why is this granted me, that the mother of my Lord should come to me?... Blessed is she who believed that there would be a fulfillment of what was spoken to her from the Lord (Luke 1:43, 45).

In its sound teaching on the true devotion to Mary that has existed through all the Christian era, the Church makes due distinction between the adoration we owe to God in the Holy Trinity and the reverence due to Mary: "The various forms of piety towards the Mother of God, which the Church has approved within the limits of sound and orthodox doctrine, according to the dispositions and understanding of the faithful, ensure that while the Mother is honored, the Son through whom all things have their being (cf. Col. 1:15-16), and in whom it has pleased the Father that all fullness should dwell (cf. Col. 1:19), is rightly known, loved and glorified and His commandments are observed" (*Lumen Gentium,* 66). In our devotion to Mary, then, there must be sound doctrine, nothing merely pietistic, sentimental or superstitious. For me, in particular, it should be based on an absolutely strong and filial love that recognizes in her a true mother who is deeply interested in me, as an individual, and as a Christian, and is ever anxious to be of practical help to me. Let me recall now some of the instances in my life when I felt very tangibly the influence of Mary. O Mary, Help of Christians, my Mother and benefactress, I thank you sincerely for all you have done for me throughout my life and especially on those more notable occasions I have just recalled. Please help me to show my gratitude constantly in practical form, e.g., today I shall....

Henceforth All Generations

For he has regarded the low estate of his handmaiden. For behold, henceforth all generations will call me blessed; for he who is mighty has done great things for me, and holy is his name. And his mercy is on those who fear him from generation to generation (Luke 1:48-50).

The Magnificat has been called "an explosion of the joy of poverty" and the Vatican Council II decree on the Church says that Mary "stands out among the poor and humble of the Lord" (*Lumen Gentium,* 55). She lived in Nazareth, an insignificant little town of Galilee. In all probability her own home was poor, but the spirit of her poverty lay, above all, in her complete trust and abandonment to God's providence—and of this there is ample evidence in the Magnificat. So complete was her spirit of abandonment to God that she had already determined to give up the joy and, what was considered by the Hebrews, the privilege of bearing children in the ordinary way. She knew only too well, from the sufferings of her childless cousin, Elizabeth, how much she was sacrificing in order to offer God her virginity. This fitted in perfectly with the plans of divine Providence from all eternity. We have here combined, then, for our own practical application the three virtues that underlie and underline our three vows: the holy abandonment that makes us give up all things in poverty; the purity that obviously calls forth our vow of chastity; the humility based on faith that is the only sure foundation for our obedience. O Mary, my model, help me to dwell on these aspects of my holy vows in the light of your own wonderful example.

Behold, henceforth all generations will call me blessed.

Had we not studied Mary, had we taken this statement of hers in sheer isolation, there might well have seemed to be a note of pride in her Magnificat. But it is obvious from what we know of her that there is no triumphalism whatsoever in what she says, for she asserts right from the start that her soul magnifies not herself, but the Lord, to whom she attributes all the praise and glory, even that which she now prophetically sees will come to herself throughout the ages: "For he who is mighty has done great things for me, and holy is his name." How often occasions arise in our lives when we feel that we have accomplished something fine, something good, something really praiseworthy, but how anxious we become for these things to be publicly acknowledged. For the sake of one brief flash of glory we are so thoughtlessly careless about damaging the delicate virtue of humility. We are not expected, however, to deny what has been accomplished, for humility is essentially a lover of truth. No, humility demands rightly that we should acknowledge, even publicly, that without God behind us nothing good could have been achieved. What deep feelings of humility should also inspire me at the thought that God has actually used such a poor creature as myself to be His instrument in their accomplishment! Are not these thoughts of practical application in my life? O my God, forgive me the pride that has spoiled so much of the good You have wished to do through me. You have indeed done great things for, in, and through me. May all praise be Yours now and forevermore!

His mercy is on those who fear him from generation to generation.

In her profound humility, Mary groups herself with the multitude of sinful humanity in need of God's mercy, echoing the frequent thankful cries of the psalmist: "Surely goodness and mercy shall follow me all the days of my life; and I shall dwell in the house of the Lord for ever.... For the Lord is good; His mercy endures for ever, and his faithfulness to all generations." How much need I too have of the mercy of God. I have only to think of the many calamities of my past life in order to stir up some kind of fear of His judgments, but what God wants from me is not that, but a deeper humility in realizing my utter weakness, my sheer helplessness without Him in all things, even in avoiding sin. Perhaps He also wishes to remind me of the later admonition of His Son: "Be merciful, even as your Father is merciful" (Lk. 6:36). Mary, dear Mother of Mercy, help me to admit my spiritual needs with deep humility. Help me this day to be kind and merciful to others.

Bethlehem

In those days a decree went out from Caesar Augustus that all the world should be enrolled. This was the first enrollment, when Quirinius was governor of Syria. And all went to be enrolled, each to his own city. And Joseph also went up from Galilee, from the city of Nazareth, to Judea, to the city of David, which is called Bethlehem, because he was of the house and lineage of David, to be enrolled with Mary, his betrothed, who was with child (Luke 2:1-5).

God the Father had ordained that His Son should be born at a time (one of those extremely rare times) when the whole world was at peace. The Emperor, Caesar Augustus, having just completed his victorious conquests in Gaul and Spain, dedicated a special new altar on the Campodoglio in Rome to "the God of Peace." After seven centuries of war there was now, unbelievably, peace. Shortly afterwards the real God of Peace Himself was born at Bethlehem, a town five miles south of Jerusalem called "the city of David," where he too had been born and in the late Hebrew times it was the expected birthplace of the Messiah. Notice how God's Providence made use of the censorship whim of the far-off Roman Emperor to bring about the unexpected transfer of Joseph and Mary to Bethlehem from Nazareth, so that the prophecy might be fulfilled: "But you, O Bethlehem Ephrathah, from you shall come forth from me one who is to be ruler in Israel, whose origin is from old, from ancient days" (Mi. 5:1). Both Joseph and Mary were descended from David and hence they had to register at his city, Bethlehem. How marvelous are the ways of divine Providence that can make use of seemingly very ordinary events to achieve its own sublime purposes!

When things happen, therefore, that we cannot help or avoid, it is wise to resign oneself completely and confidently into the hands of God's loving Providence. Don Bosco said: "Material means are in the hands of God, who knows how to do much with little. He has even effected all out of nothing, and sometimes makes use of worthless instruments to bring out His sublime purposes" (*M.B.*, II.) Do I allow myself to become unduly upset when the unexpected happens? Do I keep calm and pray? Do I abandon myself confidently to God's Providence? Let me now do so through the hands of Mary.

Bethlehem means "house of bread," hence it was a fitting place for the birth of Him who was to call Himself "the Bread of Life" and to give Himself to the world in the form of bread. From the very earliest ages, as far back as can be traced, bread, made from various cereal grains, seems to have been the staple food of mankind. This no doubt was precisely why God chose it for the outward form of the Blessed Eucharist as a common bond of unity for all mankind. Born in the "house of bread," our Savior made His final sacrifice on the cross begin with the breaking of bread at the first eucharistic supper with His apostles. Let me consider now how much I owe to the Incarnation of Christ together with the Holy Eucharist. Is my Holy Communion not merely a bond of union with Jesus but also with all His disciples, including my community, as well as those with whom I come in contact? O Sacrament most holy, O Sacrament divine, all praise and all thanksgiving be every moment Thine!

A further thought on Bethlehem concerns obedience. No doubt our Lady would have preferred to remain in her own home town of Nazareth for the birth of her child. It would have been so much more convenient; she would have been sure of the help of her own mother, relatives and friends. Bethlehem was so very far away for travel in those days. Yet here again we see exemplified Mary's implicit confidence in God's providence. We read of no murmur or dissent on her part or that of Joseph. In the decree of the distant Roman Emperor they obeyed also the authority of God who knew that thereby the scriptural prophecy would be fulfilled regarding the Messiah's birth.

How often things occur in my life which I so readily dub a "nuisance," "most inconvenient," "downright inconsiderate," and so on, things that upset my comfort or convenience, my sense of regularity or my well-arranged plans. It is so easy to make a fuss on such occasions. Sometimes objections may be necessary but surely never a fuss, which only shows lack of self-control, a mind too easily disturbed. Is there not much room for improvement in me here? Let me pray now to our Lady, Help of Christians, asking her assistance that I do something practical about it this very day.

The Birth of Jesus

And while they were there, the time came for her to be delivered. And she gave birth to her first-born son and wrapped him in swaddling clothes, and laid him in a manger, because there was no place for them in the inn (Luke 2:6-7).

At a time of extraordinary peace in the world, the Prince of Peace was born at Bethlehem. It would seem that because of the Imperial Census the little town was crowded with others who, like Mary and Joseph, had come from their ordinary homes to register in this place of family origin. Hence "there was no place for them in the inn." Just outside the town, on a hillside, Joseph found shelter in a rock grotto or cave, used as a stable: this tradition comes down to us strongly from St. Justin Martyr, who lived there only a century afterwards. Here at least, even if there was no comfort or luxury, there was privacy. And so, in the silence of that first momentous Christmas night, Mary "gave birth to her firstborn Son and wrapped him in swaddling clothes, and laid him in a manger." In a very few simple words the evangelist amazingly describes the tremendous fact that the Son of God was born as man. If we think of the full significance of the role of the second Person of the Blessed Trinity, we cannot but be deeply amazed at the mystery of His condescension in actually becoming a man while remaining God. Let me thank God now for this tremendous gift to mankind. O little Babe of Bethlehem, I adore You as my God and Savior with feelings of deepest reverence and gratitude.

Picture for a moment the actual scene in that humble birthplace at Bethlehem. Look at the tiny baby in the straw of the crib or, better, in Mary's tender arms, while Joseph gazes ecstatically upon Him in bewilderment. How helpless the child must have seemed, how trusting, how dependent! What were Mary's thoughts? Surely those of any mother whose love pours forth when she actually sees the child she has carried nine long months in her womb. What joy to see the little eyes upon her, already full of instinctive love, the tiny fingers curving about her own.... Mary must have experienced all this and more, for she knew this was no common child and she herself no ordinary mother. This was the very Son of God, she was His extraordinarily privileged Mother, called by God's angel "full of grace." May I always treat Jesus within the poor stable of my heart with exactly the same tender care as Mary then did! Dear Mother....

There is always a fascination about seeing a new-born baby, noting its utter dependence and helplessness, its first strivings to understand what is going on about it, recognizing those who are more closely associated with itself so that it can stretch out its tiny hands toward them for help or a better relationship. What joy must have filled the hearts of Mary and Joseph when they saw all this happening in their own regard! Perhaps Mary's understanding of what lay behind it all was greater than that of her husband, but he too must have felt deeply consoled. In becoming a tiny, helpless, dependent babe, Jesus wanted to teach me to have a similar relationship with my heavenly Father, quite secure that He will look after me if I abandon myself with total confidence to Him as I go about my daily duties faithfully. Jesus, help me....

Let my mind go in spirit to Bethlehem's cave to look upon my newborn Savior. Surely I am filled with awe at the thought that God, Creator of the world, actually became a tiny human baby, detaching Himself from the rights of His divinity in order to do so. A baby arouses immediate sympathy and even delight as we watch it stretching out its little hands to make contact and share its love. Such was Jesus, too, stretching out His infant hands to make contact with me, to invite me into the closest possible intimacy with Him throughout my life—I protecting Him, He protecting me! What confidence in Him this thought should inspire! Dear Jesus, I give You my heart now with all its thoughts and desires and I ask You to make it entirely Yours for ever.

Let Us Go Over to Bethlehem

Glory to God in the highest, and on earth peace among men with whom He is pleased (Luke 2:14).

The astonishment of the simple shepherds of Bethlehem must have been great indeed when they heard the angelic voices singing the first Christmas carol. Quite obviously God the Father was extremely pleased with these poor people because of their simple lives, but above all because of their genuine virtues. To them, therefore, He gave a great reward in return for the glory they were already giving Him in their own simple way: the reward not merely of hearing the angelic song but also of great and lasting peace once they had seen the Infant Savior. The type of life we religious lead should also be a simple one, characterized not only by a spirit of evangelical poverty and detachment, but also by spiritual simplicity which makes us look automatically in all things toward God and His will and peace, determined always to do whatever He wishes. The more peace there is in my soul, the greater will the light of God shine in it, through it, and about it. Am I an apostle of peace in my own surroundings? O Prince of Peace, come to my heart and mind to remove all obstacles to Your perfect reign within me. Help me to be an example and an apostle of true peace to others.

When the angels went away from them into heaven, the shepherds said to one another, "Let us go over to Bethlehem and see this thing that has happened which the Lord has made known to us." And they went with haste, and found Mary and Joseph, and the Babe lying in a manger (Luke 2:15-16).

Notice the eagerness with which the shepherds go to find God. We too should have the same spirit of eagerness in seeking for Him and His will every single day. However, let us not neglect His physical presence among us in the Blessed Sacrament. Surely that is where our steps should lead us frequently, not merely to attend Holy Mass and other community exercises of piety, but also on occasions for our own private visits to the Friend we deeply love and appreciate. Even a few brief moments before the Blessed Sacrament can bring a great sense of peace. It is not even necessary to have to recite prayers. Just to be there is already a wonderful privilege. How often do I pay Jesus such visits? O Jesus, hidden in the feebleness of the Eucharist, help me to become a person of great faith in all things, for You have said: "The righteous shall live by faith" (Rom. 1:17).

We can imagine the excitement and happiness of the shepherds as they crowded into the humble stable to see the Infant Savior and to explain to Joseph and Mary why they had come. What joy must then have flooded the heart of Mary on hearing this from those simple shepherds; how happy they must have been to see the holy child lying there in all beauty and simplicity! Did Mary allow them to take Him up and hold Him a little while? What a lovely reward that would have been for them, or even merely to gather around Him and gaze in rapture at God made Man! The shepherds undoubtedly followed the age-old custom of those parts, still surviving today, of bringing gifts to the mother of the new born child, especially eggs and milk. How gratefully Mary must have received them, these humble gifts from rough and simple people. Our gifts to her may bear close comparison, but let us be generous with them for she passes them all on to Jesus. What gifts can I offer Mary today for her Son? O Mary, accept above all my rough and simple heart and make it worthy of your Son, whom I adore in spite of all the roughness of my character and life....

Epiphany

Now when Jesus was born in Bethlehem of Judea in the days of Herod the king, behold, wise men from the East came to Jerusalem saying, "Where is he who has been born king of the Jews? For we have seen his star in the East, and have come to worship him." When Herod the king heard this, he was troubled, and all Jerusalem with him; and assembling all the chief priests and scribes of the people, he inquired of them where the Christ was to be born. They told him, "In Bethlehem of Judea; for so it is written by the prophet: 'And you, O Bethlehem, in the land of Judah, are by no means least among the rulers of Judah, for from you shall come a ruler who will govern my people Israel'" (Matthew 2:1-6).

The word *Epiphany* means "appearance" or "manifestation" and here in St. Matthew we read of the star, a symbol of faith, leading the Gentiles to the discovery of Jesus as their King and Savior. Scientists and astronomers try to calculate or even explain away the particular celestial phenomenon seen by the Magi (a "magus" was a member of an ancient Persian priestly caste, or simply a wise man). Let us, however, take the Gospel account on faith and meditate on the lessons God wishes us to learn from this extraordinary visit. Wherever they came from (Matthew has them say "the East," but tradition gives them different origins and races) and whatever the form of the star, they obeyed what they took to be a special call from on high and set out to find the newborn "king of the Jews." To them the obvious place to go was the renowned Temple of God at Jerusalem. Their arrival and questions caused quite a sensation and the news soon reached King Herod himself: "he was troubled and all Jerusalem with him." What need was there for Herod or anyone else to be troubled? Surely if the expectation of the coming Messiah was as great as it should have been, the hearing of the actual news should have caused great rejoicing. What do we find instead? Apparently several uneasy consciences, an unwillingness to believe truth, a resentment of something good.

How often we find the same thing down through the ages, even in our own day. Rulers can get so obsessed with ambition and power that they either forget God or mention Him only in pious platitudes as a camouflage. How true that power can corrupt! Not only those in authority, however, but others also can—in practice if not theory—forget God, resent truth, and seek only their own will, comfort and advantage. How often too one finds resentment and even jealousy concerning the good achieved by others. This horrible spirit can enter even into religion and is something surely most displeasing to God. Is there no trace of it in my own character? If there is, let me now beg God's strong grace to help me root it out once and for all, to be ambitious only for God's honor, not my own, and to rejoice sincerely in the good of others. Jesus,...

It would certainly seem that the Magi traveled a good distance, and probably at great cost and inconvenience. That did not seem to worry them however. For them the main thing was that they had received a call from God to seek and find His Son. The execution of that will of His was their only preoccupation. Even when the guiding star temporarily disappeared they did not give up the search, though it must have been a moment of great anguish and hesitation. What should they do next? Rightly are they called wise men, for they consulted. If I am really anxious to do the holy will of God in all things, I should allow nothing at all to stop me from searching for it, finding it, doing it. Do I not sometimes, however, allow my own comfort and convenience the upper hand, preferring my own will to His? And when—as happens to practically everyone—those moments of doubt and hesitation come, am I sensible enough to seek the advice of prudent people? Or do I just blunder along, overconfident in myself, my vision blurred by egoism, pride, ambition? In such moments let me rather "look to the star, call upon Mary," as St. Bernard advises.

O Mary, Seat of Wisdom, Mother of Good Counsel, Help of Christians, let me forget my own worldly wisdom. Shine the light of your example on my way to Jesus.

At first it is edifying to see that Herod too actually did consult others, the chief priests and scribes—a wise choice, for they were the very ones to give the correct answers. Unfortunately, however, we know that his motives were not sincere. There was in this man no desire to seek and fulfill God's will. He was foolish enough, stupid enough in his worldly wisdom, to think that he could actually disdain it. When the will of God was confirmed by the quotation of scriptural prophecy, he at once set about opposing it in a subtle manner. Am I one of those so-called clever people who seem to think they know all the answers, are forever dogmatizing about practically everything, with an apparent horror for the simple, saving phrase "I think..."? Such people are an unnecessary trial in community relationships. Do I realize, then, the advisability and frequent need of consultation—but with the right people, not with the grumblers, the chip-on-shoulder critics who can only do my soul and spirit real harm? Looking at the day ahead, can I foresee any dangers for me in this line? If so, what should I do to avoid them discreetly? Let me pray to Jesus and Mary about it—because it's very important! O Jesus,...

They Rejoiced Exceedingly

Then Herod summoned the wise men secretly and ascertained from them what time the star appeared; and he sent them to Bethlehem, saying, "Go and search diligently for the Child, and when you have found him bring me word, that I too may come and worship him." When they had heard the king they went their way; and lo, the star which they had seen in the East went before them, till it came to rest over the place where the child was. When they saw the star, they rejoiced exceedingly with great joy; and going into the house they saw the child with Mary, his mother, and they fell down and worshiped him. Then, opening their treasures, they offered him gifts, gold and frankincense and myrrh. And being warned in a dream not to return to Herod, they departed to their own country by another way (Matthew 2:7-12).

"Where is he? For we have seen his star in the East, and have come to worship him." For these wise men, the only thing that mattered was the will of God. The Magi seem to have been the disciples of the ancient sage, Zoroaster, whose dominant theme was to strive always to cooperate with the Holy Spirit of the Divinity. These disciples of his had certainly learned this lesson well, and here, Gentiles though they were, following their consciences faithfully, they were rewarded so magnificently by the true God with the gift of true faith. What really matters in life is the fulfillment of God's holy will. Neglecting it, disobeying it, can only bring final disillusionment and a great lack of peace. God, after all, in His total wisdom, knowledge and understanding, knows what is best in every case and in every circumstance. Our very limited intelligence can so easily deceive us into thinking that our own way is infallible, and, as experience should by now have shown us, pride is so easy and so subtle in leading us to this immature conviction about ourselves. As the great de Caussade used to say, we must never try to dictate to God what should or should not be done, nor should we ever set limits to the action of His holy will, for it is all-powerful. Those holy wise men, the Magi, sought for Christ and Him alone. So should I at all times. How do I measure up to their standard? Do I, like them, strive always to cooperate with the Holy Spirit which is constantly whispering the direction I should take in order to find Christ in my life?

Come, Holy Spirit, fill my heart, which wants to be faithful, and enkindle in me the fire of Your love....

Imagine their tremendous sense of relief when, after leaving Herod, the Magi once again saw the star leading them on to Bethlehem. Rightly, then, "they rejoiced exceedingly with great joy." For them that star was the will of God and that was the only thing that mattered. It would have been most natural for them *en route* to have had doubts, so human to think of returning home in case their whole long and inconvenient journey was just a wild-goose chase. But no, they overcame all doubts and human weakness and fears; they persevered on to victory, rejoicing at the appearance once again of God's pointer, the star. Mere human wisdom can be such a dangerous obstacle on life's way; the human mind is one of the most awesome of God's creations but how wayward it too can be at times! Well-controlled, trained always to seek only the will of God in all things, then indeed our mind is thoroughly attuned to the wisdom of God's Holy Spirit. Well then may it, like the Magi, rejoice exceedingly with great joy. What is my own experience in this line? Have I not always felt a great sense of peace, even of joy, when I have tried fully to abandon myself to God and His holy will? Let me pray for an increase in this spirit, for it is so crucial if I am to be a true and worthy religious.

Father in heaven, let me not merely say each day "Thy will be done," but let me mean it, and prove it....

The Magi had brought with them symbolic gifts fit for a king, three of the gifts then considered most valuable in the East. Imagine their surprise, then, when the star stopped "over the place where the child was." Scripture simply states: "...going into the house, they saw the child with Mary his mother, and they fell down and worshiped him. Then, opening their treasures, they offered him gifts, gold and frankincense and myrrh." How often when we say we are most anxious to do God's will, we show not only surprise but even resentment when eventually it is manifested in a way contrary to our likings. Do we then refuse Him our gifts of resignation, submission and acceptance?

When was the last time I put up a struggle against the manifest will of God? Was it worth it? Did I gain peace of mind by kicking against the goad? Perhaps in the future it may help me to bring Mary into the picture. The Magi, we read, "saw the child with Mary his mother." If I find obedience difficult, any duty or task awkward, something hard to accept, let me ask Mary's help to bow down humbly to the wise will of God underlying it, and then do it cheerfully. Let me reflect now on what attitudes of my mind should correspond with the Magi's gifts of gold, frankincense and myrrh when I find the will of God confronting me. What practical form can I give these points for the day ahead?

Mary, dear Mother, help me in this useful search, so that I may return to my own country of God's will by a way that is completely other than any previous obstinacy and self-will....

Flight into Egypt

Now when they had departed, behold, an angel of the Lord appeared to Joseph in a dream and said, "Rise, take the child and his mother, and flee to Egypt, and remain there till I tell you; for Herod is about to search for the child, to destroy him." And he rose and took the child and his mother by night, and departed to Egypt, and remained there until the death of Herod. This was to fulfill what the Lord had spoken by the prophet. "Out of Egypt have I called my son." Then Herod when he saw that he had been tricked by the wise men, was in a furious rage, and he sent and killed all the male children in Bethlehem and in all that region who were two years old or under, according to the time which he had ascertained from the wise men. Then was fulfilled what was spoken by the prophet Jeremiah: "A voice was heard in Ramah, wailing and loud lamentation, Rachel weeping for her children; she refused to be consoled, because they were no more." But when Herod died, behold, an angel of the Lord appeared in a dream to Joseph in Egypt, saying, "Rise, take the child and his mother, and go to the land of Israel, for those who sought the child's life are dead." And he rose and took the child and his mother, and went to the land of Israel (Matthew 2:13-21).

What tremendous anxiety must have first seized Joseph when he realized the imminent danger of the Child Jesus after the departure of the Magi! What dread must have filled his mind at the thought of the long and perilous journey ahead! How were they to get to Egypt? The long and wearisome Sea of Sands stretched between them and safety. But we can well imagine that these very human and likely apprehensions, even if they kept arising, were stilled by Joseph's eminently practical common sense and his tremendous reliance on God's Providence. For him the two went hand in hand. He did not adopt a mere quietist attitude, sitting back and letting things happen, confident in God. In such an emergency the will of God obviously demanded prompt action, and Joseph took it. We can feel sure that he at once sold at least part of the Magi's providential gifts in order to obtain the means for making the journey safely, possibly even paying to join one of the larger caravans which was one of the few safe means of traveling through the bandit-ridden desert. Legends galore have sprung up about this sacred journey but we have no facts to prove them. The anonymity of a large group traveling in caravan would probably have appealed most to the ever practical-minded Joseph. The journey from Nazareth to Bethlehem, anxious as it must have been, would have seemed a mere nothing compared with this one of over 600 miles to Egypt. It is estimated that it could have taken from ten to twenty days. Only when they had crossed over Herod's border into the Roman province of Egypt could Joseph and Mary feel safe, knowing that the Father would see to all their needs now that they had done all that was humanly possible.

It is sometimes cynically said that no sense is so uncommon as common sense, and yet it is a God-given talent that should be used to its fullest as part of the fulfillment of God's will. Can I rightly say that I am noted for my common sense in practical life? C. E. Stowe says that "Common sense is the knack of seeing things as they are, and doing things as they ought to be done." Coleridge caps this by adding: "Common sense in an uncommon degree is what the world calls wisdom." St. Joseph certainly evidenced this gift in an eminent degree. I might therefore pray to him now to improve in this important matter myself.

The ancient Jews had fled from Egypt as a land of slavery, but during the past few centuries its role had been reversed, for it became for many a place of refuge and liberty. Such it was for the Holy Family. At that time there were flourishing Jewish colonies in Egypt. Somewhere among these Joseph must have found work—tradition says Heliopolis, a little north of Cairo and associated with the ancient Joseph, Viceroy of Egypt. Today, in its place, stands the village of Matariyeh, with legends or traditions concerning the Holy Family's residence there, e.g., an ancient sycamore tree often used by Mary for its shade, a well of sweet water, etc. Whatever the truth of these things, we may take it that the Holy Family lived an ordinary, quiet and unpretentious life, grateful to be safe there, even if poor. In this I may find a very valuable lesson of common sense combined with true holiness, and again it is the question of seeking and finding God's will wherever I am, in whatever circumstances I am placed. Wisely does de Caussade say that God makes saints as He pleases, but they are all made according to His plan, and all must be submissive to this plan. This submission is true self-abandonment, and it is the most perfect of all ways. The more absolute this submission becomes, the greater is their sanctity. Keeping in mind the example of the Holy Family in Egypt, let me apply this now to my own life. How do I measure up to it?

After the flight of the Holy Family from Bethlehem, there took place the frightful slaughter of the innocent babes at the command of Herod. Soon afterwards he himself was to die after thirty-six years of tyranny. He was buried in the sumptuous mausoleum he had had built for himself on a hillside just south of Bethlehem itself. The memory of his cruelty could have awakened no sympathy as his pompous funeral passed so close to the little town from which the Savior had been driven. In the meantime though, Jesus was safe in Egypt, grateful to those who had died in His stead. There He remained until His Father sent special word again to Joseph to return to the land of Israel. Note once again that God leaves room for Joseph to exercise his common sense in choosing a residence. Publius Syrus, a wise Roman of those times, said: "Good health and good sense are two of life's greatest blessings."

The example of St. Joseph is all the more remarkable in that he could so easily have relied entirely on God the Father's continual and immediate direction of every detail concerning His Son's welfare on earth. The very paucity of His instructions to Joseph, however, seems to bear out the fact that He expected him to use his common sense in the practical details of fulfillment. Thus it is, too, with our obedience. Usually only the outlines are given and we have to fill in sensibly. How do I show up in this combination of common sense with obedience? When faced with things to do, do I pray? Do I consult? Do I get down to business right away? Or do I forget God? Do I act senselessly, blunderingly, too independently, dilly-dallying, without orderliness—in other words, spoiling obedience by not using prayerful common sense? Wise and sensible St. Joseph, help me to become a thoroughly sensible person!

He Grew and Became Strong

He withdrew to the district of Galilee. And he went and dwelt in a city called Nazareth, that what was spoken by the prophets might be fulfilled, "He shall be called a Nazarene" (Matthew 2:22).

And the child grew and became strong, filled with wisdom; and the favor of God was upon him (Luke 2:40).

Apart from these few words, the Gospels are strangely silent about the actual life of Jesus, Mary and Joseph at Nazareth. It is surely safe therefore to presume that it must have been a very ordinary life, that not only Joseph and Mary fitted once again into the usual routine of their previous life there, but also that Jesus Himself followed the pattern of a child's life. We may take it that in due course Jesus went to school and learned there to read and write, to say the verses of the Law by heart, to study the Scriptures. It seems reasonable, too, to presume that He helped Joseph at his carpentry and Mary with her household tasks. The home itself was doubtlessly poor, but what peace and happiness surely reigned in it. All these conjectures can find their basis in the few words of Scripture quoted above. We call it the Hidden Life, but there is the danger of losing in its apparent obscurity most valuable lessons surely intended by God for us. Our own lives, generally, are very ordinary; there is a routine of duties and tasks that can, if allowed, numb the true spirit that should underlie them if they are to be pleasing to God. What is needed is to keep in mind the motives and purposes at the basis of our actions, plus a constant recall to the will of God. Notice, too, the specific Gospel mention of growth and strength in Jesus. Maturity and health are also important parts of God's wise plans for each of us. Due care of these can also win God's favor. Can I find here useful points for consideration—and reduction to sensible practice?

Health is an important part of our life and it has been wisely said that without health all men are poor. Our own experience has frequently pointed out the truth of that. The practical deduction from it should be that it is part of our faithfulness to our vocation to take due care of our health. After all, when we enter religion, part—a very important part—of our donation to God is our body as well as our spirit. It is through that body, with its various abilities and capabilities, that we can hope to fulfill the apostolic desires and holy ambitions that fill our minds in regard to the spread of God's kingdom in whatever sphere He assigns to us. God can, of course, use even ill health to effect great things, but He will never condone neglect or downright carelessness—nor any form of hypochondria. Care of health is not necessarily synonymous with a private pharmacy! The old Roman poet, Horace, says wisely in his *Satires:* "Now learn what and how great benefits a temperate diet will bring along with it. In the first place you will enjoy good health." Even more wisely, Vatican Council II exhorts religious: "They should take advantage of those natural helps which favor mental and bodily health" *(Perfectae Caritatis,* 12). Am I being really sensible about my bodily health? Am I careless about it or, on the other hand, inclined to make mountains out of molehills? Let me think now and pray about it to the young Christ who "became strong, filled with wisdom, and the favor of God was upon him."

What of maturity? Maturity is another way of saying that growth in wisdom is attributed to the growing Christ. In its call for a sound renewal of the religious life, how often Vatican Council II referred to this necessity. What it says of seminarians, for example, can apply to all religious: "By wisely planned training there should also be developed in seminarians a due degree of human maturity, attested to chiefly by a certain emotional stability, by an ability to make considered decisions, and by a right manner of passing judgment on events and people. They should be practiced in an intelligent organization of their proper talents; they should be trained in what strengthens character; and in general, they should learn to prize those qualities which are highly regarded among men and speak well of a minister of Christ" (*Optatam Totius*, 11). All religious are ministers of Christ, and hence we all need these qualities, which can be summed up neatly in the one word "maturity." Let me now examine myself closely on each in turn, seeing how I measure up to them, making suitable, sound resolutions. O Jesus, who grew in strength and wisdom, help me also to mature and thus win God's constant favor.

Growth of Jesus

And Jesus increased in wisdom and in stature, and in favor with God and man (Luke 2:52).

Especially for the young, it is good to meditate further on the natural growth of Jesus as man; for those who are older it is good, too, to revise their notions about youth in the light of God's will, without undue pessimism, only anxious to help tactfully in every way.

Jesus came down on earth not merely to redeem the whole man, body and soul, but also to give us a pattern of life, to show us how to live in such a way that we can always be sure of fulfilling God's will and ensuring His pleasure. For this purpose He followed exteriorly all the stages of physical and natural growth of an ordinary child and adolescent. We are told too that He "increased in wisdom." A whole book of the Bible is full of the praises and advantages of wisdom. St. James gives a fine description of it: "The wisdom from above is first pure, then peaceable, gentle, open to reason, full of mercy and good fruits, without uncertainty or insincerity" (3:17). Let me now at this point of my meditation examine each of these qualities in turn, applying them honestly to myself. Am I friendly, a lover of peace, ready to give way easily in matters not of principle? Do I really contribute towards peace in the house and in the community? Am I gentle in my speech and manner, even down to such a fine point as to avoid making unnecessary noise? Am I amiable in my way of dealing with others, even those under me? Am I open to reason? or am I inclined to obstinacy and stubbornness? Am I full of mercy, especially regarding the faults and mistakes of others? What are the obvious good fruits of my love of God as seen in my life? Regarding uncertainty, do I dilly-dally about things, e.g., work, decisions? Is this not perhaps through a lack of confidence in and cooperation with God? Am I always sincere? How can I put right any of these things that have gone wrong in my human and spiritual growth? Let me now consult Jesus on this.

Jesus increased in stature. St. Luke uses the same Greek word here for height as when he later describes the size of Zacchaeus (19:3). From the Holy Shroud in Turin (for which there appear to be very many proofs of authenticity) it seems that eventually Jesus became quite tall—a fact also supported by tradition. As a boy grows in height and strength, so he gradually assumes his duty of work, and we may be sure that Jesus led no idle life in Nazareth. He learned, probably at school, to read and write. Did the schoolmaster ever guess what lay ahead for this pupil of his (a point here of great importance for all teachers)? At home, no doubt, He learned carpentry from Joseph. St. Justin Martyr, the great Christian apologist (died c. 163) says: "He was in the habit of working as a carpenter when He was among men, making ploughs and yokes" (*Trypho*, 88). Later we find Jesus Himself saying: "My yoke is easy" (Mt. 11:30), and the Greek word used by Matthew means also "well-fitting." Is it not possible to read into this not only the confirmation of His craft but also His thoroughness at work? Interesting, too, is the other Greek work *tekton* used by St. Mark (6:3) to describe Jesus, for it means not a limited carpenter but one capable of doing many useful related jobs with strong yet gentle hands. Here let me apply a Vatican Council II exhortation to myself: "Let them perceive as well the superiority of virginity consecrated to Christ, so that by a choice which is maturely thought out and magnanimous they may attach themselves to God by a total gift of body and soul" *(Optatam Totius,* 10). Do I look upon my physical condition, growth and care, in the light of God's will also, trying to imitate Christ growing and maturing, endeavoring always to include my whole body in my daily self-donation to God and His service?

"Jesus increased...in favor with God and man."

Obviously, being God as well as man, Jesus already possessed interiorly the fullness of grace. Here, in fact, in the Greek original, the term *cáris* conveys the sense of a person being dear, courteous, lovable in the eyes of all. Such a description, we feel, can only have come from Mary's own lips to St. Luke himself, and it gives a lovely picture of the growing Jesus, our model. In His home, at school, in the workshop, and further afield, Jesus must have come into contact with a great variety of people and characters: the nice as well as the not-so-nice, the courteous as well as the uncouth and rough, the reasonable and the downright unreasonable. His reaction to those who were less pleasant was not one of rebellion and a counter-awkwardness that achieves nothing worthwhile, but a gentlemanly courtesy and respect for everyone's human and spiritual dignity, for in everyone He saw a soul to be saved. Here at Nazareth He learned not merely to tolerate but even to love people, all people, and also all the things of creation, some of which He mentioned later in His public parables and advice...the sower sowing his seed, the ripening cornfield, the birds of the air, the mustard bush, the lilies of the field.... Life was constantly full of interest for Him, we can be sure, for He made it so, for everyone and everything was part of His apostolate—no narrow bounds of self-interest or selfishness, no lazy boredom but always an outgoing, apostolic look beyond self so as to be a helpful and integral part of mankind and God's splendid creation. And we can be sure of His constant spirit of union with God the Father as well as with mankind through an habitual state of prayer deep down in His sacred heart. Oh how much I can learn from the growing, maturing Christ! Let me see now how I can imitate Him on these points in a practical manner. O Jesus and Mary, help me to grow in every way that God wants, so that I too may find true favor in the eyes of God and men and thus assist You in Your redeeming work on earth.

Baptism of Jesus

Then Jesus came from Galilee to the Jordan, to John, to be baptized by him. John would have prevented him, saying, "I need to be baptized by you, and do you come to me?" But Jesus answered him, "Let it be so now; for thus it is fitting for us to fulfil all righteousness." Then he consented (Matthew 3:13-15).

The rite of baptism denoted a form of purification in Israel, but as preached by our Lord's extraordinary cousin, John, it had an extra feature: the confession of one's own sinfulness and due repentance. The Greek word for "repent" *(metanoia)* means a change of mental attitude. With great humility added to his forthrightness, John also foretold that someone else far greater than he was about to come. And now we see Jesus, grown up and mature, actually coming to John and asking to be baptized, as though He too were a sinner in need of purification, repentance and conversion of life. John protests but Jesus insists. Later we find John the Baptist referring publicly to our Lord as "the Lamb of God, who takes away the sin of the world" (Jn. 1:29), and that was doubtless what Jesus had in mind. What could be more innocent and spotless than the sacrificial lamb offered on God's altar in the temple? Yet it was killed and offered up as though guilty, in lieu of sinners themselves. Later Jesus Himself would declare quite simply that no one could accuse Him of sin, but here we find Him already assuming the burden of the sins of mankind by undergoing baptism. He was the victim of expiation for sin, yet even before His final act of holocaust on Calvary He underwent in His lifetime various forms of penance for sin: e.g., His earlier life of mortified poverty; here the public acknowledgment of the sinner's state in baptism; later the fasting in the desert, followed by a life of constant mortification, poverty and expiatory prayer. These thoughts must surely move me to marvel at the deep humility of Jesus on the one hand and at His spirit of mortification on the other. If I think of my own past, have I not more than ample grounds for cultivating both these virtues, not just superficially but with intensity? Morbidity about past sins is of no help, but what I need is the humble realization that I have offended God's goodness badly, perhaps very often, yet He has not struck me down as He could have done, but in His mercy He is allowing me now further chances to make up for my past by a brave, generous, and even cheerful spirit of sound and sensible mortification that will help cleanse away the last vestiges of past sins and act at the same time as a preventive for the future. Lamb of God, You take away the sins of the world, take mine away also and fill my heart with that peace that is synonymous with love of You.

> *And when Jesus was baptized, he went up immediately from the water, and behold, the heavens were opened and he saw the spirit of God descending like a dove, and alighting on him (Matthew 3:16).*

I can fittingly recall here the importance of my own baptism and the lasting effects it should have on my whole life. Baptism incorporates us into the Mystical Body of Christ, and thereby imposes on us the duty and responsibility of striving to become Christlike in our manner of thinking, speaking, and behaving. Jesus Himself gave this magnificent start to my Christian vocation by calling me to baptism, baptizing me personally through the minister of the sacrament, incorporating me into His Mystical Body publicly and solemnly. He expects me to live up to that vocation and to cultivate assiduously throughout my life those plentiful seeds of the various virtues planted in my soul at holy baptism, so that I might become indeed "another Christ" in every way possible. In my own case, according to God's wonderful plans, one tremendous development of my baptismal vocation was His call to become a religious. Here again the Church speaks: "It is true that through baptism he has died to sin and has been consecrated to God. However, in order to derive more abundant fruit from this baptismal grace, he intends, by the profession of the evangelical counsels in the Church, to free himself from those obstacles which might draw him away from the fervor of charity and the perfection of divine worship.

Thus he is more intimately consecrated to divine service" (*Lumen Gentium*, 44). Have I ever looked upon my religious vocation as an intensification of my baptism? Does it not demand of me a really sincere and fervent sense of duty in my love and service of God and souls? Let me pray about this now, so that for me too, as a result of my fidelity, the heavens may be opened.

> *And he saw the Spirit of God descending like a dove, and alighting on him; and lo, a voice from heaven saying, "This is my beloved Son, with whom I am well pleased" (Matthew 3:16-17).*

These words of God the Father echo almost identical words earlier in the Bible, and contain a significance that could easily be missed. King David, a prototype of Christ, was in the throes of much adversity, a time of great trial, when he wrote the second psalm, but then he records that God said to him, "You are my son, today I have begotten you" (Ps. 2:7). Again in Isaiah we are given a prophecy of the Messiah as the Servant of God: "Behold my servant, my chosen, in whom my soul delights" (Is. 42:1). The baptism of Jesus marked the start of His public life and the words of the Father signify at once His twofold role of suffering and serving as well as the divine delight in His presence on earth. It was for Jesus at once an identification with mankind and with the Father's redemptive will. In the dove, moreover, we see the symbol of the third Person of the Trinity, the Holy Spirit. Here, then, we have an almost tangible evidence of the most Holy Trinity. At my baptism the same elements were present, not merely the water but the three divine Persons effecting the essential sacrament. On that day too, the Father proclaimed: "This is my beloved son with whom I am well pleased." But have I remained faithful to the grace and opportunities then received? Have I never taken away God's pleasure from my soul? Have I tried to exclude suffering and serving in the cause of God and my fellowmen? Baptism was meant to make me "another Christ." How am I measuring up to that ideal? O Jesus, baptized for me, cleanse my soul from the last vestiges of accumulated sin. Help me to start again, generously, to be faithful to my baptismal vocation. Let me start today to be constantly pleasing to you. To this end I shall....

The Three Temptations

And he fasted forty days and forty nights, and afterwards he was hungry. And the tempter came and said to him, "If you are the Son of God, command these stones to become loaves of bread." But he answered, "It is written, 'Man shall not live by bread alone, but by every word that proceeds from the mouth of God'" (Matthew 4:2-3).

Satan was not at all sure of the exact status of Jesus, but he obviously suspected that He was someone out of the ordinary, certainly in some ways a privileged man, called by God to some special, high vocation. In spite of the very ordinary life Jesus had lived in Nazareth, Satan could not have been unaware of His supreme purity and goodness, His eminent practice of all the virtues. Possibly he had tried over and over again to tempt Him and failed, and so, gradually, he had come round to the idea that quite possibly this man might actually be the promised Son of God, the Messiah, the Redeemer—to whose coming Satan always looked with the utmost dread. And now he saw Him go out into the desert. Satan stayed about Him, noticing keenly His amazing endurance in that rugged, lonesome wilderness of craggy hills and sand, overwhelmed at the length of His fasting. In many ways a sound psychologist from long centuries of experience, Satan realized that when a man is physically weak and very hungry, his morale is generally at a low ebb and he will do practically anything to obtain relief. Seeing Jesus now so desperately weak, Satan approaches Him and points to the many limestone rocks lying about in that area, round stones that look remarkably like little newly-baked loaves of bread. If this man was the Son of God, then surely He could quite easily perform a miracle, changing some of those stones into real bread in order to break His long fast. Jesus could quite lawfully have done so, but because the suggestion came from Satan it was at once taboo. He quietly counters it with God's own words in Deuteronomy, reminding His Chosen People how He had fed them on manna in the desert and that "man does not live by bread alone but by everything that proceeds out of the mouth of the Lord" (8:3). In other words, no matter how important the things of the body, far more important are the things of God, who, if necessary, can provide even contrary to and above the needs of nature. Being God, Jesus could have performed the actual miracle and still defeated Satan. But He contents Himself with the moral victory of humility and prudence in not revealing His true identity. Satan must have begun then to feel an ever-increasing sense of annoyance and frustration that made him even bolder.

As for myself, I must be very careful to avoid any juggling about when it comes to a choice between material and spiritual values. For me the supernatural should always predominate and motivate. Bodily and material things have their own due measure of importance, but when the things of God are at stake I must be ready to give up everything—even food and comfort—in order to follow bravely the example of Jesus. Have I at times tried to compromise? With what results to my conscience? O Jesus, my model, feed my mind and heart on the bread of Your word, especially when they are tempted to crave after earthly pleasures or satisfaction in the hungry desert of temptation.

> *Then the devil took him to the holy city, and set him on the pinnacle of the temple, and said to him, "If you are the Son of God, throw yourself down; for it is written, 'He will give his angels charge of you,' and 'On their hands they will bear you up, lest you strike your foot against a stone.'" Jesus said to him, "Again it is written, 'You shall not tempt the Lord your God'" (Matthew 4:5-7).*

Having tried in vain to make Christ give in to the mere needs of the body, Satan turns now to tempt the very spirit which Jesus had just said was superior to the body. If this man is indeed the Son of God then he hopes to trick Him into showing His own independence in the manner suggested—and again, in itself, it would not be wrong for Jesus to do so. Coming from Satan, however, the suggestion was essentially vile and reprehensible, an attempt to make Him boastfully show pride in a spectacular miracle—especially since there was always a crowd in the Temple precincts who would witness it and proclaim the prodigy. In other words, "Win the people over now by acting as a kind of glorified Superman—if you are in fact the promised Messiah!" Wisely Satan took into account the mob mentality that always loves the spectacular and so easily gives its allegiance to the grand outward show. It still is so today. But again the quiet, scriptural, humble retort: "Again it is written, 'You shall not tempt the Lord your God.'" Once more Satan is furiously frustrated and his own pride more than ever deeply wounded! In the world of today how widespread is the almost frenetic seeking after novelties and sensations by the immature of mind and heart.

Vatican II very wisely acknowledged the definite need in the Church and in religious orders for a process of sound and sensible updating to ensure a more effective modern apostolate, but it stressed equally well "a continuous return to the sources of all Christian life and to the original inspiration behind a given community" (*Perfectae Caritatis*, 2). In calling this important modern Council, Pope John XXIII expressed his longing for "fresh air" in the Church, a "New Pentecost" and hence, obviously, for the wisdom and prudence of the Holy Spirit in all forms of renewal. Pope John was too old and wise and experienced to wish just boyishly for a whole long list of sheer novelties without solid basis or lasting values. Am I being sensible in these matters within my own order and community? Do I always go by sound and reasoned guidance on the part of those who have the chief responsibility in determining the details of renewal and adaptation? O Jesus, save me from my own pride, especially intellectual pride; help me to follow You only, with the guidance of Your Holy Spirit.

Again the devil took him to a very high mountain, and showed him all the kingdoms of the world and the glory of them; and he said to him, "All these I will give you, if you will fall down and worship me." Then Jesus said to him, "Begone, Satan! for it is written, 'You shall worship the Lord your God and him only shall you serve.'" Then the devil left him, and behold, angels came and ministered to him (Matthew 4:8-11).

It would almost seem as though Jesus was making fun of Satan at each stage of the three temptations, for by His humility each time He seems to lower the devil's opinion of Himself and His status, thus keeping him entirely in the dark, his curiosity unsatisfied. First he asks Jesus to perform by Himself an absolute miracle; then, since He apparently cannot do that, he asks for something just spectacular, relying on the help of God's angels; and now, finally, practically convinced that Jesus is, after all, just an ordinary human (even though with some extraordinary qualities), he goes to the limit of offering Him the whole world (a promise he could never fulfill—"the father of lies," as Jesus later calls him!) if only He will show him some form of worship. Subtle and clever as he undoubtedly is, Satan can also betray that supreme weakness of pride which shows itself so often in utter stupidity. Jesus rebuffs Satan openly: "You shall worship the Lord your God and him only shall you serve." Let me go away from this meditation with that divine text engraved indelibly in my memory and heart, so that no happening will ever find me in doubt about choosing between the things of Christ and those of Satan. Perhaps this very day there will be more than one occasion. Can I foresee any? How am I going to react? With the help of God's grace, I shall firmly.... O Jesus, help me to keep this resolution bravely!

The Testimony of John

And this is the testimony of John, when the Jews sent priests and Levites from Jerusalem to ask him, "Who are you?" He confessed, he did not deny, but confessed, "I am not the Christ." And they asked him, "What then? Are you Elijah?" He said, "I am not." "Are you the prophet?" And he answered, "No." They said to him then, "Who are you? Let us have an answer for those who sent us. What do you say about yourself?" (John 1:19-22)

As with all religious superiors, the Temple authorities had not only the right but also the responsibility to keep an eye on religious trends and behavior. When, therefore, they sent a delegation of priests out to the banks of the Jordan to interview this new religious phenomenon, John the Baptizer, they were in fact doing their duty in a quite lawful way. They had in mind, too, we may be sure, the prophecy of Malachi (4:5) which foretold that Elijah, or someone like him, would precede the Messiah's coming. Here, in fact, was a man who, after a four-hundred-years absence of prophets, not only acted like a prophet but even dressed as Elijah had done and was baptizing people in a strange new rite. At this point, let me take this view of maturity regarding the responsibility of my superiors to ensure not only the regularity of community life but also that all the members, as a whole and as individuals, are indeed living up to their public and private consecration to God. Sometimes this necessitates their asking questions.

If I am over-sensitive I probably show resentment and thus make their task more difficult, forgetting, as Don Bosco said, that "a superior must be a parent, a doctor, a judge" (*M.B.*, VII). I may possibly consider their questions as tactless or too probing, or think they suspect and do not trust me. This may even be so, but perhaps in the latter case I have caused it by my attitudes. Let me also remember that superiors remain human and have faults, but so do I! The task of superiors is by no means an easy one and they can only act according to the light they receive. They need the cooperation of their community as well as their sympathy in their very difficult task. St. John Bosco says: "Let us consider our superiors as brothers, even as loving fathers who have no other desire than the glory of God, the salvation of souls and the good progress of our society" *(M.B.,* XVIII). On analysis I will find that this is true, in spite of human deficiencies and faults. Let me be not only sympathetic and cooperative, but even merciful when faults appear. No matter how great their faults may seem, I can never be a judge of their motives, and the authority of Christ is always there in spite of faults. Have I been rather harsh and critical heretofore on these points? Abbot Marmion used to say: "I look above the head of my superior and there I see Christ." Let me prayerfully now resolve to do precisely this in the future.

> *He said, "I am the voice of one crying in the wilderness, 'Make straight the way of the Lord,' as the prophet Isaiah said" (John 1:23).*

All the conjecturing of John's interrogators was wrong and he made no pretense to be anything other than what he was. He stated clearly that the Christ, the Messiah, had already come and, implicitly, that He was a king. Oriental custom dictated that whenever the emperor or ruler's coming was announced it was expected of the local inhabitants that they should make comfortable the roads along which he would travel, fill in the holes, level the bumps, do away with unnecessary curves, etc. John had probably seen this happening and he uses this theme from Isaiah for the new king of the world, Jesus Christ, already born but soon to travel about among these very people. He exhorts them, in other words, to a spirit of truth at all times, to fill their somewhat empty hearts and lives with the love of God and neighbor, flatten the spirit of pride, straighten out any crooked habits, so that the King of Peace may find easy access into their hearts. He would bring with Him the supreme gift of true peace so that He might set up His permanent kingdom there. There are quite a number of practical points for my consideration here. How strict am I about truth? It has been wisely said that any time you find that truth stands in your way, you may be sure you are heading in the wrong direction. President Woodrow Wilson said: "Truth is the most robust, indestructible and formidable thing in the world." Do I regard and treat it as such? Are there no selfish gaps or pitfalls in my life, waiting for me to fill them up with the love of God and neighbor? What bumps of pride are still very obvious in my way of thinking and acting? Am I always upright with God and others? Let me answer these and other relevant questions quite honestly, since God already knows the answers! Jesus, meek and humble of heart, make my heart like Yours!

Now they had been sent from the Pharisees. They asked him, "Then why are you baptizing, if you are neither the Christ, nor Elijah, nor the prophet?" John answered them, "I baptize with water; but among you stands one whom you do not know, even he who comes after me, the thong of whose sandals I am not worthy to untie." This took place in Bethany beyond the Jordan, where John was baptizing (John 1:24-28).

It has been maintained that the first test of a truly great person is his humility. John the Baptist, therefore, who refused any opportunity to enhance his own importance, was remarkable because of his obvious humility and lack of human respect. Although six months older than Jesus, John made no account of this, considering himself as not even fit to be His slave, to do the meanest of personal tasks for Him. And why? Because he recognized in Jesus his Lord. That wiped out at once any equalities or superiorities in which he might have allowed himself to indulge. He wanted to get that idea across to the people too, saying, "Among you stands one whom you do not know." Later, St. Peter was to write: "You that are younger, be subject to the elders. Clothe yourselves, all of you, with humility toward one another, for 'God opposes the proud, but gives grace to the humble.' Humble yourselves therefore under the mighty hand of God, that in due time He may exalt you" (1 Pt. 5:6). How resentful people can be at times of those in higher authority than themselves, forgetting that in them, precisely because of their God-given authority, stands "someone whom you do not know," God Himself, who says to them in our regard, "He who hears you hears me, and he who rejects you rejects me, and he who rejects me rejects him who sent me" (Lk. 10:16). One of the marks of immaturity is an almost automatic suspicion about those who are older, especially if they are superiors. The basis of this may be jealousy, or just deep pride. What is my own attitude toward those in authority? Am I ever on the lookout for their human faults, perhaps criticizing them publicly or even holding them up to ridicule, passing judgment on them, never giving credit to possible saving motives? If so, I must really get down to a serious conversion from such immaturity to the laying of a solid foundation of saving humility such as John the Baptist possessed, who had far more to boast of than I. Jesus, meek and humble of heart.... Let me say this *often* today, and every day.

They Followed Jesus

The next day he saw Jesus coming toward him, and said, "Behold the Lamb of God, who takes away the sin of the world! This is he of whom I said, 'After me comes a man who ranks before me, for he was before me.' I myself did not know him; but for this I came baptizing with water, that he might be revealed to Israel." And John bore witness, "I saw the Spirit descend as a dove from heaven, and it remained on him. I myself did not know him; but he who sent me to baptize with water said to me, 'He on whom you see the Spirit descend and remain, this is he who baptizes with the Holy Spirit.' And I have seen and have borne witness that this is the Son of God" (John 1:29-34).

From what John says here, it seems likely that there had been little or no direct contact between Jesus and himself since the time of the Visitation. Quite probably his parents, being already so old at his birth, died while he was still young, and it has been strongly suggested that he went to live with the monastic Essenes in the desert, possibly even in the very Qumran caves where the now famous manuscripts recently came to light. This would explain his statement "I myself did not know him." The baptism of Jesus, however, made clear to him at once that this was indeed the Son of God, the Messiah. Once Jesus departed, he began loudly to proclaim the fact, giving witness to what he had seen after he himself had received his own mandate. After Vatican Council II we have heard so much about witnessing to Christ. What should it mean for me? *Lumen Gentium* itself tells me: "All the disciples of Christ, persevering in prayer and praising God, should present themselves as living sacrifices, holy and pleasing to God. Everywhere on earth they must bear witness to Christ and give an answer to those who seek an account of that hope of eternal life which is in them" (10). It refers then to St. Peter's first epistle: "In your hearts reverence Christ as Lord. Always be prepared to make a defense to any one who calls you to account for the hope that is in you, yet do it with gentleness and reverence; and keep your conscience clear, so that, when you are abused, those who revile your good behavior in Christ may be put to shame. For it is better to suffer for doing right, if that should be God's will, than for doing wrong" (3:15-17). Let me now prayerfully take each of the points in those two quotations and apply them to my own state of mind and behavior in order to see if I am as fearless as John the Baptist in giving my own worthwhile witness to Christ.

The next day again John was standing with two of his disciples and he looked at Jesus as he walked, and said, "Behold, the Lamb of God!" The two disciples heard him say this, and they followed Jesus (John 1:35-37).

As a result of the heavenly sign when Jesus was baptized, John was in such awe and reverence of Him that in his public proclamation of His coming he had described Him as a king. On the next occasion, however, he sees Jesus walking nearby and is so struck by His meekness and humility that he points Him out to those about him, saying, "Behold, the Lamb of God!" Did he realize at the same time the fuller significance in that description, a prophecy of His sacrifice ahead? Quite probably he did, for in the Hebrew mind the lamb was always associated with sacrifice for sin, and every year in Jerusalem literally thousands upon thousands of lambs were offered up in expiation for sin. Perhaps there flashed into John's mind, too, the prophecy of Isaiah concerning the Messiah: "He was oppressed and he was afflicted, yet he opened not his mouth; like a lamb that is led to the slaughter..." (11:19). Here was Jesus, then, in the flesh, walking along with all the meekness of a lamb destined for slaughter, and yet within Him was the strength and constancy of will that made Him a powerful man. The lamb does not know what lies ahead. Jesus does, but He goes along calmly, meekly, with perfect self-control, manfully, too, we can be sure, for at once two of John's own disciples left him to follow Christ. Let me not, then, associate any idea of weakness with meekness. And when at Holy Mass and Communion Jesus is presented to me under the title of the meek Lamb of God, let me recall that He comes to me then as strength for my body, mind and soul, to take away my sins and to give me the peace which can only come from a conscience founded strongly on the inherent strength of Christ. Can I say that I possess the virtue of meekness to any marked degree? "My child, perform your tasks in meekness; then you will be loved by those whom God accepts. The greater you are, the more you must humble yourself; so you will find favor in the sight of the Lord" (Eccl. 3:17-18). "Learn of me, for I am meek and humble [gentle and lowly] in heart" (Mt. 11:29).

The two disciples heard him [John] say this, and they followed Jesus.

We know from St. John the Evangelist's account that one of these was Andrew, whom he takes care to mention, as obviously it was a tremendous thing, spiritually and historically, to be the very first two to follow Jesus. Why, then does he not mention the other one? For the simple reason that it was himself and he did not wish to draw attention to himself or his privilege. This attitude we find throughout his Gospel and often it is only when he mentions tiny details (e.g., very briefly he mentions "the tenth hour," i.e., about 4 p.m.) that we realize that only someone actually there would have noticed and remembered such finer points. The psalmist David, in his lovely Psalm 42, sings: "As a hart longs for flowing streams, so longs my soul for thee, O God. My soul thirsts for God, for the living God. When shall I come and behold the face of God?" The young John was no doubt familiar with those words which were probably used often in prayer. This longing for God had drawn him to follow the Baptist. Later in the same psalm David says: "Deep calls to deep" and when John the Baptist pointed out Jesus, suddenly those words became very true for his young disciple, who then left, with the Baptist's implicit blessing, to follow Jesus. The abyss of humility in Jesus recognized at once and called out to the great depth of humility in young John, telling him that here indeed was the living water, the living God for whom his soul thirsted; that now at last the prayerful question, "When shall I come and behold the face of God?" was answered. Eagerly he answered the smiling invitation that flashed from the face of the young man, Jesus, into the heart of the younger John. The youth of the whole world was represented on that historic occasion in the privileged, generous youth of high and noble ideals founded on deep humility. "He who is humble and amiable will always be loved by all, by God and men" (St. John Bosco, *M.B.*, VI). Does not the example of young John inspire me to a brave imitation of this great virtue of his in mind and heart, and suggest a practical resolution regarding my own behavior today?

Come and See!

And he [John the Baptist] looked at Jesus as he walked (John 1:36).

Andrew and young John Zebedee may not have realized their historical importance in being the very first to follow the Messiah, but Jesus did, and hence we may naturally assume that when He turned as they came after Him it was with a smile. Never once in the Gospels is smiling or laughter mentioned regarding Jesus, but that is surely no justification for saying that He never smiled or laughed. Is it not more reasonable to suppose that, being perfect man as well as God, He possessed to a high degree these two very natural and even lovable characteristics of mankind? The lack of actual mention may simply be because the evangelists took it for granted. In any case, even though Jesus was to be outstandingly the Man of Sorrows, His Gospel or message is rightly called "the good news," with the word "rejoice" occurring frequently, as it did in the Old Testament. Jesus Himself said He had come to fulfill the Old in the New—including, therefore, rejoicing! Ecclesiastes exhorts: "Rejoice, O young man, in your youth, and let your heart cheer you in the days of your youth." This advice, however, is balanced with these further words: "Walk in the ways of your heart and the sight of your eyes. But know that for all these things God will bring you into judgment" (11:9). At any rate, let us try to get a complete and helpful picture of Jesus, one that does not exclude His handsome smile and gentle laughter. Here, then, smiling no doubt, Jesus turns around to the two eager followers and asks them kindly, "What do you seek?" What a thrill for them to hear that perfectly modulated, manly voice of His for the first time! Almost boyishly, they (or probably just young John himself) burst out: "Rabbi, where are you staying?" It should have been some other more formal introductory phrase, but this was the almost irrelevant question that shot out and probably made Jesus smile even more. Is there any harm in suggesting that it was at that very moment young John stole the heart of Jesus as "His favorite disciple"? Surely there was a definite twinkle in His limpid, all-seeing eyes as He smilingly parried the boyish question, saying, "Come and see" – in other words, "We are friends already. Come to my home!" John's reverence for Jesus began on that day and endured through all his life, as evidenced in his writings, for he saw then, on that occasion, for the first time the smiling face of the living God. Is there any encouragement and consolation for myself in all this? Any scope for imitation and resolution? Or have I grown too old and cynical already? Even that can be remedied! Ever-young Jesus,...

What do you seek?

That was the question Jesus put to us also when the time came for us to make a decision to follow our religious vocation. We weighed the matter carefully, perhaps went through a hard period of doubts and indecision, possibly even great obstacles, but finally we felt ready to say "Yes" to the call of Christ. No doubt we consulted wisely and felt that we knew the correct answer to that question "What do you seek?" Looking back now to that time, what exactly did I myself expect then? What was I really seeking? For whom was I searching – Jesus or myself? Surely I was anxious to follow Christ as generously and as zealously as possible. But has the picture changed since that time? Has it become dimmed and dulled? Is my generosity less now? My zeal? Youth can be such a wonderful period in life and, thanks be to God, a time of great generosity. What a pity, then, that it should fade. Young John followed Christ eagerly, generously, and yet we may be sure that he little guessed all that lay ahead of him because of his choice of Christ. The time would come when he too must suffer, mentally and physically (No fun being thrown into boiling oil!) and eventually live out his old age in exile on the rocky island of Patmos. But do we find in his writings, even sixty years after today's incident of his older boyhood, any trace of disillusionment with Christ or His teachings, any lessening of zeal or generosity? No, even to the last line of the solemn Apocalypse, Jesus was for him still "the First and the Last—the Alpha and the Omega." The ecstasy of his faith-filled reverence for the God-Man was then as fresh and youthful as on the day he left the Baptist to follow the gentle Lamb of God. Why should it be any different with me? Have I in any way lost my youthful enthusiasm and contact with Christ, my ideal? Let me pray now that my love of Him may be reinvigorated and my zeal never diminish as I seek to imitate Him.

Come and see.

We have seen Jesus saying this with a smile, and we have noted that He playfully dodged giving a direct reply to John's boyish question. John and Andrew went with Him to where He was staying, and even though we can be quite sure it was a poor place, we read that "they stayed with him that day." It wasn't the place that mattered to them, it was Jesus. If only John had given us a fuller account and told us the details of the long conversation they had with Jesus during those many hours, the way He spoke and acted, His gestures, smiles, gentle laugh or serious look, questions and answers, advice, and the thousands of things we still do not know about that virile young personality that was Christ, both man and God. We feel that these details would help us tremendously and make us more keen and enthusiastic in our love and service of Christ. And the answer is a disconcerting silent mystery. Surely there must be a reason for this? And surely the answer is that God wants more from us than just ephemeral youthful enthusiasm that can vanish too easily like the froth on a glass of beer. God appreciates our youthfulness and its ardors and enterprises, for He too was young throughout His whole life on earth. But He wants, above all, our spirit of faith and solidarity. To have shown us in detail all that lay ahead when we first set out to follow Him might have brought a disillusionment too heavy for youth to bear. But Jesus had looked deep into our souls, as into the heart of young John. He saw the goodness and love in our hearts and He knew that if we could be tided over the times of trial ahead, all that essential goodness within us would be of tremendous value to ourselves and to Him in our more mature work of spreading His kingdom. "Come and see," He said therefore to us too—"take it as it comes, not expecting too much, or even anything except that I shall always be there with you, helping you, staying close by your side all the time, unless you yourself send me away or walk off by yourself!" At this stage of my life can I say I have responded so far? Is there anything to remedy? O Jesus, still my Ideal, awaken in me once more my youthful faith, love and boundless trust in You, for You are still to me the First and Last, my Alpha and Omega, and I accept trustfully even Your hidden plans for me, including trials.

We Have Found the Messiah

One of the two who heard John speak, and followed him, was Andrew, Simon Peter's brother. He first found his brother Simon, and said to him, "We have found the Messiah" (which means Christ). He brought him to Jesus. Jesus looked at him, and said, "So you are Simon the son of John? You shall be called Cephas" (which means Peter) (John 1:40-42).

On leaving Jesus, the first two disciples, John and Andrew, must have been eager to tell others about Him (Andrew was probably fairly young too). Andrew at least told his brother Simon, and we can be sure that John told his own brother, James, even though in his modesty he does not say so in his Gospel. The Baptist had announced that the kingdom of God was at hand, and these two young enthusiasts had the privilege of being the first to enroll followers of Christ. Do I ever think of my own individual importance as a religious, and as a member of a community? Vatican Council II speaks clearly on this point: "By the charity to which they lead, the evangelical counsels join their followers to the Church and her mystery in a special way. Since this is so, the spiritual life of these followers should be devoted to the welfare of the whole Church. Thence arises their duty of working to implant and strengthen the kingdom of Christ in souls and to extend that kingdom to every land. This duty is to be discharged to the extent of their capacities and in keeping with the form of their proper vocation. The means chosen may be prayer or active undertakings. It is for this reason that the Church preserves and fosters the special character of her various religious communities" *(Lumen Gentium*, 44). And again in another decree: "By their prayers and active labors, religious men and women play an indispensable role too in rooting and strengthening the kingdom of Christ in souls, and in causing it to expand" (*Ad Gentes*, 15). All that may be clear enough in its intent, but what about my own individual part in it? There is always the danger of the routine of duties gradually rendering the ideal less attractive, obscuring the real purpose behind those very duties considered as part of my apostolate in spreading the kingdom of Christ. Constant reminders are necessary. How anxious and zealous am I to awaken in others an interest in Jesus Christ, Christian ideals and behavior, priestly and religious vocations, a dedicated laity? Does my life and conduct say loudly to others, "I have found the Messiah"? The world is still looking for Him, and perhaps it looks often to *me* to see if I know where He is. What has been my answer so far: silence? a mystified look? a shake of the head? What is going to be my answer henceforth?... But how? Obviously I need to pray now, don't I?

> *The next day Jesus decided to go to Galilee. And he found Philip and said to him, "Follow me." Now Philip was from Bethsaida, the city of Andrew and Peter. Philip found Nathanael, and said to him, "We have found him of whom Moses in the law and also the prophets wrote, Jesus of Nazareth, the son of Joseph" (John 1:43-45).*

Here in quick succession we see the first disciples arriving, one after the other, and again it is a question of the word spreading from one to another. John and Andrew told their brothers. Andrew and Simon Peter probably told Philip, for the Gospel makes note that he came from the same place as they did. Philip in turn finds Nathanael. In our age of extreme scientific progress and advanced technology, uncountable millions are spent on sending satellites into outer space, but how much energy and zeal is spent on sending the message of God's kingdom throughout our own tiny planet? True, much is being done by many, but proportionately little. Nor is it necessarily a case of having to go directly to the foreign missions, for the seed of the word of God is waiting to be sown at our very own doorstep. Souls only a few paces away are lying in a parched field that waits for God's water from our hands. When a soul sincerely gives itself to Christ, it gives itself to others implicitly also, for it is anxious, like the apostles, to take Christ to others, to be a witness of Him and His teachings in example, word and deed. That is my inherent duty, too, but I must remember that my witnessing must be totally Christlike, not just a projection of my own pious, apostolic or zealous image. If it is a camouflaged self I am trying to project, the world will only smile cynically and move further away from the kingdom of Christ. In God's eyes what is my image as a disciple of Christ, anxious to spread His kingdom? Let me think now, resolve, and pray "Thy kingdom come...."

> *Nathanael said to him, "Can anything good come out of Nazareth?" Philip said to him, "Come and see." Jesus saw Nathanael coming to him, and said of him, "Behold an Israelite indeed, in whom there is no guile!" Nathanael said to him, "How do you know me?" Jesus answered him, "Before Philip called you, when you were under the fig tree, I saw you." Nathanael answered him, "Rabbi, you are the Son of God! You are the King of Israel!" Jesus answered him, "Because I said to you, I saw you under the fig tree, do you believe? You shall see greater things than these." And he said to him, "Truly, truly, I say to you, you will see heaven opened, and the angels of God ascending and descending upon the Son of man" (John 1:46-51).*

Nathanael (Bartholomew) was evidently a young man with his head screwed on the right way! He was not one to be rushed off his feet by the mere praise or excitement of others; he was not just a mob follower. Hence even when his friend Philip tells him enthusiastically about finding Jesus, he takes it quite coolly and counters it with what might have been considered a rather disdainful or pessimistic question were it not denied by Jesus' praise of him. Nevertheless he allows himself to be persuaded to come along and see this new prodigy. There is a lesson for me here also: to make sure that my convictions are solid and that my behavior is based on sound Christian and religious principles, not just passing whims and enthusiasm. Jesus sees Nathanael coming and utters words of high praise about him, saying he is one "in whom there is no guile." If he had been over susceptible to praise, the young man might well have blushed and showed his thrill, but he keeps quite cool and challenges His reasons for such a statement. It is only when Jesus tells him some particularly intimate detail that only God could have seen, that this solid, upright young man is completely won over and becomes enthusiastic himself about the Son of God and His kingdom. His was an allegiance that endured right through the long years ahead and met its culmination in a particularly painful martyrdom, for we are told that he was skinned alive. What are my own reactions to praise? Do I purr inwardly even when I attribute success to its true source by some such phrase as "Thanks be to God!"? My reactions to praise (and blame) can also play their part positively or negatively in the spread of Christ's kingdom, for those about me always observe the ways and example of the so-called apostle. Resolution? "O Jesus, all praise and all thanksgiving be every moment Thine!" *Deo gratias* for....

The Mother of Jesus Was There

On the third day there was a marriage at Cana in Galilee, and the mother of Jesus was there; Jesus also was invited to the marriage, with his disciples (John 2:1-2).

Jesus had invited His first followers to "come and see." Here we find them already "on the third day" in such great intimacy with Him that they are present, all five of them at least, at a wedding feast. And tucked away in the opening sentence above is the lovely presence of Mary, His mother: "And the mother of Jesus was there," surely one of the most beautiful sentences in the Bible! How like John the Evangelist to bring her into the picture so lovingly, so delicately, he who loved her so much and represented all mankind as her son when Jesus died. If we read carefully, we shall recognize in the Gospel story that Mary was always there in the humble, quiet background of the life of Jesus. It was a presence, we can be sure, that He deeply appreciated, for He loved His mother tenderly, perfectly, otherwise He would neither have been the perfect man nor the perfect God. Any failing here in this most elementary of man's natural instincts would be an unforgivable contradiction of the whole purpose of the Son of God becoming man not only to redeem us at the end of His life but to be "the Way, the Truth, and the Life" by His own example in all things. How the bigoted and prejudiced fail to grasp such elementary reasoning is more than amazing. It is said that we honor Mary too much and that our devotion to her detracts from the worship due to God. Did Jesus honor His mother too much, that mother whom God the Father had specially chosen and prepared for her high dignity? Can we ever hope to attain to even a degree of His love and respect for her? How can sensible and sound devotion to Mary detract from the worship of God when its primary object is precisely to honor God through an instrument so much worthier than ourselves? Whatever honor we pay to Mary she passes on at once to God, knowing it is intended for Him. Jesus, her Son, is my model, but do I imitate Him as fully as I should in the love and honor I show to her who is also constantly there in the background of my life, as in His, and has been present at all its major events? Is my devotion to her really sincere and practical? Do I have recourse to her at all times, or perhaps *only* in my needs? Let me consider this carefully now—and pray.

> *When the wine failed, the mother of Jesus said to him, "They have no wine." And Jesus said to her, "O woman, what have you to do with me? My hour has not yet come." His mother said to the servants, "Do whatever he tells you." Now six stone jars were standing there, for the Jewish rites of purification, each holding twenty or thirty gallons. Jesus said to them, "Fill the jars with water." And they filled them up to the brim. He said to the servants, "Now draw some out, and take it to the steward of the feast." So they took it (John 2:3-8).*

Early in his own Gospel, St. Luke told us that "his mother kept all these things in her heart" (2:51). Now we find Jesus, so many years later, at the start of His public life, a physically and intellectually mature young man who was also God. How much must have filled the heart and memory of Mary about her beloved Son! How anxious she must have been especially in these early days to do all she tactfully could to help His kingdom get off to a good start. Now at this homely social feast she comes to know of the young married couple's embarrassment and she takes it as a God-given opportunity. Notice her supreme tact in presenting the situation to Jesus in a simple way that is not even a direct suggestion. Our English translation of Jesus' reply is rather rough but the term "O woman" was actually a formal, even ceremonial, term of respect, not a direct and public brush-off of Mary by our Lord, for how could He ever be callously discourteous in public to the mother who had borne, reared, loved and served Him so tenderly for so many long years! Let us concentrate on the sound fact that Jesus at once did the very thing He knew Mary desired, and in a miraculous way—in fact, His first known miracle. Have there been no "miracles" in my life, even minor ones? Mary's presence and intercession were certainly there, I can be sure, and influential, had I but realized it. Let me now thank Jesus and Mary for their joint interest in me, with special regard to particular occasions I should recall. For practical action, let me resolve never to separate them in my mind and heart. Jesus and Mary, please....

His mother said to the servants, "Do whatever he tells you" (John 2:5).

If indeed Mary had been publicly rebuked or rebuffed, how could she possibly have turned right away—smiling kindly, no doubt—to the servants and said, "Do whatever he tells you"? Beautiful words, but, sadly for us, the very last words of Mary to be recorded in the Gospels. But what wonderful words those were! How we treasure someone's last words before dying, but even though Mary did not, of course, keep actual silence until her death, let us treasure these last recorded words of hers as such, for the marvelous message they give to each of the souls entrusted to her motherly care. She wants me, then, to do whatever Jesus tells me. Jesus tells me many things, in the Scriptures, through the Church, through my superiors, at meditation, spiritual reading and prayer, in a thousand different ways. Let me try to listen carefully and to obey to the very best of my ability, confident in His ever-abundant, ever-helpful grace. But let me not forget what He tells me also, by His own example, about my own attitude to His holy mother and mine. He Himself gave her to me in that role in the person of young John at the foot of the cross. He wants me to stand by Mary throughout all my life, as John did, protecting her if need be, loving and serving her. The love of Jesus for His mother infinitely surpassed the love of any other man for the woman who bore him. Surely He expects from me as close an imitation as possible in every practical way. This should be also out of a sense of gratitude for all she has done for me in so many ways. Let me, then, cultivate the habit of thinking of Mary often, doing my various activities carefully out of respect for her presence and attentive eye, asking her to suggest to Jesus what she knows to be best for me. Let me be eminently practical, not vague, in seeing to it that Mary is not a forgotten background figure but an intimate companion in my life as an apostle, a mother to whom I pray often, knowing she understands and loves me and will do all in her power to help me to be constantly pleasing to Jesus and to lead me straight into heaven. "Do whatever he tells you!" Prayer. Resolution.

Whip of Cords

The Passover of the Jews was at hand, and Jesus went up to Jerusalem. In the temple he found those who were selling oxen and sheep and pigeons, and the money-changers at their business. And making a whip of cords, he drove them all, with the sheep and oxen, out of the temple; and he poured out the coins of the money-changers and overturned their tables (John 2:13-15).

Right after the homey but striking event at the Cana wedding feast, we suddenly find Jesus plunging into His role of divine authority in a way that must have occasioned much talk, comment and contention. By starting off His public life at a happy social occasion, our Lord doubtless wanted us to take due note of our social responsibilities—perhaps even of our recreational periods sensibly used—but here we find Him much more solemn and even severe regarding our spiritual obligations. From writers of those times other than the evangelists we are given a good background for this particular incident. From them we learn that although from a distance the temple seemed to pilgrims like a mountain of shining white snow (Josephus Flavius), from close up one's attention was at once drawn from its external magnificence to the sordidness and frightful smell that surrounded it and even penetrated a good distance into some of the sacred courtyards. Jesus must have noticed this even as a boy, but now was His first opportunity to do something about it. He first made a whip out of cords in order to drive out the animals and at once there must have been a protest. We can imagine that handsome, manly face of His dead serious, those marvelous eyes blazing with righteous indignation, and that resonant voice sounding clear and authoritative above all the noise. The extraordinary thing is that He got everyone's attention. They saw the look of determination on His face, the whip in His authoritative hand, heard the ring of command in His voice, and with that they fled in terror, together with their animals and birds, out of God's desecrated temple of prayer and worship. This indeed must have been a quite startling event in Jerusalem that day, attracting tremendous interest in this extraordinary young man who had spoken and acted and punished as one having authority.

Let me stop here for a moment and consider its personal application. Just as the Hebrews in the temple precincts had allowed trade and merchandise to become more important than actual worship (for we are told by historians that exorbitant prices were generally charged), is there not in me the danger of putting a price on things concerning God? In other words, do I perform various religious and spiritual duties through inferior motives, e.g., because I must, or because it's safer, or it's good to have a routine? In this way is there not the awful possibility that my piety and love of God is not fully genuine? Do I really try to concentrate on the love of God and His true worship when I am performing my practices of piety and religious exercises? O Jesus, help me to drive out from my life all that is sham, and to revitalize all that has become numbed through sheer routine.

> *And he told those who sold the pigeons, "Take these things away; you shall not make my Father's house a house of trade." His disciples remembered that it was written, "Zeal for thy house will consume me" (John 2:16-17).*

Picture the confusion on that amazing occasion! With the animal traders Jesus seems to have been quite rough, because they needed it. This picture alone should prove His essential manliness and courage, His lack of human respect. But notice the contrasting gentleness towards the poor pigeon-sellers. The others He had driven out forcibly, but He merely speaks to these solemnly. Why? For the simple reason that the others were rich and these were poor: they hadn't the money to buy and maintain large animals in number; all they could do was to use their wits, catch doves and pigeons and sell them. How often indeed poverty drives towards wrongdoing, and for this reason Jesus was gentle with the poorest traders, gentle, but still reprimanding, for they too were at fault. Perhaps He was trying to tell them that even though being poor was a great problem, trying to get rich was not the true answer. Throughout the Gospels we see the compassion of Jesus for the poor, but it is well to keep today's incident in mind also. Abbé Pierre, "the ragpickers' priest," has said that each time we stretch out a hand to help the poor we should try also to seek a remedy. The remedy may lie with themselves or in their attitude, and here perhaps we can tactfully educate them to think and act in a Christian spirit, instead of rebelling against God or being vindictive by crimes, big or small.

How often we are told that two-thirds of the people in the world today go to bed hungry every night. This thought doubtlessly makes us feel grateful for what we ourselves have through the kindness of divine Providence and its generous instruments, our benefactors. At the same time we should frequently question ourselves as to what we can do in some way to alleviate the sufferings of the poor. At the very least we can pray for them and for a speedy solution to the world problems of poverty, hunger and suffering, but there is a definite need for religious to set a public example also of concern and anxiety which takes on very practical forms. Is there some way I can bring this matter up for discussion in community? What can I myself do about helping the poor? Jesus, You set us an example of poverty; help us to....

> *The Jews then said to him, "What sign have you to show us for doing this?" Jesus answered them, "Destroy this temple, and in three days I will raise it up." The Jews then said, "It has taken forty-six years to build this temple, and will you raise it up in three days?" But he spoke of the temple of his body. When therefore he was raised from the dead, his disciples remembered that he had said this; and they believed the scripture and the word which Jesus had spoken (John 2:18-22).*

The furor eventually died down and it is surely logical to think of Jesus meanwhile praying in the temple, making reparation to the Father for the sins of disrespect and dishonesty. Certain people now approach Him for an explanation of His conduct, possibly quite unfriendly because of their own vested interests in the temple trade. That there were temple authorities among them is more than likely, because later, at His Passion, they were to recall His astounding answer to their present question. But they, because of their hardness of heart, were on an entirely different wavelength and completely misunderstood His reply. The disciples alone saw the full sense of it afterwards. How often we too misinterpret the ways of God, forgetting that He is all-wise and all-knowing, that He can see into the future and knows what is going to turn out for our eventual good. But because our minds do not at once grasp all this and we see only the immediate bleak picture of what is happening, we rebel or sulk or kick against the goad. This may be especially the case when it concerns correction. I myself should be the very first to make a whip of cords to drive out from God's temple of my heart all that is unworthy there, so that even this body of mine may one day be fit for the glory of total resurrection in Christ.

What, then, is my attitude to correction, whether self-imposed or coming from others? Surely this is something very important in my life if I am really trying to strive after Christian perfection. Let me try, then, to adjust my mind to Christ's and try to do something concrete about it this very day. Lord Jesus, I recall now gratefully those words: "My son, do not regard lightly the discipline of the Lord, nor lose courage when you are punished by him, for the Lord disciplines him whom he loves, and chastises every son whom he receives" (Heb. 12:5). Help me, Lord, never to forget this.

He Must Increase

Now a discussion arose between John's disciples and a Jew over purifying. And they came to John, and said to him, "Rabbi, he who was with you beyond the Jordan, to whom you bore witness, here he is, baptizing, and all are going to him." John answered, "No one can receive anything except what is given him from heaven. You yourselves bear me witness, that I said, I am not the Christ, but I have been sent before him.... He must increase, but I must decrease" (John 3:25-30).

John the Baptist had already given public acknowledgment to Jesus as the Messiah and here he does so again, for his virtue of humility is solid, not sporadic. He recalls his testimony of Christ to his questioners and points out the valuable lesson for me also that "no one can receive anything except what is given him from above." This is something I must very frequently recall to mind. God has given me all my talents to be used for His greater glory and the good of souls (including my own) and yet how natural the temptation may come for me to feel proud of them or even boast of them as though I were self-made. St. Ignatius of Loyola admitted that he suffered from this inclination for long years but by dint of perseverance in sound reasoning with himself he kept the tendency in strict control. Hence I should not feel too discouraged at having such an unworthy inclination, though God still wishes me to put up a constant brave fight in the matter of controlling it sensibly. When we feel that we have done something really well, it is natural enough to feel happy about it if we are praised, natural enough even to feel a bit hurt if it goes totally unacknowledged. Taking either of these to a point of exaggeration is where danger enters. If the praise that comes our way tends to swell our head, we are called upon by Christ to imitate more closely His own spirit of humility which gave all praise and thanks to the Father. If we become oversensitive about not receiving the praise or acknowledgment we think we deserve, then we have a very definite area for improvement also and should aim at an ever greater spirit of humility which will help us to overcome it.

Let me pray now about this, conscious of how easy it is to slip into vanity. I have before me now the fine example of John the Baptist and his sincere anxiety that he himself should diminish so that Jesus alone might increase in glory. What wonderful self-control! I too must strive after that. In what ways do I still fail? How can I improve? Jesus, You have given us John the Baptist as a wonderful model of true humility; please help me....

He must increase, but I must decrease (John 3:30).

John the Baptist had been given a tremendous mission to fulfill in introducing the Messiah to the world. He had fulfilled his task well and courageously so far and would continue to do so until God's will directed otherwise. In the process he could have exalted his own importance but he constantly abased himself before the stature of Christ, saying: "He must increase, but I must decrease." When Msgr. Rumeau, the Bishop of Angers, paid his first visit to Pope St. Pius X, he remained on his knees, but, he says, "my attitude visibly distressed him, and bidding me to rise at once, he protested, saying, 'Not on your knees, Monsignor, for I am the least of God's priests.' And when I pressed him for advice upon a grave matter, I noticed that before replying he invariably turned his eyes to the crucifix on his table as if seeking counsel there." Here indeed was the profound humility of the Baptist renewed again in the Vicar of Christ who, not in mere words, but in deeds was saying the same thing: "He must increase; I must decrease."

I may well recall also the words of the psalmist: "O Lord, my eyes are not raised too high; I do not occupy myself with things too great and too marvelous for me, but I have calmed and quieted my soul" (Ps. 131:1-2). Let me compare my own attitude of mind and my actual behavior with all the foregoing, then adapt the psalmist's prayer to my own particular needs in this regard.

The humility of John the Baptist—soon to pass out of the scene, his task accomplished—deserves deep study and imitation if I am to be a worthy follower of Christ, a worthy religious. Vatican Council II stressed the importance of this virtue for religious, priests and lay people alike. What it says of priests can apply to me also: "Conscious of his own weakness, the true minister of Christ labors in humility, testing what is God's will.... By such responsible and voluntary humility and obedience, priests make themselves like Christ, having in themselves the attitude which was in Christ Jesus, who 'emptied himself, taking the nature of a slave...becoming obedient to death' (Phil. 2:7-9)" *(Presbyterorum Ordinis*, 15-16). St. Francis de Sales teaches that the quiet, constant effort to control our look and tone, our words and manner, in our ordinary everyday life will in time effectually remove every real hindrance to perfection. The same applies to humility. "Hold tight to holy humility," he says. "The heart that loves God must be attached solely to His love. It is a false interpretation of the word 'courage' to give in to pride and vanity. Christians call them cowardice and meanness of spirit, whereas patience, meekness, gentleness, humility...to these they give the name of courage. For such has been the courage of our Captain, of His Mother and His Apostles, and all the most valiant soldiers of the heavenly army." His close disciple, St. John Bosco, confirms: "Our help must come from on high, but in order to get it we must descend very low. The lower we stand, the more help will come from on high" *(M.B.*, XIII). And in his own humility he could aver: "Remember always that Don Bosco was not and is not anything else but a poor instrument in the hands of a most able and all-powerful artist, God—to God, then, all praise, honor and glory" *(M.B.*, XVI).

The sentiments of these two similar-minded servants of God should encourage me in my humble endeavors to give God at all times credit for any good that seems to be accomplished through me. I am only God's poor instrument. Without Him I am utterly useless: "He must increase; I must decrease." Resolution? Prayer?

Living Water

He left Judea and departed again to Galilee. He had to pass through Samaria. So he came to a city of Samaria, called Sichar, near the field that Jacob gave to his son Joseph. Jacob's well was there, and so Jesus, wearied as he was with his journey, sat down beside the well. It was about the sixth hour (John 4:3-5).

As a result of the Syrian occupation some time before, the Samaritans were a mixture of peoples. Their religion also was a mixture of worship of the true God and others, with an adherence to part of the Bible only. They expected the Messiah and had their own special temple at Mount Garizim in rivalry to that of Jerusalem. Because of this, they were deeply resented by the Jews, especially since, shortly before the time of Christ, some Samaritans had profaned the temple at Jerusalem. All contact between Jews and Samaritans was considered unholy, even to the drinking of water, for that of the Samaritans was considered more impure than a pig's blood (cf. G. Pace, *Antologia Biblica II*, p. 120). This background gives an extraordinary significance to the gesture of Jesus in asking the Samaritan woman for a drink, and she herself points this out. However, I must first recall that Jesus was very tired. He allows this very human condition to be perpetuated in the Gospel for our encouragement, so that we may know that He appreciates what it is like to be really tired and weary after a hard day's work, or after a long and wearisome journey. Let me picture Him, then, as I myself have often been, slightly weary or really tired, as He sits so humanly on the edge of the well wall, leaning against the upper structure, eyes closed, mind on His Father in whose cause He has tirelessly labored. He could have drawn the water Himself but He has a purpose in waiting. Here, then, we see Jesus actually relaxing for a short span of time. Modern man has become very much enslaved by almost ceaseless activity, which has found its way quite readily into religious communities under the plausible disguise of zeal. It would be well, however, for the matter to be examined in the cold light of reason to see whether over occupation is leading to over preoccupation with matters of far less importance than union with God. Some people cannot bear to relax for a single moment, but that attitude is not necessarily virtuous. If we are not at peace with ourselves and with others when thus busily occupied, it might well be merely a mania. St. Francis de Sales used to warn firmly against allowing any such thing to enter into our lives, for, as we hear often enough, "God is not in the whirlwind."

When we find ourselves becoming over occupied, generally tension sets in and should be taken as a providential warning to stop deliberately, to pray for light to God's Holy Spirit, and then to try to decide calmly how best to unwind a bit, to get better organized, to get our duty priorities in right order. I have the example of the tired Jesus before me in the Gospel. Let me now ask Him to help me sort out this matter sensibly. Jesus,...

> *There came a woman of Samaria to draw water. Jesus said to her, "Give me a drink." For his disciples had gone away into the city to buy food. The Samaritan woman said to him, "How is it that you, a Jew, ask a drink of me, a woman of Samaria?" For Jews have no dealings with Samaritans. Jesus answered her, "If you knew the gift of God, and who it is that is saying to you, 'Give me a drink,' you would have asked him, and he would have given you living water" (John 4:7-10).*

The kingdom of God knows no boundaries and does not exclude even the generally despised Samaritans. Jesus sees approaching Him a soul to be saved, to be helped, to be raised to a better life. All uncharitable conventions set aside, He pretends it is He who needs help: "Give me a drink." A nice lesson of tact here in my approach to others, especially the more awkward or difficult or despised. One thing I must be on my guard against in all apostolic works is that of a superior or even condescending attitude. At times I must be ready even to make myself lower than those I serve in the name of Christ. I am only God's instrument. When He sees someone in need,

He is like a good father who hands his little child a coin to drop into the beggar's hat. Whatever I have to give comes from God, my Father. Let me give it, then, with childlike simplicity and goodness, tact and kindness.

Let me review my attitudes to see whether I have been imitating Jesus and what I can do in practice to improve. Dear Master, I am often weary myself from labors and traveling, sometimes weary of myself. Give me, please, to drink of the abundant, sweet and living water of Your saving grace, so that I may persevere in trying to be good and to do good in Your own tactful manner. Resolution.

> *The woman said to him, "Sir, you have nothing to draw with, and the well is deep; where do you get that living water? Are you greater than our father Jacob, who gave us the well, and drank from it himself, and his sons, and his cattle?" Jesus said to her, "Every one who drinks of this water will thirst again, but whoever drinks of the water that I shall give him, will never thirst; the water that I shall give him will become in him a spring of water welling up to eternal life." The woman said to him, "Sir, give me this water, that I may not thirst, nor come here to draw" (John 4:11-15).*

There is so much goodness and kindness in the world. In my endeavors to help others I might well make this my starting point instead of the negative one of criticism, fault-finding and reproach. The Samaritan woman's goodness of heart at once responded to Jesus' appeal for help, even though she manifests her surprise that He, a Jew, should ask her, a despised Samaritan, for a drink of water. I must be ready for that, too, in my apostolate...rejection, scorn, or doubting of motives...but let me not be put out by it.

Let me try to be supremely tactful, as Jesus was, smile away the rebuff and try by kindness and humility to win people's confidence. I must not give that first impression that so often turns people off, viz., that of being a rather loud and showy "do-gooder." That was not Christ's way. It must not be mine. There may have to be publicity at times, but let me not lose my sense of proportion and values. Let me not forget that Christ is the one who handles me as an instrument and can only make use of that instrument if it is pliable in His hands. Let me be the docile, ever-ready cup into which He can pour the living water with which to satisfy the thirst of others. The world (in spite of denials) really thirsts for Christ. Let me try to be as large a cup as I can by using all the talents He has given me to their fullest extent, but always humbly, tactfully, thankfully. In this way, the living water that Jesus will pour into my cup will become a wonderful spring of water for others as well as myself. Jesus, help me....

Cure of the Ruler's Son

So he came again to Cana in Galilee, where he had made the water wine. And at Capernaum there was an official whose son was ill. When he heard that Jesus had come from Judea to Galilee, he went and begged him to come down and heal his son, for he was at the point of death (John 4:46-47).

Once again we find Jesus at Cana. He had come now into His own territory, for Nazareth was nearby and Jesus Himself had testified that "a prophet has no honor in his own country." In spite of that He returns and proceeds at once to work another miracle at the very same place where He performed the first one, Cana. This time He does so in an even more remarkable way, hoping to convince the hardhearted unbelievers who should have been the very first to support Him but were probably impeded by pride and jealousy. The changing of the water into wine was still very vivid in the minds of those privileged to have been present when it occurred, and the fame of it had doubtless spread through Galilee, at least. Hence when the grapevine telegraph brought news to Capernaum (Capharnaum), sixteen miles away, that Jesus had returned to Cana, it must have been spoken of quite a bit, so that even this high-ranking official heard of it. He makes a point of coming himself to see Jesus personally, arriving in the very late evening. In his example we may see two things: first, a deep anxiety for the welfare of his dying son that made him go to what must have been quite an extreme for him in the hope of obtaining a cure; and secondly, the profound act of faith he made in Jesus. From the first point I can draw the thought that when it concerns the spiritual welfare of those in my charge, who should be particularly dear to me in Christ, I should be ready to sacrifice my own convenience, no matter what the cost.

If the laity are urged by the Council to be "led by the light of the Gospel and the mind of the Church, and motivated by Christian love" *(Apostolicam Actuositatem,* 7), then surely this applies to me, for I am also an active apostle of Christ. The overflow of the love of God in my own heart will naturally want to give itself especially to the more needy of my neighbors, without counting the cost.

Let me examine prayerfully, with Jesus Himself, my own mental attitude and behavior towards the needy. When I do my good deeds, are my motives always pure, i.e., for the sole love of God seen in my neighbor, or are there not sometimes strings attached for my own benefit? How really disinterested is my so-called charity and helpfulness?

> *Jesus therefore said to him, "Unless you see signs and wonders you will not believe." The official said to him, "Sir, come down before my child dies." Jesus said to him, "Go; your son will live" (John 4:48-50).*

Jesus seems to receive the ruler with a certain amount of aloofness, but that, we can be sure, was only in order to test his spirit of faith, for He is pleased indeed when the man shows it by insisting. His faith may not have been perfect—if it had been he might just have asked for Jesus to perform the miracle at a distance (which is precisely what He did), but he insists that Jesus accompany him in order to heal his son. Perhaps he even had a carriage or a horse ready to take Him there at once, for the boy was "at the point of death" and sixteen miles by foot is a fair distance to travel along a winding road, especially at night, to the lakeside.

Perhaps Jesus smiled seeing such a luxurious conveyance awaiting Him, the poorest of the poor. This may have been His major motive in performing the cure at a distance, rather than give any cause for talk against His professed poverty. Since this suggestion is by no means improbable and even if we seem to be stretching the idea somewhat, let me avail myself of it as a reminder of my own vow and virtue of poverty that should be based not on a weak or vacillating faith but on the solid example of Jesus Himself and the firm teaching of His Church. Vatican II loudly praises "poverty voluntarily embraced in imitation of Christ" as a "witness which is highly esteemed, especially today.... By it a man shares in the poverty of Christ, who became poor for our sake when He had been rich, that we might be enriched by His poverty" *(Perfectae Caritatis,* 13). But surely neither Christ nor His Church wish us to interpret that as material riches and comforts! As St. John Bosco says: "Let us not forget that we are poor, and we must have this spirit of poverty not only in our hearts and in our interior detachment from material things but we must also show it exteriorly to the world" *(M.B.,* V).

Jesus has given me the example but does my spirit of faith measure up to it in actual fact? In what definite ways do I give external witness to my interior spirit of poverty? Let this be a ruthlessly honest examination, for it is most important nowadays.

> *The man believed the word that Jesus spoke to him and went his way. As he was going down, his servants met him and told him that his son was living. So he asked them the hour when he began to mend, and they said to him, "Yesterday at the seventh hour the fever left him." The father knew that was the hour when Jesus had said to him, "Your son will live"; and he himself believed, and all his household. This was now the second sign that Jesus did when He had come from Judea to Galilee (John 4:50-54).*

Now the man's faith comes to perfection for he accepts the word of Jesus, no longer insists on His accompanying him and returns home. What joy for him, then, when he meets his excited servants hastening to meet him in order to tell him the wonderful news of his son's cure. He asks the time of the actual happening and deep gratitude puts the joyful seal on his faith when he hears it took place at the exact time Jesus had promised it. When he tells the others, naturally "all his household" believed with him and he became an apostle in his own sphere.

How necessary faith is for me too in my apostolate and witnessing for Christ. Vatican II speaks of "the witness of a living and mature faith, namely, one trained to see difficulties clearly and to master them.... This faith needs to prove its fruitfulness by penetrating the believer's entire life, including its worldly dimensions, and by activating him towards justice and love, especially regarding the needy" *(Gaudium et Spes,* 21). This brings me right back to the point of helping those who are in need. In order to do so effectively as a witness to Christ I must have that fellowship of feeling based deeply on my own spirit of poverty ("The poor help the poor") and perfect faith in Jesus who uses me as His instrument. O Jesus, I have so much still to learn in these vital matters of poverty, faith and effective witnessing. Help me by Your example and words soon to live up to these standards.

Rejection at Nazareth

And Jesus returned in the power of the Spirit into Galilee, and a report concerning him went out through all the surrounding country. And he taught in their synagogues, being glorified by all. And he came to Nazareth, where he had been brought up; and he went to the synagogue, as his custom was, on the sabbath day. And he stood up to read; and there was given to him the book of the prophet Isaiah. He opened the book and found the place where it was written, "The Spirit of the Lord is upon me, because he has anointed me to preach good news to the poor. He has sent me to proclaim release to the captives and recovering of sight to the blind, to set at liberty those who are oppressed, to proclaim the acceptable year of the Lord" (Luke 4:14-19).

The fame of Jesus was spreading fast and He was actually invited to His own nearby town of Nazareth to speak publicly in the synagogue. His coming must have been eagerly awaited by many who knew Him so well, having seen Him grow up in their very midst, marveling sometimes at His splendid manly qualities and virtues. Since He had left them, word had come back of many wonders performed by Him which seemed to confirm the great future that the more discerning must have surely foreseen. At last He came. The synagogue was packed that day. Unfortunately, however, not all had the same high esteem of Him. Many were there also from sheer curiosity, and, it seems, many were of a malicious mind. At any rate none of this appears at first. They listen keenly as Jesus reads from the prophet Isaiah. Notice His own choice for that day, with its emphasis on the poor and needy as the acceptable ones of the Lord, chosen especially for "the good news."

Let me pause here to reflect. Since these are the predilection of Christ, so too ought they to be that of His

Church. Great emphasis was put on this in the debates and discussions of Vatican Council II where more than one high dignitary stressed the need for the Bride of Christ to be actually recognized by the world as "the Church of the Poor." In its decree on the Church it was declared that, in imitation of Christ, "similarly the Church encompasses with love all those who are afflicted with human weakness. Indeed she recognizes in the poor and the suffering the likeness of the poor and suffering Founder. She does all she can to relieve their needs and in them she strives to serve Christ" *(Lumen Gentium,* 8). Why this anxiety? Because the Church recognizes precisely that in the poor she finds the same Christ who said, "You did it to me!" She wants the poor to be consoled at the thought of their strong link with Christ: "Those who are oppressed by poverty, infirmity, sickness or other hardships, as well as those who suffer persecution for justice' sake—may they all know that in a special way they are united with the suffering Christ for the salvation of the world. The Lord called them blessed in His Gospel" *(Lumen Gentium,* 41). Is my attitude to the poor and needy that of Christ and His Church? Do I feel an actual fellowship and solidarity with them? Can I improve in this?

> *And he closed the book, and gave it back to the attendant, and sat down; and the eyes of all in the synagogue were fixed on him. And he began to say to them, "Today this Scripture has been fulfilled in your hearing." And all spoke well of him, and wondered at the gracious words which proceeded out of his mouth; and they said, "Is not this Joseph's son?" And he said to them "Doubtless you will quote to me this proverb, 'Physician, heal yourself; what we have heard you did at Capernaum do here also in your own country.'" And he said, "Truly, I say to you, no prophet is acceptable in his own country" (Luke 4:20-24).*

At the end of His talk, (surely not by any means fully reported by the evangelist), the babble of voices that broke forth seemed to be all in His praise until the more spiteful among them deftly switched it into the flow of their own uncharitableness. It should be part of my program of imitating Christ to cultivate as He did that courtesy of behavior and those "gracious words which proceeded out of his mouth." It is said that nothing costs so little and goes so far as Christian courtesy. It is contagious (though not at Nazareth on this occasion, unfortunately!) and can be understood in any language.

True to His home upbringing, Jesus, on His return to Nazareth, showed that He had not forgotten the exquisite courtesy taught Him by Joseph and Mary, and even when His foster-father's name was sarcastically mentioned (after all, Joseph was only a poor carpenter!), notice the tactful way Jesus replied: "Doubtless you will say...." A gentleman never lowers himself to the level of his adversary.

What they were saying or implying seems to have been a reproach that He who came of such poor stock should dare follow the vocation He had chosen, should dare be a public preacher, should dare perform miracles, etc. This kind of meanness can unfortunately crop up where least expected. Perhaps in the past I have experienced some of this myself, on account of my youth, the exercise of my talents and abilities, my success in some undertaking.... Our Lord suffered the same and hence I should try not to be over sensitive, simply endeavoring to keep my motives pure in all I do. Can I now say that this is always so? Let me pray about it. Jesus,...

> *"But in truth I tell you, there were many widows in Israel in the days of Elijah, when the heaven was shut up three years and six months, when there came a great famine over all the land; and Elijah was sent to none of them but only to Zarephath, in the land of Sidon, to a woman who was a widow. And there were many lepers in Israel in the time of the prophet Elisha; and none of them was cleansed, but only Naaman the Syrian." When they heard this, all in the synagogue were filled with wrath. And they rose up and put him out of the city, and led him to the brow of the hill on which their city was built, that they might throw him down headlong. But passing through the midst of them he went away (Luke 4:25-30).*

What Jesus says now infuriates the people because, even though politely said, it was a very clear hint of God's displeasure at the way they were treating His Son, whom they refused to accept as the Messiah in spite of signs and miracles. Jealousy was at the root of it all. In those regions of the Middle East there is a saying that sticks and stones are only thrown at fruitbearing trees, and these people, in trying to put on a show of moral indignation, were crudely trying to fit a halo onto jealousy. Can I truly say that there is no taint of jealousy in my heart at any time? If I cannot, let me pray about it earnestly because this is something really serious. If, thank God, I am free of it, let me ask myself about obstinacy, for this was part of the trouble of the people of Nazareth in refusing to change their views about Jesus. Obstinacy is one of the worst advertisements of pride and yet some people are even obstinate in denying their obstinacy! Especially let me be on my guard concerning obstinacy when corrected. No matter who corrects me, or how, such a one is always my benefactor and I should humbly accept and examine the correction to see if I am really guilty *before God* or not. If I am obstinate about it, I am no less guilty than the Nazarenes in rejecting Jesus, jostling Him out of the city of my heart, trying to throw Him out of my life. "Learn of me for I am meek and humble of heart!" Let me pray about this and make some suitable resolve.

Unclean Demon

And leaving Nazareth he went and dwelt in Capernaum by the sea, in the territory of Zebulun and Naphtali.... And he was teaching them on the sabbath (Matthew 4:13; Luke 4:31).

Rejected by His own, Jesus adopts Capernaum instead, on the northwestern shore of the Sea of Galilee, or Lake Genesareth. At that time it was a garrison town (Mt. 8:5), an administrative center (Jn. 4:46) and a customs station (Mt. 9:9). Peter, Andrew and Matthew lived there. Many of the things told in the Gospels happened in this very district. Jesus probably chose Capernaum as His headquarters because it was the most populous and important city in Galilee and would thus give more people the chance of hearing the good news of the coming of God's kingdom. It was also said to be a city in need of conversion because its economic wealth had brought much corruption. Naturally that would make the Good Shepherd all the more anxious to come to its spiritual assistance. Significantly, then, we find Him now driving out an unclean devil. Notice, too, that this occurred right in the synagogue itself. Satan and his minions have no respect for persons or places. I should not be surprised, therefore, that their presence can be felt even in the mind of a religious, in a religious house, in the chapel itself. We remain human in spite of our high vocation, for, as Vatican II says: "Man is split within himself. As a result, all of human life, whether individual or collective, shows itself to be a dramatic struggle between good and evil, between light and darkness" (*Gaudium et Spes*, 13). That is a rather bleak fact but the constitution continues: "Indeed, man finds that by himself he is incapable of battling the assaults of evil successfully, so that everyone feels as though he is bound by chains. But the Lord Himself came to free and strengthen man, renewing him inwardly and casting out that prince of this world who held him in the bondage of sin." Satan deeply resents my human and Christian dignity as a child of God and special follower of Christ, but I need not fear his assaults if I combine sensible precaution with a deep faith and trust in the power of Jesus to cast him and his temptations far away from me. Have I recently shown any lack of precaution or trust?

And they were astonished at his teaching, for his word was with authority (Luke 4:32).

My sense of faith and trust in Christ should rest on the solid basis of a good knowledge of Him, especially through a reverent reading and practical meditations of the Gospels. On the other hand, lack of contact is bound to weaken both faith and confidence. If we lose contact with the living God, how easy it becomes to get distracted by other things, to cultivate them to excess, and finally almost to idolize them. How easy it is, for example, to exaggerate and then finally worship our own intellect, forgetful that it comes from God, and that whatever wisdom or knowledge we have is but the faintest reflection of His. People can make too much fuss over their own body, pampering and indulging it, giving way to vanity and exaggerated ideas about its beauty, strength, or abilities. How easy it is to become too attached to material things, a room, tools, equipment, books.... All these can become difficulties, but instead of letting them remain such, why not use them as stepping stones toward closer union with Christ? Let me now prayerfully ask Jesus to help me in this.

And in the synagogue there was a man who had the spirit of an unclean demon; and he cried out with a loud voice, "Ah! What have you to do with us, Jesus of Nazareth? Have you come to destroy us? I know who you are, the Holy One of God." But Jesus rebuked him, saying, "Be silent, and come out of him!" and when the demon had thrown him down in the midst, he came out of him, having done him no harm. And they were all amazed and said to one another, "What is this word? For with authority and power he commands the unclean spirits, and they come out." And reports of him went out into every place in the surrounding region (Luke 4:33-37).

This is the first instance we read of concerning contact between Jesus and the evil spirits since His glorious defeat of Satan in the desert. In this case we are told that it is an unclean demon, which is generally believed to mean impurity. Notice the use of the plural when the demon cries out against Jesus, for the strength of this vice is indeed most powerful. At the same time the devil implicitly voices recognition of the stronger power of Jesus ("Have you come to destroy us?") by virtue of His being "the Holy One of God." Satan had left the unconquered Jesus in the desert not quite sure yet as to His real identity, but the things that had happened since (and he must have been all eyes and ears!) seem to have convinced him that Jesus was indeed the Son of God and the Messiah. This must have made him and his satellites dread another crushing defeat, for immorality is one of Satan's strongholds. Jesus treats the demon with the curt contempt he deserves, for there is no point in arguing: "Be silent and come out of him!" Knocking the man down as a last gesture of rebellion, the unclean devil obeys but by the power of Jesus the man suffers no harm. Picture his tremendous sense of relief at finding himself once again clean and pure in the sight of God. The question of temptations and sins against the holy virtue of purity can be a source of great worry if I am not sensible in my outlook on life and in my supreme trust in the help of God's grace with which I try to cooperate by avoiding the occasions of sin. While Jesus does not want me to live in fear, constantly worrying lest I fall, He does expect me to try and think positively about the greatness and worthwhileness of this splendid virtue and to rely heavily on His abundant grace to help me preserve it as something precious which I have given to Him at my profession. Even if there have been past falls and wrong thinking, let me henceforth be much more sensible and positive in the future. O Jesus, Your own splendid purity is my ideal. Help me always to live up to it so that my chastity may be a source of deep joy and positive fulfillment for me as it was for You.

Cure of Illness

And when Jesus entered Peter's house, he saw his mother-in-law lying sick with a fever; he touched her hand, and the fever left her, and she rose and served him (Matthew 8:14-15).

When Jesus bade His apostles follow Him He did not tell them coldbloodedly to have nothing further to do with their families. Here we see Him actually entering Peter's home, where his mother-in-law was suffering with fever. Notice His extreme kindness and sympathy. Matthew says He touched her hand. Mark goes further saying He "took her by the hand and lifted her up"; Luke's account is slightly aloof: "He stood over her and rebuked the fever." Perhaps there is a lesson for me in all three versions: the lesson of tact and prudence, according to circumstances. "And they besought him for her" (Lk. 4:38). This at least I can do for all my relatives and friends, and my prayers for them will be the very best means of helping them, something which they will definitely appreciate. How many indeed are the fevers of life, not merely physical ones...the fever of worry and anxiety, of lack of security, of loneliness.... The touch of a kindly hand in prayer can definitely help, and if God allows me in some way to stretch out my hand to lift someone up, let me do so with tact and prudence, relying on His help without being anxious to draw attention or affection to myself.

At times I too suffer from my own fevers and have need of help. Let me then rely not so much on the sympathy and understanding of others (valuable though these are) but on those of Christ, to whom I can stretch out my hand with confidence. Is there any such fever in my heart or mind just now? Let me beg Jesus confidently for the cure I need and promise Him to minister even more faithfully to Him hereafter as a mark of my gratitude. Let me seek the God of consolations and not the consolations of God.

That evening they brought to him many who were possessed with demons; and he cast out the spirits with a word, and healed all who were sick. This was to fulfill what was spoken by the prophet Isaiah, "He took our infirmities and bore our diseases" (Matthew 8:16-17).

At one time or other, sickness falls to the lot of most people. Right at the outset of His preaching on the kingdom of God come upon earth, Jesus insisted on the need of penance. Not many, however, seem to look upon illness in this light, as something really worthwhile to offer up precisely for the spread of Christ's kingdom. The advance of science has made the modern person acutely aware of many things loudly and often exaggeratedly advertised by the mass-media. The enormous varieties of medicines, antibiotics and cure-alls spoken of and advocated in the newspapers, on radio and television, can become so bewildering as to drive simple people to hypochondria! It can be pathetic when a bedroom becomes a pharmacy! If a person gets ill, it is an obvious duty to take the means to get well again, but surely there should be no exaggeration about the process. In the Gospels we see Jesus very much as a healer also, and to Him we should automatically turn with the same spirit of deep faith and trust He always demanded before He cured anyone. By all means take the necessary human remedies, but never neglect the spiritual side.

What is my own attitude during personal illness? Am I inclined to be careless or to be a hypochondriac? The Bible says: "My child, when you are sick do not be negligent, but pray to the Lord, and he will heal you. Give up your faults and direct your hands aright, and cleanse your heart from all sin" (Sir. 38:9-10).

"He took our infirmities and bore our diseases."

Let me consider my own attitude towards the sick and suffering. Some people make quite a fuss when they are ill, but their own attitude to others who are suffering can be surprisingly hard and unfeeling. There are those too who, having had little or no illness in their own lives, take it for granted that others are similarly constituted and they are therefore always skeptical about others, hinting or saying openly that they are merely exaggerating. Does any of this apply to myself? Even if some people do imagine illnesses or exaggerate them, that in itself is another form of sickness that calls for Christlike compassion. Vatican II says: "Those who are oppressed by poverty, infirmity, sickness, or various other hardships, as well as those who suffer persecution for justice' sake – may they all know that in a special way they are united with the suffering Christ for the salvation of the world. The Lord called them blessed in His Gospel" (*Lumen Gentium,* 41).

Let me not, then, appoint myself judge of the ills of others; let me rather take people as I find them, and when they seem to be ill or suffering let my immediate reaction be one of prayer, saying: "Lord, he whom you love is ill" (Jn. 11:3). Even if there seem to be exaggerations, let me charitably disregard this and try to exercise a tactful apostolate of optimism and positive thinking. It is so easy for the ill to indulge in self pity, with long and detailed organic descriptions of their trouble, frequent flights into fantasy or pessimism. Let me gently counter this with a quiet sympathy and tactful cheerfulness that endeavors to get them to be grateful that things are not worse, encourages them to have patience and endurance united with Christ's present Passion, assuring and advising prayer and confidence in God's Providence and the intercession of her who is called Health of the Sick. Is there anyone at the moment to whom I can apply this Christlike apostolate of charity by visits, a letter, but above all by prayer? "Lord, he whom you love is ill."

Apostolate and Prayer

And he went about all Galilee, teaching in their synagogues and preaching the gospel of the kingdom and healing every disease and every infirmity among the people. So his fame spread throughout all Syria, and they brought him all the sick, those afflicted with various diseases and pains, demoniacs, epileptics and paralytics, and he healed them. And great crowds followed him from Galilee and the Decapolis and Jerusalem and Judea and from beyond the Jordan (Matthew 4:23-25).

These few lines of the evangelist sum up all too briefly what must have been an extremely busy apostolate, with an excessive amount of work for one man; an apostolate, moreover, that was made more humanly difficult by the constant crowds that pressed about Jesus with little or no consideration for His own comfort or well-being. They wanted to be on the receiving-end: to see, to hear, to be physically as close to Him as possible—but how much real love or charity did they show towards Him? How many actually thought of giving Him something in return for His utterly altruistic kindness and goodness and patience? The apostles, doubtless, were often anxious about Him, trying to protect Him, to care for Him, to see to His needs, but it must have been very difficult. How utterly exhausting for Jesus Himself! Love alone could have carried Him through it all without a breakdown—love at its supreme level. "The greatest commandment in the law is to love God with one's whole heart and one's neighbor as oneself. Christ made this commandment of love of neighbor His own and enriched it with a new meaning. For He wanted to identify Himself with His brethren as the object of this love when He said, 'As long as you did it for one of these, the least of my brethren, you did it for me.' Taking on human nature, He bound the whole human race to Himself as a family through a certain supernatural solidarity and established charity as the mark of His disciples, saying, 'By this will all men know that you are my disciples, if you have love for one another.'" (*Apostolicam Actuositatem*, 8).

What about my own apostolate? Is it as busy as it should be? On the other hand, is there not the danger of a host of activities crowding out what should be my vision of Christ, to whom I am constantly united in mind by frequent ejaculatory prayers for help and inspiration? Is all my work done in the serene atmosphere of the presence of God? Does the routine of it make me at times forget my true motives and purity of intention, or give in to grumbling and criticism about how much I have to do? What a pity to spoil my apostolate by lowering my eyes from those of Christ to the uncomfortable dust raised by the feet of the pressing crowd of His brethren and mine. What should be my correct attitude? What can I do about it?

> *And in the morning, a great while before day, he rose and went out to a lonely place, and there he prayed (Mark 1:35).*

Jesus makes prayer the counterweight of His heavy apostolate. Others who think differently might have suggested that He could have considerably eased His labors had He performed wholesale miracles, e.g., blessing and curing all the sick in a crowd by one single sign instead of laying hands on each one in turn and letting people crowd and push Him about without consideration. Oh yes, there can be many valid grounds for grumbling about my own situation too, but that always betokens less generosity with Christ. While of course I am expected to be sensible and practical and not overdo things, still my greatest relief in my work must be the same as that of Jesus: prayer...community and private prayer.

Let me do only what I can, *now*, to the very best of my ability, calmly, without flurry or too much looking for results, no anxiety about not being able to do all I feel I should. Let me live and work prayerfully in the *present moment.* That is the only real and sensible way to accomplish an active apostolate. Only in this manner can I maintain constant union with Jesus in a spirit of perfect and holy abandonment of myself and all my activities to Him in the bosom of the Holy Trinity. Our Lord was later to correct His friend Martha for allowing herself to become overanxious about her many activities, compared with her sister's "idleness," and Jesus told her only one thing was necessary. For me that "one thing necessary" is always the present moment, prayerfully fulfilled as God wants it. Have I of late been forgetting this old but ever new and ever necessary lesson? What resolution can I take for the day ahead? Jesus,...

He rose and went out to a lonely place, and there he prayed.

Realizing the essential need of both community and private prayer in my life as a balance to my active apostolate, surely I appreciate also the tremendous boon of the occasional period set aside for direct recollection or retreat. I should let nothing interfere with my fulfilling these duties at the regular times and with all exactitude. Notice how the apostles, anxious as they were for Jesus, were nevertheless the very ones to go and seek Him out in His retreat in order to bring Him back to the crowds: "Everyone is searching for you."

At times I may get an exaggerated notion of my own indispensability, feeling that things can never carry on (at least adequately) without me, and so gradually I can get into bad habits about prayer times, perhaps often omitting them altogether on the plea of being busy, shortening them or begrudging the time demanded for setting all things aside in order to make a good monthly, quarterly or annual retreat. Again it is a question here of lowering my sights, letting the vision of Christ in my work become obscured by the dust of the crowds, letting even people become more important to me than Christ, getting so absorbed in the works of Christ that I forget Jesus Himself. What an imbalance! A whole apostolate out of focus! A dead loss! Have I nothing with which to reproach myself? At the very least let me resolve to give full importance to my various retreats and to keep Christ steadily before my eyes. O Jesus....

Launch Out Into the Deep

While the people pressed upon him to hear the word of God, he was standing by the lake of Gennesaret. And he saw two boats by the lake; but the fishermen had gone out of them and were washing their nets. Getting into one of the boats which was Simon's, he asked him to put out a little from the land. And he sat down and taught the people from the boat (Luke 5:1-3).

Some very active people like to put on the appearance of being martyrs because of having so much to do, grumbling that they get so little help, etc. Often the solution could be quite simply more use of common sense. Our Lord here sets us an excellent example. When the pressure of people and duties was so great, He simply stepped onto a boat and continued to teach the crowd from a safe distance—evidencing, incidentally, that He must have had a fine manly voice of some resonance. Notice too that He sat down to do so. Overwork is always dangerous, leading often to physical or mental breakdown, sometimes both, and such can never be the direct will of God. When life becomes one long general feeling of fatigue it means I've already gone beyond the red line of warning. The only thing I can do then, even by way of apology to God for disregarding His signals, is to rest or try somehow to re-organize or coordinate my work on a better, more common sense basis. Isn't it possible, for example, to intersperse my work here and there with brief rest pauses, when I can really relax, even prayerfully? That gives both body and mind a chance to recover and will probably prove far more effective than drugs and stimulants. My body and mind closely resemble the makeup of a car. If I drive myself too fast, too long, almost always under pressure, then I'm simply wearing out my God-given motor in a way not intended by its Maker.

Let me not, therefore, play the martyr or the reckless person who persuades himself he never has a moment to stop along life's highway. God intends me sensibly to stop quite deliberately (calmly, of course, without need of screeching tires!) at convenient resting points. These need not be long or really idle but at least let me re-nourish my hungry soul with short, timely prayer, completely relaxed in the arms of God. Have I neglected these important wayside stops?

> *And when he had ceased speaking, he said to Simon, "Put out into the deep and let down your nets for a catch." And Simon answered, "Master, we toiled all night and took nothing! But at your word I will let down the nets." And when they had done this, they enclosed a great shoal of fish; and as their nets were breaking, they beckoned to their partners in the other boat to come and help them. And they came and filled both boats, so that they began to sink (Luke 5:4-7).*

His talk over, His present duty done, Jesus proceeds now to strengthen the faith and vocation of His apostles. Peter could so well have insisted on the uselessness of going out again after they had tried in vain all night long. In any case he was a professional fisherman and knew the lake and its fish like the palm of his hand. His reply shows that while he feels the need of giving Jesus the full picture, he will still obey with good grace. How often it happens in religious life that we feel a natural repugnance to do things we are ordered, either through sheer disinclination or because we know of good reasons which seem to militate against the wisdom of the thing commanded. Jesus shows no annoyance at Peter's remark, and the Church, similarly, has always upheld the right of subjects to make lawful and respectful representations to their superiors. This, after all, is only sensible because when those in authority order things to be done they surely wish for a successful outcome and should be grateful if things are pointed out that they are unaware of and which could spoil the whole issue.

It is then a real charity towards my superiors when I respectfully point out such things, even my disinclinations, but assure them of my complete willingness to obey.

After all, it could well be that Jesus wishes to test me, as He did Peter, and I can be certain that whatever happens, I shall not fail in trying to do my very best, leaving the outcome to Him. He is quite capable of working a miracle if He so desires and even modern times have shown instances of such in the line of obedience. But let me make sure that I really launch out right into the deep, i.e., wholeheartedly, not with resentment. Only then, through my strong faith and hope in Christ, strengthened by my love for Him and my superiors, can I expect great things to happen—and they will! O Jesus....

> *But when Simon Peter saw it, he fell down at Jesus' knees, saying, "Depart from me, for I am a sinful man, O Lord." For he was astonished, and all that were with him, at the catch of fish which they had taken; and so also were James and John, sons of Zebedee, who were partners with Simon. And Jesus said to Simon, "Do not be afraid; henceforth you will be catching men." And when they had brought their boats to land, they left everything and followed him (Luke 5:8-11).*

The haul of fish must have been quite extraordinary to have had such an effect on a professional fisherman like Peter. It wasn't simply the slippery harvest of fish on the deck that brought him to his knees but a deep humility before the goodness and power of the Master whom he had obeyed even when odds were right against him. His reaction? He felt overwhelmed by the stupendous things he had seen happening since he first joined Jesus and felt that he could not possibly be worthy of the companionship and trust of such a hero. How Jesus must have loved Peter at that moment, sprawled there before Him on the slippery deck, arms outstretched, eyes dim with tears of manly emotion: "Depart from me, for I am a sinful man, O Lord." Jesus stretches out both strong hands to help him up and embrace him, saying kindly with cheek to his, "Do not be afraid." The whole incident was another way of telling Peter and the other apostles in a most effective manner: "Trust me and you can always expect great things to happen." He promises them that what they have seen happen will be as nothing compared with the harvest of men they will win over to Him. And so much did they trust Him now that they didn't even bother about the sale of the fantastic haul, which they left to Zebedee: "They left everything and followed him."

What deep faith and humility I need in order to be a wholehearted apostle and confident fisher of men! Let me not be discouraged or fainthearted. Let me keep on trying to launch further and further out into the deep in my efforts to measure up to the standard Jesus expects of me. I can be quite sure of His sympathy, kindness and help. Let me give Him the chance to prove it. O Jesus, help me, please, to launch out into the deep regarding....

Scribes and Pharisees

Now some of the scribes were sitting there, questioning in their hearts, "Why does this man speak thus? It is blasphemy! Who can forgive sins but God alone?" And immediately Jesus, perceiving in his spirit that they thus questioned within themselves, said to them, "Why do you question thus in your hearts? Which is easier, to say to the paralytic, 'Your sins are forgiven,' or to say, 'Rise, take up your pallet and walk'?" (Mark 2:6-9)

Here for the first time we come officially across the Scribes and Pharisees (cf. Lk. 5:17) in direct contact with our Lord. It seems likely that the temple authorities, worried by all the publicity surrounding Jesus, had sent certain of them to watch and listen to Him and they will do their job extremely well from now on, constantly supplementing the biased dossier now being diligently kept in the temple files. They even entered Peter's house, where Jesus had taken refuge from the crowds. They seem to have been a very self-righteous gang of highbrows and one immediately suspects the worst kind of jealousy made them so resentful of one who was putting on such a magnificent show without having had their own formal and specific higher education. They were cowardly too, indulging their criticisms in the luxurious caverns of their minds instead of speaking out, as they should have done if they were really men of conviction. But no, when Jesus tells the paralytic that his sins are forgiven we find them "sitting there, questioning in their hearts, 'Why does this man speak thus? It is blasphemy!'" The first question was a perfectly lawful one; the following statement was an unforgivable judgment of condemnation. But they failed to reckon with the divinity of Christ, who read their minds and proclaimed their uncharitable thoughts, and as though to children (and they were really immature) He says surely He could not be blamed for saying such a simple thing rather than performing the big miracle expected of Him. He teases them really, with a good sense of humor, trying to break down that Jansenistic severity and outward bluff of theirs, almost saying He felt sure that if they had been in His place they might have done the same thing as the easiest way out. But these men have no sense of humor and little if any genuine sincerity or real love of God. The corners of their mouths arch lower and their poker faces become more sour. They really felt they now had excellent dossier material up their sleeves for speedy filing way back down south!

Amused at this image, let me not miss some points for myself, however. Am I one of these awkward "righteous" types who "can never be wrong," who do a lot of immature and unkind reporting? Do I sometimes indulge in intellectual vanity, looking down on others apparently less gifted or educated? Am I resentful or downright jealous of the success of others? Do I indulge in secret criticisms and rash judgments? Have I lost my healthy sense of humor about myself as well as others? If so, my prayer now might well begin: Lord, I'm in a terrible mess with myself, with others, with You....

> *"But that you may know that the Son of man has authority on earth to forgive sins"—he said to the paralytic—"I say to you, rise, take up your pallet and go home." And he rose and immediately took up the pallet and went out before them all (Mark 2:10-12).*

Our Lord might have left it at that, knowing mainly that the paralytic would go home at perfect peace with God and his affliction, but Jesus feels that these insufferable critics need a lesson badly, and one that will incidentally bring the poor man's contentment to perfect joy. In other words He tells these lounge critics: "All right, since you are so obstinate, and since you say that only God can forgive sins, I'll prove that I am God by setting now the perfect seal on what I have just said." Then by His own power He cures the man without even referring to God as in any way distinct from Himself. If anything were blasphemy, that would have been it, and God would not have allowed the cure to take place if Jesus were an imposter usurping divine power to Himself. It was the clearest proof possible of His divinity. Obstinacy is one of the very worst faults in society and religion, extremely bad for oneself and most uncomfortable and irritating to others. If a delicate machine goes wrong, common sense suggests an inspection of the mechanism to find out where the fault lies. So too with the delicate machinery of the mind. Have I never been accused (even by myself) of being obstinate in certain matters? In nine cases out of ten the trouble is probably an idea or set of thoughts acting like grit in the wheels. Usually it's pride, that false pride that won't allow me to admit myself in the wrong, even when my better self tells me so. I must not forget, however, that one of the infallible signs of a strong Christian character is that it is never afraid to confess having made a mistake. Self-respect alone (which is always linked with respect for Christ) should never allow me to indulge in self-deception and immature obstinacy. Next time things go wrong I shall be honest enough (i.e., humble enough) to admit quite flatly that I may be wrong and even try honestly to prove it. The result may be a well-deserved shock for my pride! O Jesus....

> *They were all amazed and glorified God, saying, "We never saw anything like this!" He went out again beside the sea; and all the crowd gathered about him, and he taught them (Mark 2:12-13).*

Reading the first few words here, after what has just happened, one senses an irritation in Jesus at the continued obstinacy of the proud scribes and Pharisees, almost as though His divine presence could stand them no longer and He must get out into the fresh air again, parting from their company, knowing He can do them no good. Who exactly were these people? The scribes were the official interpreters of scripture and teachers of biblical law and ethics, and they included Pharisees and Sadducees, almost two political parties. The Pharisees claimed direct transmission of their beliefs from Ezra (Esdras), who wrote one of the books of the Old Testament. They insisted on the binding nature of oral laws which they maintained had been revealed to Moses at the same time as the ten commandments and were equally important. Major students of their works and sayings hold that they exaggerated things and did not have enough scriptural evidence for a great many of their severe tenets. They were the ultra-progressives; the Sadducees the ultra-conservatists. In either case they met with our Lord's strong disapproval, for neither sect was really honest.

While I can learn here from Jesus' example to avoid bad company, let me also examine myself honestly as to whether I am in some ways an extremist. Self-deception here is possible and it is so easy to think up a beautiful set of reasons to justify what I think, say or do. How often such "reasons" are merely an after-thought. I must really try to study myself and the workings of this mind of mine dispassionately. What I need is a sound mind, a disciplined mind, an open mind that thinks always on a true Christian level, observes, weighs, ponders and bases its opinions on facts, refusing to deceive itself or others. I've a lot to think about here, haven't I?—honestly, with Christ alongside me, and to pray to Him.... Let me start right now: O Jesus....

Pharisaical Strictness

At that time Jesus went through the grainfields on the sabbath; his disciples were hungry, and they began to pluck ears of grain and to eat. But when the Pharisees saw it, they said to him, "Look, your disciples are doing what is not lawful to do on the sabbath" (Matthew 12:1-2).

Here Jesus is up against the Pharisees again and this time they are quoting the sabbath laws. "Thou shalt keep holy the sabbath day" was all that God said directly but the scribes had expanded this to thirty-nine headings called forbidden "fathers of work" and under these again were literally hundreds of tiny ways in which the law was broken, e.g., one would be working sinfully if he drank more than a single gulp of milk, or ate more honey than was needed to cover a sore, or used more oil than was needed to cover the smallest toe of a day-old baby, or more ink than could write two letters of the alphabet, or picked up a stone big enough to throw at a bird, etc., etc. The Pharisees devoted their external lives to the precise keeping of these minutiae and considered this alone as goodness. Theirs was a religion of sheer external legalism, not of the spirit, and it swiftly degenerated into a disdainful pride, for "they were not as the rest of men." The amazing thing is that they seemed to be so deadly earnest about it all, completely deceived by the thought that they alone were right and pleasing to God. One can admire their external self-discipline but only pity their blindness. They, of course, had made a thorough study of these exaggerated laws and therefore scorned Jesus who had not been trained as either a rabbi or scribe. He was to them just one of the despised lower class, an ignorant imposter. It must have galled them particularly when they heard people addressing Jesus as *Rabbi,* which means "My Great One," so we find them constantly on the watch to catch Him in "heretical" teachings, breaking the religious or civil laws. They were indignant! Plucking the ears of corn on the sabbath day the disciples had broken no less than four laws of the scribes: reaping, winnowing, grinding and preparing food to eat! One can but pity the inhuman and unsupernatural rigidity of the self-made lawmakers who observed and upheld them so rigorously, loudly condemning those who did not.

Their counterparts unfortunately have come down through the ages: those who arbitrarily make themselves the interpreters of laws, with a grand show of external observance, while sitting in rigorous condemnation of others in the lofty courts of their own minds, forgetting altogether that God alone can judge perfectly and that He is a God of mercy and compassion. If I can truly and thankfully say that there is no trace of such rigorism in myself, at least let me pray for the conversion of such unfortunates.

> *He said to them, "Have you not read what David did, when he was hungry, and those who were with him: how he entered the house of God and ate the bread of the Presence, which it was not lawful for him to eat nor those who were with him, but only for the priests?" (Matthew 12:3-4)*

As usual Jesus sensibly avoids entering into futile scholastic argument with these odd people. He appeals instead to religious history itself in a way that disqualifies the suffocating interpretations of the sabbath by the so-called learned ones. He recalls that when God's servant David, destined for such great things in the religious history of His Chosen People, was persecuted and pursued by Saul, he took refuge with the high priest Abimelech, who thought it no sin to feed him from the twelve sacred loaves placed every week in the sanctuary as a special sacrifice. These "loaves of Proposition" were supposed to be consumed afterwards only by the priests themselves and then only in the sanctuary itself. They were placed there still warm every sabbath day in thanksgiving for God's goodness in continually providing for the Twelve Tribes in the past and present, and as a pledge of the future. Broadmindedly, on finding David without food, the high priest considered that such urgent necessity demanded that the strict law give way to true charity. In approving of the behavior of the high priest on that occasion, Jesus again condemns sheer rigorism and shows once more His own spirit of mercy and compassion.

If ever I have to wield authority let me bear in mind the example and words of Jesus. Overseverity is never Christlike; condemning without a hearing is not Christlike; considering one's own judgments and opinions infallible is not Christlike. And even when people are definitely in the wrong or remain obstinate, let me remain Christlike. Am I inclined at times to fail in some of these points? O Jesus, supreme example of mercy, compassion, understanding and kindness....

> *"Or have you not read in the law how on the sabbath the priests in the temple profane the sabbath, and are guiltless? I tell you, something greater than the temple is here. And if you had known what this means, 'I desire mercy, and not sacrifice,' you would not have condemned the guiltless. For the Son of man is lord of the sabbath" (Matthew 12:5-8).*

In His second example Jesus uses another case very close to the things considered sacred by these critical Pharisees, temple ritual. On the one hand all sabbath work was forbidden in tiniest detail, but in actual fact on the sabbath day the temple priests were engaged in most arduous work. They had first to receive and then kill the animals presented for sacrifice, prepare them individually according to strict rules and ritual and then do the actual offering, with all the cleaning up required afterwards. The obvious answer to this, of course, would be that this was in the service of God but Jesus states right away that there is now on earth "something infinitely greater than the temple," Himself, and that by His very attitude He intends to wipe out henceforth the crushing burden of narrow man-inspired minutiae without value in the eyes of God. His point of view, in other words, is simply that charity takes precedence over any ritual rules and regulations. This, of course, brought Him into a head-on clash with the scribes and Pharisees. For them the only thing that mattered was the law and its thousands of interpretations clogging up any real joy in life. For Jesus the law was the love of God and man combined sensibly. He tried to win them round reasonably but failed because they were obstinate. I must be careful not to imitate them, but at the same time not go to the other extreme of carelessness about lawfully imposed rules and regulations, nor in interpreting them too widely just for my own comfort and self-gratification. In these matters let me always follow safe guides, never extremists. Resolution for today? O Jesus,...

Withered Hand

And he went on from there, and entered their synagogue. And behold, there was a man with a withered hand. And they asked him, "Is it lawful to heal on the sabbath?" so that they might accuse him (Matthew 12:9-10).

One of the mysteries of human psychology is how apparently enlightened people can indulge in quite obvious contradictions, without seeing it. This was the case of the Pharisees. They seemed to spy on Jesus' every public word and action. We see it now again when Jesus entered the local synagogue on a certain sabbath day. They deliberatedly draw His attention to a man worshiping there who had a withered, i.e., a paralyzed hand. St. Jerome tells us that the Ebionites of his day held that this particular man was a great lover of work, a bricklayer, who had fallen off a building and suffered paralysis of his hand, but he continued to pray for a cure. At any rate, our wily "friends" seek now to use him unwittingly as a trap for Jesus, so as to collect further evidence against Him. Their inconsistency is seen too in the fact that although they wished to have nothing whatsoever to do with sinners, they nevertheless assiduously sought the company of Jesus, whom they considered a sinner and blasphemer. What a contrast between them and Him! They had narrowed the love of God right down to themselves alone as the sole perfect observers of the laws, whereas Jesus had broadened it to include all men, sinners as well as saints, and had in fact emphasized especially compassion for sinners. Their reasoning was that since He so loved sinners He must be as bad as they were!

St. Paul was later to say of these men that "they have a zeal for God, but it is not enlightened" (Rom. 10:2). I cannot be careful enough to avoid the faults of these Pharisees, especially that of self-righteousness, blindness to the obvious, obstinacy, and I must be rigidly honest in searching out my faults and ruthless in eliminating them by firm discipline. Let me pray to Jesus now for a clear vision of myself.

> *He said to them, "What man of you, if he has one sheep and it falls into a pit on the sabbath, will not lay hold of it and lift it out? Of how much more value is a man than a sheep! So it is lawful to do good on the sabbath" (Matthew 12:11-12).*

The scribes and Pharisees maintained that on the sabbath day one could only use medical remedies if a person's life was actually in danger, but even then only enough steps should be taken to prevent him from getting worse, not better. There was to be no question of a cure; one could put on a bandage to stop bleeding but no ointment to help cure! Gently Jesus ridicules this viewpoint by the example He gives, saying how man is of far more value in God's eyes than a mere animal, for man has a soul to be saved, and anything that helps him to get closer to God is not only lawful but should be done as a duty. In that case, since a cure would certainly bring a man much closer to God because of his spirit of joy and gratitude, then surely "it is lawful to do good on the sabbath."

We are told that there were about six thousand Pharisees in Israel at the time of Jesus. They were considered the spiritual aristocracy but they could have had little real admiration from the ordinary people. So it is always when those in high places warp the ways of God into their own Jansenistic modes of thinking and acting. I must remember, too, that the eyes of the laity are constantly on religious and priests, many of them extremely ready to criticize and condemn—and woe betide us when we give them something to start with! Worse still if it is a question of scandal. The responsibility here is absolutely frightening. If I can find no trace of honest worry about myself on these scores, at least let me thank God and pray for the Church, its leaders, ministers and my superiors that they may be at all times Christlike in their authority, teachings and conduct.

Then he said to the man, "Stretch out your hand." And the man stretched it out, and it was restored, whole like the other. But the Pharisees went out and took counsel against him, how to destroy him (Matthew 12:13-14).

St. Mark adds the detail that Jesus "looked around at them with anger, grieved at their hardness of heart" (3:5), before actually performing the cure. The anger of Jesus is always frightening because it is so rare in the Gospels, and here we find it caused by hardness of heart as one of the greatest of faults. If anything should have converted them it should have been the miracle that followed. But no, it makes them worse, and surely at that moment the heart of Jesus wept for their obduracy, for they too were sinners whom He desperately wanted to save. Now they, who because of their higher spiritual training should have been the very first to follow Him, were deliberately opposing Him. Worse still when they went out (with fury, St. Luke says) to start a definite plot against His very life. The great Fenelon wrote: "A soul that belongs wholly to God never remains dry, cramped or closed in by narrowness and the inconsistencies of self-love. Since it lives only for God, it does so with a tremendous love. Love bears all, endures all, hopes all things for its neighbor...consoles, compassionates. It knows how to adapt itself: to be little with the little ones, to rise with the great, to weep with those who weep, to be happy with those who rejoice.... Nothing is so dry, so cold, so hard, so closed as a heart that loves only itself in all things. Nothing is so tender, so open, so alive, so kind, so loving and so compassionate as a heart that is possessed and animated by divine love."

In those words we can see the chasm of difference between Jesus and the Pharisees. May I never arouse His just anger by hardness of heart, unkindness to others, or narrow outlook. Let me resolutely pray to Him about each of the qualities mentioned by Fenelon. O Jesus,...

Poor in Spirit

Seeing the crowds, he went up on the mountain, and when he sat down his disciples came to him. And he opened his mouth and taught them (Matthew 5:1-2).

On a previous occasion we saw Jesus trying to get the attention of the greater crowd by addressing them from a boat off shore. Now we find Him up a mountainside near Capernaum not merely for the vantage point it gave Him, but doubtless to stress the loftiness of His thoughts and words. The Sermon on the Mount is very important, for in it Jesus assumes the public role of an official legislator in His own right, giving all men a newly expressed and perfect moral code of thought, word and behavior that opens up vast horizons. There seems, from St. Luke's account, to have been an exceptionally large crowd present. Since they came from neighboring towns, they too would be helpful in broadcasting the message. Matthew uses the phrase "opened his mouth," a special Hebrew term signifying that something important was to be said. In the beatitudes, Jesus placed special emphasis on the role of the poor and lowly in the kingdom of God.

How easy it is for religious to get lulled into a false sense of poverty simply because of a publicly expressed vow. There is a certain sense of security and perhaps even of comfort on which religious can easily rely, but which the economically poor lack. Since we may not be able to live exactly the same life of enforced deprivation, we should at least not take too comfortable advantage of the security we have by a neglect of the things entrusted to us, wastefulness, abuse, etc. For everything we religious are given by divine Providence we shall have to render a strict account. May God preserve us from any spirit of carelessness about this. Jesus,...

Blessed are the poor in spirit, for theirs is the kingdom of heaven (Matthew 5:3).

At most the four evangelists have given us only a résumé of the full life and teachings of Jesus—the very last verse of St. John's Gospel admits it broadly. Hence we can be sure that even St. Matthew's three-chapter account of the Sermon on the Mount is only a condensation of all that Jesus really said. At any rate let me concern myself now with the consideration of the beatitudes in order that I at least may try to do what Christ intended in proclaiming them, i.e., reduce them to practice in my own life. The emphasis in the first beatitude is on the *spirit* of poverty, not just the effective lack of things. The more a balloon is weighed down, the more difficult it is for it to rise. When we are really detached from the things of earth we do not make a fuss when we have to part with them, even though we may naturally feel the inconvenience of not having them. What Cassian of the fourth century said still holds good for the twentieth: "What is the use of having left great things, if afterwards one should grow attached to things of no importance? They have turned the affection which they can no longer have for great things to other things small and contemptible; the evil is in the heart and in its ill-regulated affections, and not in the nature of things. You may say that the things you are attached to are small and of little value. But it is precisely this which makes your fault the greater, that having been able to detach yourself from things of value you allow yourself to be tied up by things of no value. A renunciation such as this will not lead you to perfection, because while you wish to be considered poor you harbor in your heart the desires of the rich."

If a fire were to break out in my living or working quarters what are the things I would try to rescue first, even at a risk? What would I be most upset at losing? This might give me an indication of my attachments. O Jesus, teach me the true spirit of interior as well as exterior detachment so that my spirit of poverty may never be weighed down.

"There are many unhappy people who endeavor to take back with one hand what they give with the other.

In small things they procure for themselves a recompense for the general sacrifice they made at their profession. They are always afraid of being without what they need, and they grasp at little things like a drowning person. They find a thousand excuses, invent new needs, are terrified at a small privation. In a word, they wish to possess nothing and yet have everything, even what is superfluous. They attach their heart to a room, to an article of clothing, to a mere nothing, and they keep these things by some wile or device, doing neither more nor less than what a miser does for the treasures he idolizes. How much must these religious be pitied! How deplorable to see a person bound by the slightest thread who, in order to enter religion, has broken great chains such as the bonds of blood, love of one's country, and one's free will" (Bl. Michael Rua, SDB). St. John Bosco said he wished to die without a cent in his pocket. I never know when death may overtake me. Were it to come now, in what state would it find my room, my wardrobe, my desk, my trunk, my pockets, my wallet, and, above all, my heart? Perhaps I need an immediate resolution on at least one or more of these points. O Jesus, You who have blessed the poor in spirit....

Blessed Are the Meek

Blessed are the meek, for they shall inherit the earth (Matthew 5:5).

The sight of someone really angry is never pleasant: his facial expression and attitude is something fearsome. Anger and self-control are not Siamese twins. Fierce words, that will later be regretted, splutter or flow. Perhaps there are violent blows or kicks. It is always a terrible thing, for not only the angry person is suffering but also all those who witness it or are its direct object. "Anger and wrath," says Sirach, "these are abominations, and the sinful man will possess them" (27:30). What Proverbs says can apply equally to men: "It is better to live in a desert land than with a contentious and fretful woman!" (21:19) "Do not be like a lion in your home" (Eccl. 4:30). "The vexation of a fool is known at once, but a prudent man ignores an insult" (Prv. 12:16). "Jealousy and anger shorten life, and anxiety brings on old age too soon" (Sir. 30:24). "As charcoal to hot embers and wood to fire, so is a quarrelsome man for kindling strife" (Prv. 26:21). Anger is just one letter short of danger and is never worthwhile because, for the very least of reasons, when one's temper boils over one only lands in hot water!

Let me judge myself honestly on these points to see whether I have yet reached that point of self-control so necessary in any good Christian, never mind a religious. It is very much a matter of will power. Like muscles, will power has to be exercised regularly for there is no use having a half-hearted idea about that. Let me now think out in detail this matter of temper, anger and self-control in the light of Christ, which will give me a clear idea of what I should do about it all. Let me ask Him now for a strong determination to see this matter through with perseverance, confident that with His abundant help I shall constantly improve.

Meekness is an often misjudged word associated with weakness, but there are many synonyms for it that place it in a much better light as meant by our Lord, e.g., imperturbability, inexcitability, even temper, tranquil mind, humble patience, gentle kindness, equanimity, composure, placidity, calmness, serenity, endurance, self-possession, self-control, etc. St. Paul exhorts: "Let all bitterness and wrath and anger be put away from you, with all malice, and be kind to one another, tenderhearted, forgiving one another, as God in Christ forgave you" (Eph. 4:31-32). "A soft answer turns away wrath, but a harsh word stirs up anger" (Prv. 14:34). Anger, as we know, is a very powerful emotion, and to use all the self-control needed in order to keep it in check is precisely that equally powerful virtue called "meekness." Am I inclined to flare up too easily about things, even small things? Let me examine myself carefully and see what resolution I need to make. Jesus, meek and humble of heart, make my heart like Yours!

Before the Sermon on the Mount, revenge and petty vindictiveness were considered by the generality of people as quite lawful in order to restore the balance upset by those who had done wrong. Today this mentality persists only among more primitive tribes and among "civilized" people who are immature. Christ canceled out all that. If God is so magnanimously good and patient even with the tremendous offenses of man, surely it behooves man himself to be patient with others. Jesus was man as well as God and He gave us the perfect example of true manly meekness, which is infinitely removed from weakness: "Learn of me for I am meek and humble of heart and you shall find rest for your souls." The Scriptures have many exhortations to cultivate this strong virtue so dear to the strong Christ. "My son, perform your tasks in meekness; then you will be loved by those whom God accepts. The greater you are, the more you must humble yourself; so you will find favor in the sight of the Lord" (Sir. 3:17-18); "It is better to be of a lowly spirit with the poor, than to divide the spoil with the proud" (Prv. 16:19); "The meek shall obtain fresh joy in the Lord" (Is. 29:19). This indeed is part of that inheriting the earth promised by our Lord in the beatitude, and what greater reward can there be than that deep peace of mind and soul that allows not even an earthquake, spiritual or material, to upset it, because it places full trust in the meek and humble heart of Jesus Himself? Let me take this beatitude very much to heart, then, and recall also that exhortation of St. Paul: "I therefore beg you to lead a life worthy of the calling to which you have been called, with all lowliness and meekness, patience, forbearing one another in love, eager to maintain the unity of the Spirit in the bond of peace" (Eph. 4:1-2). Jesus, meek and humble of heart,...

They Shall Obtain Mercy

Blessed are the merciful, for they shall obtain mercy (Matthew 5:7).

Mercy in its biblical sense refers to every form of charity on behalf of the physical or moral sufferings of others, and not simply the compassion shown by one to another who is in his power and has no claim to kindness. There is a wide range of synonyms for it, including: pity, compassion, commiseration, sympathy, fellow-feeling, tender-heartedness, forbearance, humanity, clemency, leniency. All these words are different facets of the word "mercy" canonized by our Lord Himself after innumerable examples of divine mercy in the Old Testament. "Thus says the Lord of hosts, render true judgments, show kindness and mercy, each to his brother" (Zec. 7:9). In order to better understand how to practice mercy, let me first look at God's own mercy. It will be useful to consider one of the many psalms on this subject, i.e., Psalm 117. It was originally a processional hymn, with the priests and people alternating as they entered the temple to thank God for victory or for the renewal of their national life as His Chosen People on the great feast of Tabernacles. It can easily be paraphrased with a slant towards religious life. "Give thanks to the Lord; the Lord is gracious, his mercy endures for ever. Echo the cry, children of Israel: Echo the cry, all you who are the Lord's worshipers." Imagine the liturgical scene: the strong choir of levites, all chosen by privilege from the tribe of Aaron, the first high priest, and all clad in solemn vestments made strictly according to the design described in detail by God Himself to Moses: all these priests singing aloud in their strong voices the repeated exhortation to thank God for His goodness; and at the very end of each verse the whole multitude of people would cry out joyfully: "His mercy endures for ever." They kept repeating this refrain gladly, its thundering roar echoing about the local hills, including Calvary. The first few verses of this psalm of gratitude are based, then, on God's great mercy to His Chosen People. Well then may they find a grateful echo in my own heart as one of God's chosen people of today. My gratitude for His mercy should make me resolve to avoid mediocrity and to aim at being, at all times and in all things, a first class man of God. In spite of, or because of His mercy, have I not perhaps lowered my sights since I first became a religious?

"Echo the cry, all you who are God's worshipers, for I called on the Lord when trouble beset me, and the Lord listened and brought me relief. With the Lord at my side, I have no fear of the worst that men can do: with the Lord at my side to aid me, I shall yet see my enemies baffled." Even in the utmost extremes of temptation, God will mercifully come to my aid and save me if I trust Him and abandon myself to Him. There is hope of salvation right until the gates of hell clang fast behind a soul, and therefore as long as life lasts, Christ is on my side, fighting in and with me to save my soul. "I reeled under the blow and had well-nigh fallen, but still the Lord was there to aid me." How often perhaps I was on the verge of the precipice or even slipping over and God saved me even by the hair of my head, His loving eyes of mercy ever on me: "I wish not the death of the sinner but rather that he be converted and live." The Curé d'Ars used to spend up to fourteen hours a day hearing confessions. He knew what sin was and yet he maintained, "Our sins are just a grain of sand compared with the mountains of the mercy of God." Through that infinite mercy so many millions have been saved. Fr. Faber says, "There is a wideness in God's mercy like the wideness of the sea." Modern science can measure the depth and width of the oceans with fair accuracy but never the depth and width of God's infinite mercy, in which I also share so abundantly. Let me make then my own the psalmist's concluding lines: "You are my God, mine to thank you. You are my God, mine to extol you. Give thanks to the Lord, for the Lord is gracious, and his mercy endures for ever!"

Having considered God's extraordinary mercy in general and its particular application to myself, I should now consider how to practice the beatitude itself. Perhaps here I could fittingly look over again the synonyms given for mercy at the beginning of the first point, take each in turn and see how I can apply them individually to particular people or cases within my own environment. That alone should give me ample matter for meditation, resolution and prayer. "Judgment is without mercy to one who has shown no mercy; yet mercy triumphs over judgment" (Jas. 2:13).

Pure in Heart

Blessed are the pure in heart, for they shall see God (Matthew 5:8).

In Hebrew psychology the heart was considered the source of intelligence and a pure heart meant one that acted according to strictly upright intentions: "Love righteousness, think of the Lord with uprightness, and seek him with sincerity of heart...for perverse thoughts separate men from God" (Wis. 1:3). From this state of mind and heart springs chastity as a natural part of sincerity and purity of intention. "Let your heart therefore be wholly true to the Lord our God, walking in his statutes and keeping his commandments" (1 Kgs. 8:61). "You shall be blameless before the Lord your God" (Dt. 18:13). "My son, give me your heart, and let your eyes observe my ways" (Prv. 23:26). The heart is always considered figuratively as the seat of love, and it is precisely on love that our religious vow and virtue of chastity is founded. The word "love" has become very much debased in ordinary common parlance, in degrading movies and songs. What a great pity, because the plain fact of the matter is that each one of us was created by God out of and precisely for love, and life without love is utterly incomplete and unfulfilled. Jesus Christ, our model, established His whole law and kingdom on those two great commandments of love: love of God and love of neighbor intimately combined. Love was the very theme of the whole life of Jesus. Before He died, He instituted a specially helpful sacrament of love in the Eucharist, and finally He expired of love. Hence it is warped thinking to say that chastity automatically cancels out human love—not at all. Chastity raises, sublimates our love of others to the level of the love of God. Through it we love others in, through and for God alone—again following the sublime example of Christ Himself who did not allow even His most beloved Mother to come between Him and the Father. That was why He could demand from His closest followers that they leave all things—father, mother, brothers, sisters, home and all—to give themselves up solely to the love of God, knowing that all these dear people and things can still be contained and carried on safely in the love of God. We, as religious, try to intensify this love and bring it to its highest perfection by leading a life devoted expressly to a chastity based on the life and love of Christ. His love was most exalted, sublime and free from all selfish self-seeking, divorced from mere uncontrolled emotional stirrings of the flesh. It is a love that penetrates to that innermost living consciousness at the very center of the heart of mankind and finds there *God.* This is the gift I offer God and mankind by my vow of chastity. Let me meditate on this.

By my vow of chastity I give something truly wonderful and sublime, something really joyful to God—not something negative and repressive, frightening or awful. Surely on my profession day when the whole court of heaven rejoiced with me and my friends on earth, God did not chuckle with malicious glee at the prospect of all the worry and anxiety my vow of chastity would cause me. That vow is not meant by God or His Church to be an instrument of torture, a thing of such frightening aspect that it must keep me forever apprehensive and fearful lest I violate it at every turn, so that my life becomes a chain of worries about preserving or losing purity. That wasn't the way of Christ—it should not be mine either. People who live constantly alarmed about chastity lack balance and maturity. An ordinary, normal, balanced, sensible Christian should be able to know at once what is sin and what is not. If there *is* sin, I must quietly and sincerely get rid of it at once by as perfect an act of contrition as possible—but not with a flood of shame and self-pitying worry that *I* of all people could do such a horrible thing. Let me concentrate rather on the fact that God's loving goodness has been offended and resolve to make up for it by loving God more, not by endless nagging remorse. If I am doubtful whether there is sin or not, again let me deal with it calmly and sensibly, with self-discipline not despicable self-pity unworthy of a mature person. I must not torture my mind with endless examinations of possibilities and probabilities. Let me pray rather: "Lord, I'm not sure at all, but in case I did offend You, please forgive me, because I do love You." What a compliment that is to the mercy and loving kindness of the forgiving Christ who compassionates our human weaknesses! Through such an act of trust and abandonment we merit the grace of greater prudence in the future, greater maturity of personality, greater love of God.

Constant worry about a possible or even probable sinful failure about which we can give no dogmatic statement can be a downright insult to God as a negation of His mercy, kindness and forgiveness. Many souls needlessly torture themselves about holy purity and the vow of chastity. Christ meant our vow to be something positive, not negative; something consoling, not a misery; something happy, not a constant worry; something splendid and magnificent, not a handicap. Let me feed my mind on good, wholesome, nourishing thoughts of trust and hopefulness in God's love, mercy and ever-abundant help and power to save me from sin. Let me cast out rigorously all the old thoughts and fears which are morbid and unhealthy. Let me think positively of God's goodness and tremendous willingness to help me to be chaste and pure.

Let me meditate on this great beatitude and its reward.

My mind, unclouded by unhealthy pictures, doubts and desires, will see God in all the strength and loveliness of nature in the world in which I live; I shall find it much easier to see God in other people, even the awkward and difficult, poor or ugly, good or unkind, for God has many disguises. My whole outlook on life will be wholesome and healthy. In my fellow-religious I shall see other apostles of Christ in spite of their faults, trying like myself to see and love and serve God. In my charges I shall see the flock of Christ I am privileged to serve, even the black sheep. In all I shall see and love and serve God alone.

Chastity is "a surpassing gift of grace...it liberates the human heart in a unique way and causes it to burn with greater love for God and all mankind.... Religious should be trained to make a celibate life consecrated to God part of the richness of their whole personality" (*Perfectae Caritatis*). Henceforth, then, I will look upon my vow and virtue of chastity most gratefully in a positive way: a thing of splendor, a gift of constant joy, strength, and deepest consolation. O chaste Christ, who....

Persecution

Blessed are those who are persecuted for righteousness' sake, for theirs is the kingdom of heaven (Matthew 5:10).

The history of persecution for justice' sake goes right back to the dawn of mankind when Satan's jealousy made him determine to undermine the virtue of our first parents. That done, soon afterwards it raises its ugly head again in Cain who was driven to murder his virtuous brother. And so it has gone on through all the ages of mankind's checkered history. It seems an almost inexplicable perversity in human nature. One would think that if a person is good, tries to love and serve God and his neighbor to the best of his ability and minds his own business, then all should be well with him, everyone should admire and even love him. But it is not so. Inevitably some tongue or mind will be stirred at its roots by a foul jealousy that can find no peace until it can discover something to criticize. In cases of greater malice this can lead to petty or even violent persecution. At times the perpetrators are even able to persuade themselves or others that thereby they are doing a good thing. "They will put you out of the synagogues: indeed the hour is coming when whoever kills you will think he is offering service to God" (Jn. 16:2). These words of our Lord to His apostles were a reflection of both past and future history for all the "just" of God.

In the Old Testament the prophets were persecuted by their own: Moses by Pharaoh, David by Saul, John the Baptist by Herod and his family. Jesus Himself was to be the supreme example of all times. The apostles soon felt the force of His warning and ever since, in every age, the saints and good people have found the same experience because of their righteousness in the sight of God which provoked the malicious and satanic jealousy of others.

The same thing happens in this very day. How often others could repeat the words of Paul, adapted to their own circumstances: "We do not want you to be ignorant, brethren, of the affliction we experienced in Asia; for we were so utterly, unbearably crushed that we despaired of life itself. Why, we felt that we had received the sentence of death" (2 Cor. 1:8-9).

Let me pause to consider the places where, at the moment, the Church is suffering direct or indirect, sometimes subtle, persecution. Let my prayers go out to all those who thus suffer, that by faithfulness to the grace of God and the inestimable gift of faith they may soon obtain the crown of victory.

In *Lumen Gentium* the Church tries to encourage those who fall under the heading of this beatitude: "Those who are oppressed by poverty...as well as those who suffer persecution for justice' sake—may they all know that in a special way they are united with the suffering Christ for the salvation of the world" (41). There is so much unnecessary unhappiness in the world because of misunderstandings or downright malice. Are there grounds for optimism, then? Father Lombardi, S.J., of the Better World Movement, maintains that there are indeed since God can use even sin and humiliation caused by human foolishness as material for building up a better world. He therefore urges a greater stress of genuine love and charity, with the example of Jesus always before us in His dealings with all types of people. Can I think of any way I myself can implement these optimistic ideas in my own circle of charges, friends or acquaintances? Who is there having a hard time that I can cheer and help?

Possibly I myself have gone through a rather rough time which closely resembled persecution. This kind of thing can and does happen in the Church itself, even in religious families, and constitutes one of those mysteries that are quite inexplicable except in the light of the fact that even out of evil God can draw good. It is indeed a puzzling mystery that at times it is precisely the good who hurt the good. There are persons who possess many noticeable virtues and accomplish much good and yet at one tangent of their make-up give certain people a rather rough time, apparently without being aware of fault on their own side. It is an extraordinary blindspot and the very fact that they are recognized to be good in so many ways makes the injustice of their treatment painfully hard to bear. There is definitely a big weakness present, and they need many prayers, for in this matter there is a position dangerously close to that of the condemned Pharisees. I should pray that I myself may never become inflicted with such perilous myopia. On the other hand, if I myself ever become subject to apparent injustice or petty persecution, let me make doubly sure first, in candid and perfectly honest consultation with my confessor and spiritual director, that I myself am not, even in some ways, at fault. Even if I am faultless, let me keep God on my side by my spirit of humility under humiliation, fortitude under trial, patience under stress, and charity in avoiding harsh judgments on those who, please God, are only temporarily blind. Let me avoid as the most evil of plagues bitterness and rancor of thought, spreading abroad even true tales of injustice, or sinking into a hopeless despair that makes me give up, if not my vocation itself, at least that spirit of observance and regularity, of good example and of piety, and above all of charity that can help me overcome prejudices and, by my prayers, convert those who wrongly persecute my righteousness in the sight of God. No tunnel ends in a wall. By my faith, hope and charity, God will see me safely through into the light of happiness and peace again. Is there someone for whom I should now especially pray?

Blessed are you when men revile you and persecute you and utter all kinds of evil falsely on my account. Rejoice and be glad, for your reward is great in heaven, for so men persecuted the prophets who were before you" (Mt. 5:11-12).

Salt and Light

You are the salt of the earth; but if the salt has lost its taste, how shall its saltiness be restored? It is no longer good for anything except to be thrown out and trodden under foot by men (Matthew 5:13).

From time immemorial salt has had special value to men and animals alike and today the production of salt is one of the world's most widely distributed mineral industries. In the book of Leviticus we find even God ordering that all cereal and other offerings for sacrifice were to be seasoned with salt (Lv. 2:13). In the book of Numbers we read again of "a covenant of salt" (18:19). It would seem that its preservative qualities made it a specially fitting symbol of an enduring compact and sealed the obligation to fidelity signified by the sacrifice itself. There is a Persian phrase, *namak haram*, meaning "untrue to salt," i.e., disloyal or ungrateful. Table-salt is usually fine-ground and of high purity. These points of general knowledge lie behind our Lord's metaphor to His apostles during the Sermon on the Mount, for it is held that He spoke especially to them on this and the next point. What He was saying to the crowds on the mountainside was of immeasurable value and the people would publish it abroad as they returned to their homes, and from there it would go yet further abroad. Unfortunately, however, there is often the danger of reports becoming either exaggerated or watered down in the process of broadcasting from one to another. It was to be the special task of the apostles and their successors to ensure the preservation of the doctrines of Christ in the course of their transmission, so that the spiritual nourishment they offered would never lose its wholesome piquancy and be forever acceptable to mankind in general. This mission involves a great deal of sacrifice also, especially when points of unchangeable principle are confronted with a weight of public opinion that considers itself more wise than that of the Vicar of Christ or the Church's official magisterium. "The Church is, by the will of Christ, the teacher of the truth. It is her duty to give utterance to, and authoritatively to teach, that Truth which is Christ Himself, and also to declare and confirm by her authority those principles of the moral order which have their origin in human nature itself" (*Dignitatis Humanae*, 14).

How loyal am I to the teachings and guidance of the Church, the Pope, the bishops? Do I defend them against disloyalty?

In talking of salt, our Lord had in mind the local salt which came from the Dead Sea. Unlike ordinary preservative salt, this one contains many other chemicals, including sulphur, and is totally unsuitable for domestic use. If by chance it came into a kitchen and were discovered, it would be thrown out as useless. We know too that the Dead Sea is connected in history with the ancient cities of sin, Sodom and Gomorrah, which were destroyed by sulphurous rain and earthquake, and to this day have left no chance of their ruins ever being restored. The implication then is that the apostles (and I, too) had to preserve their own uprightness and sound moral balance in the sight of God in order to fulfill their task of helping preserve the faith in others. If the sulphur of deadly sin were so to affect their lives as to make of them a public scandal, their so-called apostolate would be a mere sham and merit dire punishment from God as well as the scorn of men.

The responsibility of my apostolic vocation is tremendous, including the point of good example based on a sound Christian life. St. John Bosco says that our every word "should be the salt of eternal life in every place and for every person.... As long as you correspond to the graces of God by work, morality and good example, God will use you, and you will be amazed not only at how much is accomplished but how much you yourself can do." Is there any single point in my life on which I fail to give good example? Jesus, please help me....

You are the light of the world. A city set on a hill cannot be hid. Nor do men light a lamp and put it under a bushel, but on a stand, and it gives light to all in the house. Let your light so shine before men, that they may see your good works and give glory to your Father who is in heaven (Matthew 5:14-16).

Light is an extremely complicated form of energy and essentially more primitive than any of the things in terms of which one tries to define it. It is best described therefore by its behavior and effects. In the very third verse of the Bible we read: "God said: 'Let there be light' and there was light" (Gn. 1:3) and the transformation from the utter darkness of the second verse to the glorious illumination of the third never fails to fill the imagination with awe at God's tremendous creation at its dawn. Now our Lord calls His apostles "the light of the world"—not "you should be" but "you are"—by their very vocation. By the apostolic vocation (come right down charismatically to myself) they are as a city, made up of many houses and mansions according to variety of talents and temperaments, in a prominent position in the eyes of those on the vast plains below. The light of that city will act as a beacon, strong or weak according to the amount of faith in each household.

There are many pointers for a religious here. First the matter of community responsibility in the Church and before the world: the Church rightly demands that religious orders give a corporate example to the world of a true Christian life in evangelical poverty and other matters of principle, otherwise whole sections of the city of God on the hilltop are failing to give light. It is not enough for those in religion to practice virtue just privately. Again there is a community duty of good example and also a wider obligation of apostolate. The world has its eyes on us and is only too ready to criticize when the lights are out. Our Lord even wants our good works to be seen but He underlines heavily the essential purity of intention in all our apostolate: not merely that men may see but that they be able, above all, to "give glory to your Father who is in heaven."

I must daily renew my absolute purity of intention in all that I have to do, for this will be the preservative salt to keep my various activities wholesome for souls and pleasing to God. Then by prudence in cooperating with the grace and inspirations of God's Holy Spirit the light of my good example will indeed ensure that I am doing my part in the spiritual generation of electricity in God's city set on a hill. Is *A.M.D.G.* (For the greater glory of God.) really at the bottom of my whole life and apostolate? How can I make it more effectively so? O Jesus, You who are the Light of the world....

Be Perfect

You must be perfect as your heavenly Father is perfect (Matthew 5:48).

Quite early in its dogmatic constitution on the Church, Vatican II repeats this injunction of our Lord clearly: "Fortified by so many and such powerful means of salvation, all the faithful, whatever their condition or state, are called by the Lord, each in his own way, to that perfect holiness whereby the Father Himself is perfect" *(Lumen Gentium,* 11). It is obvious then, that striving after holiness is not the monopoly of religious: however, in view of all the special graces and opportunities provided in religious life by the vows, frequent reception of the sacraments, a regular way of life, etc., it is taken for granted that religious make a steady effort at doing their utmost to fulfill our Lord's injunction perfectly. This does not imply that we must have extraordinary feelings of fervor or anything like that: it is a question of the will. We have got to *will* holiness and all the intermediate steps between us and the perfect love of God, saying with the disciples: "Lord, I will follow you wherever you go" (Lk. 9:57). A sincere desire for sanctification, holiness and perfection is something virile and it rejects all feebleness of will.

Some people can be a failure in religious life simply because they cannot get themselves to say energetically: "I *will.*" Instead, they are forever saying, "I would like to, but...." All too often this miserable "I would like to" hides cowardice. If I wish to succeed at anything I must say quite positively "I *will*—no matter what it costs me, and to this end I will use this and that particular means—no deception, no hypocrisy, no cringing or hesitation. I *will!*" It's no use wasting time in vague generalities or trying to develop willpower in general. I must concentrate on something positive. Weakness in itself is no disgrace, but there is definite shame in allowing weakness to conquer me when I know that "I can do all things in Him who strengthens me." What occasions give me a sense of shame about my willpower? What simple program of definite steps can I take in order to try better to live up to the standard Jesus expects of me?

By now it should be perfectly clear to me that religious life is essentially one of sacrifice for the love of God, the imitation of Christ walking from ordinary life up the slopes of Calvary under the weight of a heavy cross. I've known this all along. It was made clear to me right from the start. I became a religious freely and, as Père Lacordaire says, "When we become religious, it is that we may be religious right up to the neck"—in other words, complete religious, not halfhearted creatures only weakly in love with God. Inherent in my God-given makeup there are infinite possibilities, including real holiness, sanctity. With the help of God's grace, I can constantly be master of my fate, but I must be aware of the fact that faith is my sword, confidence in God my shield in the battle against a weak-willed self that would prefer a lower, more comfortable level of spiritual or religious life. St. Teresa of Avila says: "We should not limit our desires; we should, on the contrary, hope that by trusting in God, we shall be able by our constant efforts, sustained by divine grace, to reach gradually the goal attained by the saints." I like to see results, even in myself, and tend to get discouraged at my slow pace, but St. Francis de Sales says: "Have patience with everyone, but especially with yourself. I mean that you should not be disturbed by your imperfections but always have the courage to rise again after a fall. There is no better means to attain the summit of the spiritual life than always to resume our march towards perfection." Thus encouraged, let me also pray for the further help I need.

What the various spiritual writers say about striving after perfection can be summed up thus: 1) Do what God wills; 2) Do it *as* He wills. The divine will for me, as a religious, is to be found in the Constitutions and regulations based on divine and Church law, the lawful orders and wishes of my superiors, and the common sense dictates of whatever office I hold under obedience. Then God does require certain pure motives and dispositions in the performance of my duties, e.g., all for the love of God, with promptness, attention, exactness.

What is worth doing for God is worth doing well. Strict purity of intention is essential: to please God and do His will in all things. It is not a question of feelings (even though these may be lawfully there), but of a sense of duty and stability towards God, sticking at a thing no matter how I feel about it, no matter how difficult—because this is the will of God for me at the present moment and I love Him. No slackening off, therefore. Nor must I excuse myself on the grounds that the wear and tear of such an active daily life as I lead is no longer compatible with my earlier sincere desire for a genuinely full and deeply interior life of union with God. That is not so, because the grace of God is always there in superabundant measure right alongside my very hand. I can't dodge the issue. Christ's call is there before me, and I must not only heed it but do something about it—if necessary, starting from where I left off some time ago. "Be you therefore perfect as your heavenly Father is perfect." Now what exactly am I going to do? O Jesus, You have said....

When You Pray

Beware of practicing your piety before men in order to be seen by them; for then you will have no reward from your Father who is in heaven.... And when you pray, you must not be like the hypocrites, for they love to stand and pray in the synagogues and at the street corners, that they may be seen by men. Truly, I say to you, they have their reward (Matthew 6:1, 5).

If there was one thing Jesus could not stand it was hypocrisy and when it showed itself at prayer it was particularly nauseous to Him. Personal prayer is essentially genuine and has no regard whatsoever for the eyes of man. It is God's eyes and ears and heart that alone matter to the one who tries to pray well. Any kind of serving the human eye in this matter can only be an ostentatious neon-lit advertisement.

Let me therefore move out at once beyond such spectacular shows to consider once more the ever-necessary subject of real prayer. In Psalm 55 David says: "I call upon my God...evening and morning and noon." I might well think here of those regulated times of prayer in common with my brethren. Our Lord Himself tells us that where two or more are gathered in His name, He is there in the midst of them. Hence I should strive always to say my prayers in common well, feeling sure that this united front must surely pierce the clouds and be pleasing to God according to its general and individual fervor or good will.

Even if I feel no devotion, let me at least do my duty by joining in with purity of intention, because this is God's will for me at this moment and even my obedient voice is pleasing to Him, regardless of my feelings. Can I say that our Lord must really be satisfied with the way I say *all* my public prayers? Resolutions?

But when you pray, go into your room and shut the door and pray to your Father who is in secret; and your Father who sees in secret will reward you (Matthew 6:6).

St. Vincent de Paul maintained that "if we persevere in our vocation, it is through prayer; if we succeed in our business, it is only through prayer; if we do not fall into sin, it is only through prayer; if we remain in charity and attain salvation, it is all through the grace of God and of prayer."

All this implies that genuine prayer desired by our Lord. But what exactly is the quality and makeup of my private prayer? Surely if I am in a room with someone, I don't just recite pieces of poetry or speeches at him. I converse with him, according to the measure of my intimacy, even though it is possible for me quite naturally now and then to use or quote the words of others to get across what I want to say. Hence my prayers to any member of the Holy Trinity should not be just a string of Pater's (or Ave's!) but a genuine attempt to talk lovingly and aptly and in my own language—which can, of course, at times be best expressed precisely in the Our Father or some other already composed prayer. If I haven't learned this simple art yet, then I can begin by simply calling upon the Holy Spirit to teach it to me.

St. Francis de Sales says: "The sacred gift of prayer is in the right hand of God; He is only waiting until you have emptied yourself of self, of this love of your body and of your will, to give it to you." Let me ask now for the gift of genuine prayer or an increase in it. O Holy Spirit....

And in praying do not heap up empty phrases as the Gentiles do; for they think that they will be heard for their many words. Do not be like them, for your Father knows what you need before you ask him (Matthew 6:7-8).

St. Francis de Sales: "If we can speak to God, let us speak. If we are unable to speak, let us remain silent in His presence. Our patience will please Him, and presently, in wonderment we shall see Him take us by the hand, talk with us, and lead us hither and thither through the bypaths of the garden of prayer." Obviously St. Francis is not condoning laziness at prayer and what he says does not refer to prayers in common, where the matter of obedience comes in, for St. John Chrysostom says: "Your prayer is not of such efficacy when you pray alone, as when you pray with your brethren." Abbot Marmion used to say that in prayer one ought to place oneself before God in the most complete submission to His holy and all-lovable will, and then let Him do what He pleases. This man was one of the finest spiritual writers of modern times. What he says bears the mark not only of solidity but also of deep experience and practicality, and so deserves respectful attention.

Am I really content with my own personal prayer life as it stands? Where and how can I improve? "My prayer is to You, O God; at an acceptable time, O God, in the abundance of Your steadfast love answer me.... Hide not Your face from Your servant" (Ps. 69:13, 17).

Purity of Intention

When you give alms, sound no trumpet before you, as the hypocrites do in the synagogues and in the streets, that they may be praised by men. Truly, I say to you, they have their reward. But when you give alms, do not let your left hand know what your right hand is doing, so that your alms may be in secret; and your Father who sees in secret will reward you (Matthew 6:2-4).

The Sermon on the Mount, on which we are trying to meditate these days, has been likened to a musical symphony of quite majestic form. It is a good simile for the discourse is full of excellent themes, some as astounding as the sudden clash of cymbals and others quite foreign to a mere worldly point of view. It is full of contrasts and paradoxes that no one can disprove; full of tunes and melodies that linger long in the mind; the whole, one excellent theme of unison in diversity, showing mankind that true happiness consists in thinking and acting only as God wishes. The shallow-minded automatically dismissed many or most of its teachings for want of serious thought; the prejudiced or hypocrites found it unbearable because it exposed their faults on a cinerama screen. In the verses above it touched them to the quick. Every sabbath in the synagogues a public collection was made, with names and amounts duly noted, and at the end the most conspicuous donors were proclaimed aloud. Naturally this led to an almost complete overshadowing of the motive of true charity in almsgiving. The Pharisees had become noted for their vanity in this respect and our Lord condemns this spirit utterly, refusing them any heavenly reward since they have already received it...public praise and recognition. It is amazing to think that such learned men as the Pharisees allowed themselves to become so blind to their own true position before men and before God. Their hypocrisy made them abominable before God but men saw through them and despised them even when they openly lauded them. St. John Bosco said: "If we labor for our own honor, our thoughts and discoveries, our inventions and our works are worth nothing. Woe to him who works expecting the praises of the world; the world is a bad payer, it always pays with ingratitude" *(M.B.,* X). Easy as it is to condemn the Pharisees, just as easy is it for a religious gradually to lose his original purity of intention, even in the apostolate. I may start out with the best of intentions in the world to do something really fine and helpful for God or my neighbor, but the danger-point comes when people start praising what I do. That should be the warning signal for me to stop and think, and above all to make sure that I continue to do all for the greater glory of God and the good of souls—and that includes no harm to my own soul through vanity. Let me check now on my more outstanding works and see whether a slight taint of pharisaism might have entered. If so: prayer and resolution are needed!

This fine expression of Jesus about the left and right hand has become a proverb, and from it, no doubt, has sprung the lovely maxim of the Scottish Hebrides: "God gives to the left hand what the right hand gives away." The greatest philanthropists in the world are not those who give away huge sums to public or charitable causes and are upset if the newspapers do not splash the fact in striking headlines, but those who give great or little according to their means and abilities with the very minimum of publicity. Seneca of old observed wisely: "He who has conferred a kindness should be silent; he who has received one should speak of it." Referring to the spirit of hypocrisy, God Himself says through Isaiah: "When you come to appear before me, when you spread forth your hands, I will hide my eyes from you; even though you make many prayers, I will not listen. Wash yourselves, make yourselves clean; remove the evil of your doings before my eyes; cease to do evil; learn to do good" (1:12, 15-16); "They shall not please him with their sacrifices" (Hos. 9:4). In my Morning Offering let me daily renew my purity of intention: "O Jesus, I offer You all my prayers, works, actions and sufferings of this day for all the intentions of Your divine heart." But let me try to renew that intention often during the day, applying it to specific actions and especially to good works that I have to do in public and where vanity can so easily enter. In this way I shall follow the wise advice of St. Peter when he says: "As each has received a gift, employ it for one another, as good stewards of God's varied grace: whoever speaks, as one who utters oracles of God; whoever renders service, as one who renders it by the strength which God supplies; in order that in everything God may be glorified through Jesus Christ" (1 Pt. 4:10-11). Living this way, I shall realize what exactly is meant by: "God gives to the left hand what the right hand gives away."

> *And when you fast, do not look dismal, like the hypocrites, for they disfigure their faces that their fasting may be seen by men. Truly, I say to you, they have their reward. But when you fast, anoint your head and wash your face, that your fasting may not be seen by men but by your Father who is in secret; and your Father who sees in secret will reward you (Matthew 6:16-18).*

It is the same theme of contrasting hypocrisy and purity of intention. Proverbs of old has said: "There are those who are pure in their own eyes but are not cleansed of their filth.... If you have been foolish, exalting yourself, put your hand on your mouth" (30:12, 32). It is only when one is doing things solely for God that charity can exert its full reign in our hearts and lives. What our Lord says here applies not only to fasting but to all my public acts and especially my apostolate. The external apostolate can be a grand thing and automatically attract attention and praise, bringing with it that very natural but nevertheless insidious danger of vanity. But true purity of intention dissolves it, for it helps me to base all that is external and honest on what is internal. In my external works I give my time and health, the sweat of my brow, etc., but when I aim to do all these things solely for God's honor (with all which that implies) then I also give what P. Evdokimor calls "the sweat of my heart," which is infinitely pleasing to the heart of God. God doesn't want just my bodily energy and abilities—He wants *me*, the *whole of me!* Can I truly say that that is actually what I am giving Him daily? Surely I can see now the need for an intensification and extension of my daily Morning Offering. O Jesus, who have given Yourself completely to me, help me henceforth to give myself completely to You, with every single drop of the sweat of my heart.

The Poor Christ

Do not lay up for yourselves treasures on earth, where moth and rust consume and where thieves break in and steal, but lay up for yourselves treasures in heaven, where neither moth nor rust consumes and where thieves do not break in and steal. For where your treasure is, there will your heart be also (Matthew 6:19-21).

Since in these meditations we are trying to base our lives not merely on the words of Jesus Christ but also on His own example, let me here take advantage of the above words of His to give an over-all glance at His own life of poverty. During Vatican Council II an amazing number of prelates spoke out most strongly on Christian poverty, maintaining that the Church should not just help and support the poor but be actually poor herself as Christ was. In this Pope Paul VI concurred wholeheartedly, and Cardinal Gerlier of Lyons declared: "The mystery of Christ in the Church is always present, but this mystery becomes today in a special way the mystery of Christ in the poor, Christ who was poor Himself and identified Himself with the poor."

Every year at Christmas we contemplate the supreme poverty of the new-born Christ in a poor stable at Bethlehem; His first human worshipers after Mary and Joseph were poor shepherds; the offering made at His presentation in the temple was only that of the poor. Down in Egypt He was merely a displaced person, probably living in the slums; back in Nazareth He led a life of poverty and the sheer hard work of the poor. There was no splash of wealth and pomp about His public life either; He depended on others all the time for food and lodging, and we can be sure He made His clothes last a long time too. In choosing His apostles, He offered them the challenge of utter poverty: "Go, sell what you possess and give to the poor" (Mt. 19:21)—and they took it manfully, leaving all things to follow Him. So extreme was His life of poverty that He could quote the foxes and the birds of the air as being far better off than He. Let me pause here and consider my own life of poverty in its origin and perseverance. Perhaps I too had little to speak of when I "gave up all things" but have I not in the meantime accumulated many unnecessary articles that throw me out of alignment with this Man who is my model and was so utterly poor throughout His life?

> *No one can serve two masters; for either he will hate the one and love the other, or he will be devoted to the one and despise the other. You cannot serve God and mammon (Matthew 6:24).*

Our Lord's first public miracle took place at the humble wedding of a poor couple who hadn't enough money to buy sufficient wine. Jesus sympathized because He knew the pinch of poverty Himself, and that was why He listened to His own mother's plea on their behalf. Long ages before, Isaiah had given as the signs of His coming that the poor were no longer to be the despised but the privileged ones to whom the Gospel of the Messiah would be first announced. Jesus Himself over and over again warned against the dangers of riches and mammon. What a frightful thing, therefore, if religious orders should ever exemplify His solemn warning about the heavily-laden camel finding it so difficult to enter the symbolic narrow gate called the Needle in the city wall. The obstructing hump in our case might well be, if not actual wealth, a whole heap of unnecessary private luxuries and superfluities. To His disciples going out on their apostolic missions He recommended the simplicity of poverty regarding food, clothing, money and comforts. They were to rely only on the riches of divine Providence which would see to all they needed when they deserved it. The whole of His life was heavily underlined with the true spirit of poverty and detachment. And at the end it was the death of an absolutely poor man, stripped of everything. But why all this? St. Paul tells us: "For you know the grace of our Lord Jesus Christ, that though he was rich, yet *for your sake* he became poor, so that by his poverty you might become rich" (2 Cor. 8:9).

But surely Jesus never gave up the riches of heaven to become poor on earth in order to make us religious materially rich, with a whole wealth of luxury and comfort against which He Himself spoke so strongly! The Church was founded in poverty, so too my own religious order, so why should things be different now? Do I in any way contribute towards the diminishing of the true spirit of poverty in my order or community? How? Why? Jesus, You were truly poor: help me....

> *The eye is the lamp of the body. So, if your eye is sound, your whole body will be full of light; but if your eye is not sound, your whole body will be full of darkness. If then the light in you is darkness, how great is the darkness! (Matthew 6:22-23)*

If there is one thing the modern world is positively demanding it is that there be no further contradictions between words and deeds in the Church, and especially in the matter of poverty. Nevertheless Christ Himself would not wish for extremes. In certain spheres the Church and our religious orders simply must keep up-to-date and be in the very vanguard of progress if they do not want to become utterly estranged and foreign in the very world they are trying to bring to Christ. In schools and hospitals, for example, there must be the same high standards of efficiency as in any public institutions of the same nature, otherwise we shall lose both them and our apostolate. Hence it is not at all a question of not having good, solid buildings with modern and efficient equipment, but what does matter is that it should be obvious to all the world that we religious do not exclude or neglect the poor and that even in apparently comfortable religious buildings there still exists the spirit of Christ's poverty. If anything is necessary or a help towards greater efficiency, towards helping others in the name of Christ, then it can be a good instrument of apostolate and not against poverty. This covers all up-to-date even labor-saving devices and equipment to help in God's work without unnecessary difficulty and danger to health: not luxury, therefore, but apostolic efficiency. Nor is Christ totally against all comforts, for He Himself sat comfortably no doubt at Cana's wedding feast, relaxed and happy, and surely enjoyed the food and wine there as much as anybody else, for He knows that at times we need such breaks and relaxation in order to get a renewal of energies for yet greater work.

Moderation, temperance and sensible thinking on such matters put us on the same side of the room as the poor Christ. Can I say that in all things regarding poverty, and especially concerning apostolate, feast days, food, relaxation, comfort, etc., I am guided according to the mind of Christ? O Jesus, model of sensible poverty....

My Own Poverty

Do not be anxious about your life, what you shall eat or what you shall drink, nor about your body, what you shall put on. Is not life more than food, and the body more than clothing? Look at the birds of the air; they neither sow nor reap nor gather into barns, and yet your heavenly Father feeds them. Are you not of more value than they? (Matthew 6:25-26)

Perfectae Caritatis says: "Religious poverty requires more than limiting the use of possessions to the consent of superiors; members of a community ought to be poor in both fact and spirit, and have their treasures in heaven" (13). We, after all, are supposed to be the Church of the poor, followers of the poor Christ, and on no account must we by our carelessness or lack of prudence mar this image in the eyes of the world, and especially in the eyes of the poor. The fact is, however, that it is not easy to convince the generality of outsiders that we are really poor. Do we ever have to go without a meal simply because there's not enough money in the house? Do we ever have to work away in spite of illness because we can't afford a doctor? Do we have to wear our clothes right down to tatters because our income is so small? Do we have to worry about board and lodging, to skimp and scrape in order to buy some necessary item or other? Do we have to walk long distances or travel always by crowded train, bus or trolley because we cannot afford even a secondhand car? It is good to recall these things and contrast our advantages with the hardships not only of the poor but even the middle classes.

Our advantages come from God's Providence and we should show our appreciation as a community and as individuals, and do all we possibly can to live poorly and help Christ's poor. We religious are important leaders and exemplars in the Church of the poor Christ and we must make absolutely sure that by our life and example we are on the same wavelength as the poor, otherwise we help the devil himself to jam the lines of communication between them and Christ. Let me pray now to the poor Christ.

> *Why are you anxious about clothing? Consider the lilies of the field, how they grow; they neither toil nor spin; yet I tell you, even Solomon in all his glory was not arrayed like one of these. But if God so clothes the grass of the field, which today is alive and tomorrow is thrown into the oven, will He not much more clothe you, O men of little faith? (Matthew 6:28-30)*

I have a public vow of poverty affecting all material goods, their use and disposal, and the canonists can make the details quite complicated. For me, however, the easiest and the greatest saving measure in the whole matter is contained in two points: personal sense of responsibility and lawful permission. There are definitely many ways in which I can fail against either my vow or its virtue and I should cultivate a very delicate conscience in all that concerns poverty, especially as it is an important part of my Christian witnessing. There should therefore be no question of manipulating or bluff, or cheating, or downright deception—such gambles are unworthy of a follower of Christ. I must be careful too about presumed permissions, for there are strict conditions attached: 1) It must be either impossible or at least greatly inconvenient to go along and ask directly for the permission; 2) After that I must, as it were, place myself in spirit before my superior and if I can then feel quite sure he lawfully can and would, under the circumstances, grant me the permission, only then may I presume it; and 3) I still have the obligation to report and explain to him as soon as possible. Quite a delicate business? Therefore it is better to be extremely careful about using presumed permissions, isn't it? Tacit permission is even more dangerous because I can easily deceive myself into thinking my superior sees (he may not, he may be distracted), says nothing and therefore approves. (He may not approve, he may even be scared to say so—Whose fault: his? or mine, my touchy character and ways, etc.?).

I should never fall back on such a mean way of doing things, when I can or should be manly enough to weigh up the lawfulness or not. Then I should go humbly and ask permission directly, prepared even for a refusal. Why should I make things more difficult for my superior, especially by trading on his weakness? Any lack of sincerity, any kind of pretense or subterfuge, any misrepresentations of the truth are quite unworthy of a religious, and they can only stain and warp the conscience. Have I any historical blushes to record, especially on these points of presumed and tacit permissions? Resolution (a firm one, please!)?

> *Therefore, do not be anxious, saying, "What shall we eat?" or "What shall we drink?" or "What shall we wear?" For the Gentiles seek all these things; and your heavenly Father knows that you need them all. But seek first his kingdom and his righteousness, and all these things shall be yours as well (Matthew 6:31-33).*

Fr. Paul Albera, S.D.B., says: "Some religious, without perceiving it, have gradually created countless needs for themselves, and expect their superiors to supply them with comforts such as would hardly be found even in wealthy families, and they lose their peace of mind when they are denied anything they so ardently desire." Then he goes on to give two very opportune pieces of advice: "1) Love poverty and never be ashamed of practicing it, even when your house is suffering from lack of necessities; 2) Accept willingly and generously the consequences of poverty in a spirit of penance." All this fits in with our Lord's own words above. Poverty of spirit is at the very heart of my vow of poverty: I love and therefore must follow the poor Christ, trying to imitate as closely as possible His spirit of detachment even when I have all or more than I need—avoiding, however, all silly extremes. The poor Christ must always be the ideal before me as an individual religious, making me want to imitate Him in every possible lawful way. I have also a community duty of poverty, a witness to the world outside. How can I contribute? Even in such apparently small ways as not wasting; making things last longer; not expecting replacements too soon or too easily; avoiding, however, false economies (beware: plausible salesmen and advertisements!) prudent and sensible administration. Even if we seem to live comfortably on an income of almost nothing a year, let us recall the prudent Chinese maxim: "Even though we live in a forest, it is not wise to waste firewood."

Divine Providence looks after us in a truly marvelous way but we must never abuse His kindness and the charity of His instruments, our good benefactors, and certainly we should never live better-off than they do. There is a crying need today for the Church of Christ to be recognized obviously as the Church of the poor, helping the poor, being poor. In this campaign for recognition as such, we religious, as communities and as individuals, play a very important part by the manifest example of our own lives with a *public* vow of poverty. Am I really doing all I can in this matter? O Jesus, You have said: "I have given you an example, that as I have done, so do you also"; therefore....

Worry and Care

Do not be anxious about tomorrow, for tomorrow will be anxious for itself. Let the day's own trouble be sufficient for the day (Matthew 6:34).

Here we have a delightful instance of the sensible, psychological practicality of our Lord. It wasn't that Jesus was just one of those happy-go-lucky types who doesn't care about anything, knowing it will pass. It wasn't that Jesus was not concerned with the future; He quite definitely was, for how could He ever forget that Calvary lay ahead, each day closer! But there is a big difference between worry and concern. A worried person only sees problems, but a concerned person tries calmly to solve them.

The word "worry," then, is not in God's vocabulary and should not be in mine either. Jesus was the sound psychologist and psychiatrist *par excellence* and if at times any worry upsets me He will surely want me to analyze it sensibly and as calmly as possible—stretched out preferably on the comfortable couch of confidence in His kind Providence!

A problem may look big, even overwhelming in itself, but when we reduce it to its component parts, it becomes much simplified and far easier to tackle from some strategic point likely to give us victory. If we allow our minds to revolve vaguely round and round such a problem, the brain can get quite dizzy and cannot see that strategic point. The only wise thing to do is to stop quite deliberately, make a very slow act of confident abandonment to God, and then calmly set about analyzing the problem, its origin, possible results, possible solutions—keeping one hand tight in Christ's all the while! Very often what God wants one to do at that moment is something quite out of line with one's position, possibly even something as seemingly mundane as a game, or a piece of music, or a good brisk walk, or even a healthy swim! For a worried brain why not, when possible, use God's own gifts of fresh air, sunshine, water, cheerful companionship, absorption in something that seemingly is not of value but at that moment actually is, and is part of God's will too to help us fulfill His injunction about not worrying? Am I worried or concerned? How great is my trust in Christ and Providence?

Worry, we are told medically, can affect the circulation, the heart, the glands, the colon and stomach (ouch—those ulcers!), the whole nervous system—in other words it can upset one's whole health. This was never willed by God when He gave us such a splendid organism. People who give in to worry become very "nervous," and charity can be affected because they can easily upset others too—and again God never intended us to be an unholy nuisance to others. There are even people who seem proud of their nerves, judging by how often they speak about them! Perhaps they think that this denotes a certain fine temperament, sensitiveness or refinement, with a special tendency for ideas out of the ordinary. In actual fact it more generally denotes a lack of self-control.

I can either be master of my own mind or let my mind master me. So too with nerves and worry. If I haven't done so already, it's about time I really started to get down to the technique of relaxation—Christian as well as psychological and physiological. Even if I am not at present worried, let me make a very humble, sincere and confident act of loving abandonment of the future to God, my loving Father.

Our Lord tells us that each day has its own particular troubles and one should deal with those instead of possible, probable or even certain future ones. Past mistakes and future fears are alike, worthless in themselves as subjects for sound thought. The past is over and done with, unfortunate though it may have been, and if I wrap it all up in the infinite mercy of God with deep sorrow for any definite or possible guilt, I may safely place it in the wounded heart of Christ. By all means let me continue in various ways to make reparation but without any morbid raking up of the details. Leave those to God. In the last point I discovered how to settle the future: holy abandonment. And the present? Straight thinking is necessary, making an effort to see things at their true value, without making every little mouse an elephant.

Let me strive to surrender all that I am, all that I have, all that I think to God, desirous only of doing His holy will in all things. Jesus, You abandoned Yourself entirely to Your loving Father; help me....

Judge Not!

Judge not, that you be not judged. For with the judgment you pronounce you will be judged, and the measure you give will be the measure you get (Matthew 7:1-2).

St. Matthew's account of the Sermon on the Mount is the longest, for it contains far more details than the other evangelists give. In the present instance we have the golden rule of charity and judgment. Our Lord doesn't forbid the passing of judgments but He makes it clear that in doing so we must be absolutely free of any malice, prejudice, obstinacy, vindictive spirit, etc. St. Paul, writing to Timothy, says that "the sins of some men are conspicuous, pointing to judgment" (1 Tm. 5:24); sometimes malice is quite obvious, e.g., calculated murder, cruelty, torture, downright lying, etc., and we are not expected to whitewash such things in a kind of wishy-washy charity. The real charity in such cases lies in not appointing ourselves judges of other people's consciences, no matter what the appearances. God alone knows the aberrations and madness that can seize the human mind at times to make seeming monsters out of men. The supreme law of charity or love always holds good.

Vatican II: "Respect and love ought to be extended also to those who think or act differently than we do in social, political, and religious matters too. In fact, the more deeply we come to understand their ways of thinking through such courtesy and love, the more easily will we be able to enter into dialogue with them. This love and good will, to be sure, must in no way render us indifferent to truth and goodness. Indeed love itself impels the disciple of Christ to speak the saving truth to all men. But it is necessary to distinguish between error, which always merits repudiation, and the person in error, who never loses the dignity of being a person, even when he is flawed by false or inadequate religious notions. God alone is the judge and searcher of hearts; for that reason He forbids us to make judgments about the internal guilt of anyone" *(Gaudium et Spes*, 28). Clear enough, isn't it? Do I fall short at times? Why? Therefore....

> *Why do you see the speck that is in your brother's eye, but do not notice the log that is in your own eye? Or how can you say to your brother, "Let me take the speck out of your eye," when there is the log in your own eye? (Matthew 7:3-4)*

At the root of all unkind and rash judgments there is the same old criminal, pride. Pride is dreadful and no one even likes to speak much about it, for the simple fact that it is an inherent human tendency and in many cases the cancer is already rampant. Our Lord knew this and in His kindness He used the psychological method on a subject that has to be mentioned in warning from time to time by way of attempting a much-needed and always possible cure. His approach here is quite delightful and proves for all time that He did have an excellent sense of humor. He gives a word-picture caricature that He probably uttered with a smile and a lovely twinkle in His fascinating eyes. Those about Him surely laughed or chuckled with merriment at the mental picture of a man with a huge log in his own eye actually trying to search out and extract the speck of dust in someone else's. Perhaps He was also trying to tell them that a sound sense of humor is a very sane and balancing thing to have in life.

The pessimists and sour faced mostly lack sound judgment, whereas the optimist and the one who keeps his God-given precious gift of a sense of humor fresh and balanced is saved from ultimate misery even in the worst situations. He manages to turn his thoughts from the really bad things in order to concentrate on a healthy funny point he sees in the whole situation. It can indeed be a saving grace, worthy of its own special *Te Deum!* Am I a confirmed pessimist? Have I a good, sound sense of humor? If so let me thank God, and when tempted to judge others unkindly, search instead for the saving or humorous point and thus dodge uncharitableness. In this way I make fun of the devil himself, which is just what he needs—frequently!

> *You hypocrite, first take the log out of your own eye, and then you will see clearly to take the speck out of your brother's eye (Matthew 7:5).*

Although Jesus probably had the crowd smiling or laughing at His caricature, that was just to make the idea presentable; the sting lay in the tail, and, although speaking to all, He singled out each guilty person there with the sharp term "hypocrite." It must have been quite a hard blow for some. Perhaps He also meant those very superior persons—the scribes, Pharisees and Sadducees—who gave themselves such airs and were forever publicly condemning others, including Jesus Himself. Certainly the log in their eyeballs was more than obvious to everyone else. Criticism is a very dangerous piece of dynamite to handle. Sometimes, because of one's official position or sense of responsibility, it is necessary and can even be an act of charity, but never when there is malice or unkindness attached. In such circumstances, when one finds it genuinely painful to criticize, then one may feel fairly safe, but if there's the slightest feeling of pleasure in doing so, one is already walking in a minefield. There's an old saying: "Before you call the village dirty, see that your own home is clean."

Before I dare criticize anyone, let me honestly examine myself and my motives first. Have I the very same fault myself, using his to camouflage mine? If I were in his exact circumstances, might I not be just as bad—or worse? Will any good be achieved by my criticism? Is true charity, i.e., love, at the root of my criticism? etc. Isn't it much safer to mind my own business and leave all judgment to God? O Jesus, in the past I have...; in the future, especially today, help me to..., particularly with regard to....

Asking and Giving

Ask, and it will be given you; seek, and you will find; knock, and it will be opened to you. For everyone who asks receives, and he who seeks finds, and to him who knocks it will be opened (Matthew 7:7-8).

When you often converse with someone whom you really like and who really likes you, then after a while you begin to realize not only how much that person is influencing you, but also how much influence you have on him too. This seems to be behind our Lord's words—this freedom of conversation which one can have in prayer and candid demands with the God we love so much. The person who has tremendous faith and confidence in prayer comes to realize, with a joyful humility, that he has great power over the heart of God Himself. One striking instance of this, among many in the Old Testament, was Moses. How often when the people turned away so capriciously from God, Moses simply begged pardon for them or said quite bluntly yet respectfully and lovingly—"Blot me, I pray you, out of your book which you have written" (Ex. 32:32). It worked every time! There is an urgent need in the world today for many men and women of prayer of the caliber of Moses and other great saints of prayer. The worship of idols is not by any means a thing of the dim and distant past—it goes on constantly today in so many different and sometimes cleverly camouflaged ways: not merely the golden calf or its equivalent in local currency, but the worship of power and pleasure, and above all of self. There is even prevalent today, perhaps more than ever before, that worship of one's own intellect. Such people get together and declare quite brazenly that "God is dead"—no doubt implying they are His lawful successors! And how many followers they have!

How great, then, is the need for real men and women of prayer to turn back the anger or punishment of God from a world that seems not merely to disregard or spurn Him, but even deny Him altogether. How often do I think of my own personal responsibility in this regard—for I belong to the world, and have my duties in and towards it, including above all this mighty one of prayer. Therefore, even now, let me take quite literally what Jesus says: "Ask...seek...knock..."—the matter is quite urgent, frightfully urgent, in fact!

> *Or what man of you, if his son asks him for bread, will give him a stone? Or if he asks for a fish, will give him a serpent? (Matthew 7:9-10)*

Not only is the world desperately in need of prayers, and of my prayers, but there is a great part of it that not only takes them for granted but relies strongly on them. There are even flagrant or careless sinners who rely on the prayers of religious as their one solitary link between themselves and God. Heaven help them if my prayer-life is so weak that that link is so tenuous that it could too easily break! Can I disclaim all responsibility for the loss of such souls? If people ask me for prayers, does my mouth too readily say "Yes, certainly" while my heart is in strong silence, giving a stone instead of the bread of life that could re-nourish the faith of such people? Prayer can work marvels! Jesus Christ is our supreme Mediator with the Father but it is part of His plan for the spread of His kingdom on earth that I assist Him in a special way in this work of intercessory prayer.

Whenever others ask for my prayers, then, it should be for me not just an occasion for attempted humility, "Oh, my prayers are not much good, I'm afraid!" but rather a sharp reminder of the intercessory role I have in the eyes of God and man alike. This realization, of course, should never swell my head ("How highly these people think of me and my prayers!") but rather swell my heart with a greater love of God based on the even humiliating but helpful thought, "Though I'm not one bit as good as they think, I'll do my very best to pray much for them, relying on God's mercy to help me improve and also grant what they need."

Let me recall now some of the people who habitually rely on my prayers or who have recently asked for them. Has my whole attitude to this matter been a healthy one?

Will it be so in the future? How? What can I do this very day to be a helpful intercessor? O Jesus, You said, "Ask and it will be given you," so I humbly ask now that....

> *If you, then, who are evil, know how to give good gifts to your children, how much more will your Father who is in heaven give good things to those who ask him! (Matthew 7:11)*

In spite of my own personal unworthiness, then, there is one big and really worthwhile job I can do for the world: intercessory prayer. This in spite of all my sinful past and present weakness, even future failures. Confidence in the promise of Jesus is the great thing, but He also expects me to increase my intercessory power by the improvement of my own spiritual and community life. Whatever charity I do may be based not just on natural, almost instinctive kindness that will automatically stretch out to give someone what he needs, but on my own continual efforts to fill my life with the love of God. All my charity then will be the genuine overflow that I can generously impart to others without any selfishness or expectancy of return favors.

The very utmost and best that I can do for my neighbor is only the weakest possible reflection of the generosity and goodness of God. He will then eagerly seize my humble gift and electrify it with direct volts of atomic power from His own Sacred Heart. This will not only cause my own poor heart to blaze in itself but to act as a beacon-light of true charity to others, lighting the way towards heaven for some who need it badly. This is to be the person of prayer that God chose me to be, and which the world, and especially many of my friends, think me to be. Am I letting people down, God especially? At this point a sound resolution should suggest itself easily—and a fervent prayer also.

The Narrow Gate

Whatever you wish that men would do to you, do so to them (Matthew 7:12).

At a congress of religious in 1961, the following statement was made: "The world yearns to see the face of God. The world wants God to explain the riddle of life. The weary weight of this unintelligible world cannot be borne by mankind alone. The world wants to see the Christ of God yoked to the same plough it pulls. Until the world sees Him in His followers, it will continue to wallow in the slough of despondency and wander in the valley of the shadow of death." Just typical, flowery rhetoric? But Christ Himself said: "By this shall men know that you are my followers, that you show love for one another." So we can't dismiss lightly the responsibility in that statement, for the world does indeed (even if it denies it) look for that manifestation of the face of God which is at once recognizable in true Christian charity. This is a big responsibility and perhaps we have not always shouldered it properly. Over and over again the world has been able to twist the ancient compliment into scorn: "See how those Christians love one another!" and even today it makes capital out of any seeming proof of a lack of charity, unity and peace in the Church, in religious orders or groups, in communities. St. Cyprian wrote: "To break unity is to corrupt truth." The fundamental truth of the Church is in its unity based on love, by which the members are made one with Christ, the Head, and with one another. But "charity begins at home" and my first job is to ensure that I do my very best to contribute from the overflow of my loving heart my generous measure towards the peace, unity and true fraternal charity of my own most immediate group or community. "So if there is any encouragement in Christ, any incentive of love, any participation in the Spirit, any affection and sympathy, complete my job by being of the same mind, having the same love, being in full accord and of one mind. Do nothing from selfishness or conceit, but in humility count others better than yourselves. Let each of you look not only to his own interests, but also to the interests of others. Have this mind among yourselves, which was in Christ Jesus" (Phil. 2:1-5). This was precisely the way Paul tried to show the face of Christ to the world of his day. This is precisely what God expects of me today. Let there be in my life no caricature of Christ's face!

Enter by the narrow gate; for the gate is wide and the way is easy, that leads to destruction, and those who enter by it are many (Matthew 7:13).

Charity should be the widest gate of all leading into heaven—and so indeed it is really, but unfortunately it would seem that the old economic factor of supply and demand has caused charity to become a very narrow gate through which comparatively few enter. If more people practiced it truly, it would perforce extend. Uncharitableness has become such a very wide and easy gate that leads to hell and it so often seems jammed with eager entrants! It would seem that even Christians and religious have a long job ahead in order to erect a wide gate of charity. St. Paul says that whereas knowledge so often puffs up, "love builds up." Through the gifts and grace of God I may have various talents and abilities in this or that sphere and use them seemingly well, but forgetfulness of their true origin can cause my knowledge to puff up my head with pride. When, however, I try to use my God-given gifts humbly and in the true altruistic service of my neighbor then my charity is helping to build up: myself, my neighbor, my group, my community, the Church, the kingdom of God on earth. How sad, therefore, that charity can become a very cold word for some. That should certainly not be true among religious and Christians. For us it should be a warm, dynamic word, a vivid reality, the pulsating motive behind our/my every deed and word because it springs out, not from a narrow refrigerator door, but from the warm inner depths of a heart full of love of neighbor and of God inseparably united. If I do not find this a vivid picture of my group or community, am I not also in some way at fault? How? What remedy? O Jesus....

For the gate is narrow and the way is hard, that leads to life, and those who find it are few (Matthew 7:14).

Charity is undoubtedly not always easy to practice and that is why our Lord can speak of a narrow gate and a hard way. The word "love" has become so debased in literature and song that often religious men are afraid to use it, lest it seem they are just emotional. Yet the fact remains and is strongly upheld by psychologists of standing that even men are capable of a real love, one that is noble and strong, and therefore men have nothing to be ashamed of in admitting quite openly that they love God and their neighbor in this noble, strong and manly way. Certainly there is nothing unmanly or emotional in St. Paul's virile concept of charity or love portrayed so resoundingly in his short but famous 1 Corinthians, chapter 13, which I should know by heart and practice. It begins: "If I speak in the tongues of men and of angels, but have not love, I am a noisy gong or a clanging cymbal," and ends: "So faith, hope, love abide, these three; but the greatest of these is love"—a firm, unemotional verdict that seals all the wonderful things said in the intervening verses.

What a pity that charity has been made such a narrow gate, that its path has been made so hard, that so few comparatively find it, for it leads so wonderfully to life and light and peace and radiating happiness. A good resolution for today might be to read, study, perhaps learn by heart 1 Corinthians 13, but above all to practice it and see how I can help others also to be Christlike in their kindness, their love. O Jesus....

Centurion's Servant

As he entered Capernaum, a centurion came forward to him, beseeching him and saying, "Lord, my servant is lying paralyzed at home, in terrible distress." And he said to him, "I will come and heal him" (Matthew 8:5-7).

Perhaps the first striking thing about the centurion is his easy confidence in Jesus. He was a pagan, a Roman, a military officer, yet he shows great confidence in this man of another and conquered race. Well does Montaigne say that "confidence in another man's virtue is no slight evidence of one's own." Jesus is obviously pleased by the soldier's attitude of trust in Himself and charity towards a servant and at once agrees to go along with him. Early in His ministry He had been approached by another ruler from Capernaum who begged the cure of his own son and at first Jesus seemed to treat him with a certain aloofness. Here, however, He at once seems to take to this Roman centurion and readily agrees to do what he asks. It seems clear that in the earlier case Jesus sensed a lack of complete trust, but not here. Unmistakably, therefore, confidence in God is a great compliment, and perfect trust is the highest we can pay.

Why should we ever doubt the power of God, the infinite kindness and mercy of Jesus? We have every possible reason not just merely for trust but for complete, undoubting confidence. We have the inexpressible comfort of feeling safe with Jesus; no need for inhibitions with Him, for we can say things just as they are, quite sure that He understands, listens and loves us. Let me consider this prayerfully, thankfully in His regard.

But the centurion answered him, "Lord, I am not worthy to have you come under my roof; but only say the word, and my servant will be healed. For I am a man under authority, with soldiers under me; and I say to one, 'Go,' and he goes, and to another, 'Come,' and he comes, and to my slave, 'Do this,' and he does it" (Matthew 8:8-9).

Here we see the truly outstanding part of the incident, showing the perfect flower of this noble man's confidence in Jesus. So perfect is his trust that he says there is no need even for Jesus to come with him: he feels that his own home is not worthy to receive Him and that, in fact, Jesus can cure his servant from a distance. He compares his own human authority over others with the divine authority of Jesus over all things, including illness: a clear acknowledgement of the divinity in Christ. This man, remember, was no fool. The standards of promotion in the Roman army were high and firm. A centurion was an officer in charge of 100 soldiers, well trained to strict obedience, as this man himself declared; moreover, he asserts, he also has slaves. There is no boasting here of his own grandiose authority and dignity and the power he is able to wield over men. It is all told in a spirit of direct simplicity to underline the complete confidence he has in Christ. He gives examples of his own succinct orders to others and implies that he is quite sure that Jesus, even by one word of command uttered from a distance, can at once cure his servant. Here indeed was a soul that gave tremendous joy to the heart of Jesus: someone who trusted Him completely. He expects that same trust from me, but do I always give it and show it? Perhaps so many of my prayers are not answered precisely because of this lack of perfect confidence in Jesus, who is almighty.

Let me reflect now on my own remissness in this regard and try to make as perfect an act of confidence in Jesus as I can.

When Jesus heard him, he marvelled, and said to those who followed him, "Truly, I say to you, not even in Israel have I found such faith. I tell you, many will come from east and west and sit at table with Abraham, Isaac and Jacob in the kingdom of heaven, while the sons of the kingdom will be thrown into the outer darkness; there men will weep and gnash their teeth." And to the centurion Jesus said, "Go; be it done for you as you have believed." And the servant was healed at that very moment (Matthew 8:10-13).

This centurion makes a tremendous impression on Jesus, not for his fine Roman military uniform, his physical stature or noble face, but for his splendid manliness and the openness of his noble character—"He marvelled." How encouraging too to find this very human trait in the personality of Jesus and to hear Him giving open praise to the centurion, who contrasted so greatly with the cold disbelief and the subtle trap-setting of so many of the rulers of His own Chosen People. This man's vibrant faith and humble confidence filled the heart of Jesus with consolation, and yet at once He laments at the very opposite in His own—"not even in Israel." He prophesies then the entrance of the Gentiles into the kingdom of heaven itself, which hitherto the Jews had claimed to be their own exclusive right. There will be no distinction of race or color, of culture or social status: heaven lies open to all who show the same faith and confidence as this noble Roman; those who fail to measure up to the standard will be unworthy of the never-ending joyous spiritual banquet. For them instead there will be rejection by God because they first rejected Him ("outer darkness...weep and gnash their teeth"—typical Hebrew expressions of sorrow, despair, terror and fury). Quite calmly then Jesus does the very thing His petitioner expected—"the servant was healed at that very moment." The Church has adopted and adapted the centurion's humble words for the precious moment preceding Holy Communion. This should be the ideal moment, then, for me to renew and strengthen my faith and confidence in Jesus, entrusting myself to Him completely, with the fullest trust that His entrance into my poor heart can infallibly cure me of all my ills if I put myself in the right dispositions. Let this idea form part of my prayer now and of my special resolution for this day. "O Lord, I am not worthy...."

Funeral at Naim

Soon afterward he went to a city called Naim, and his disciples and a great crowd went with him. As he drew near to the gate of the city, behold, a man who had died was being carried out, the only son of his mother, and she was a widow; and a large crowd from the city was with her. And when the Lord saw her, he had compassion on her and said to her, "Do not weep" (Luke 7:11-13).

Naim was, in the time of Jesus, a beautiful town on the northern slope of one of the smaller peaks of Mount Hermon, with glorious views of Mt. Tabor and Nazareth across to the Plain of Esdraelon. It is hard to imagine Jesus not having an eye for the beautiful in nature even here, and hence in this lovely setting occurred what has been called one of the loveliest gems of Luke's Gospel. Today there is only a very small village there, but close by one can still see the ancient rock cemetery towards which the funeral cortege was proceeding when Jesus met it. The funeral seems to have been a large one, showing possibly the popularity of the widowed mother and/or of her dead son or at least a great sense of public sympathy. In Israel the death of a widow's only son was always considered a tremendous loss and three times in the Old Testament we find vivid mention of it. Perhaps Jesus had been admiring the surrounding panorama just before entering the town and, on hearing the crowd of mourners coming through the main gate, His heart was at once touched by the great contrast between the beauty and the sadness, and He felt urged to wipe out the sorrow and add joy to the grace of the whole setting. Perhaps too He had in mind the thought that not very far ahead in time there would be another sad funeral cortege of an only Son of a widow named Mary, His own beloved Mother! He goes up to this mourning mother and tells her something that perhaps many had already been telling her: "Do not weep." But there must surely have been something quite different in the way He said it, something startlingly different, with a tone of supreme, heartfelt sympathy combined with a sense of authority and power. Others must have heard Him too and, like the mother, stopped in their tracks, filled with wonder and anticipation.

It is perhaps trite to say that death must come to all, without regard to popularity or status, that it is inevitable, etc.—facts we already recall regularly and, it is to be hoped, salutarily. Here let our application be: may my death also arouse the deepest sympathy of Jesus for those who will mourn for me so that they may receive the spiritual comfort they need and not grieve unreasonably without leaning heavily on the spirit of faith and God's holy will. As regards myself, may my death be preceded by a tremendous faith in the mercy of Jesus, prompting me to perfect sorrow for all sins and a spirit of holy abandonment. Without morbidity, let me now try to contemplate my own death and funeral in this light, and pray that my passing may indeed be something beautiful in the eyes of God. O Jesus, Master of all things beautiful in the world, Master of life and death....

> *And he came and touched the bier, and the bearers stood still. And he said, "Young man, I say to you, arise." And the dead man sat up, and began to speak. And he gave him to his mother (Luke 7:14-15).*

Very briefly but so vividly Luke describes the scene—how meaningful, for example, even those two simple words "stood still." The pall-bearers seemed to know instinctively that something extraordinary was about to happen, that their sad job was over. There was no coffin, the body was borne on a stretcher, covered with the funeral shroud, such as Jesus Himself would soon have. Perhaps He lowered the shroud from the boy's face and chest before giving him the direct and authoritative order: "Young man, I say to you, arise." Surely there must have been much good in that boy's character and life that Jesus should single him out in a way that would be forever remembered in history. Note, too, his prompt obedience:

"And the dead man sat up," perhaps not knowing what it was all about, unable momentarily to contact reality, but then he "began to speak": questions? exclamations? praise? Perhaps all and more. And why does Luke say: "And he gave him to his mother"? Perhaps both son and mother were petrified with a rush of astonished and wonderful feelings and, sympathizing, Jesus Himself helps the lad to get up and leads him by the arm to his mother's embrace. The implications of the whole scene are so easy to imagine with justification, and the few words written light up brilliantly the beautiful humanity and magnetic personality of the God-Man, Jesus.

This thought should lead me to an unbounded confidence in the goodness, kindness, mercy and practical charity of my supreme Example. It should encourage me also to a firm trust in His healing power every time I try to make an act of true sorrow or go to confession. I might well examine my attitudes on these two points and take suitable resolves, including prompt obedience to Jesus' express order, "I say to you, arise!"—from the death of grievous sin, from the mud of careless habits, from lukewarmness to a better following of Christ, from mere favor and good-will to real holiness of mind and heart and life! O Jesus,...

> *Fear seized them all; and they glorified God, saying, "A great prophet has arisen among us!" and "God has visited his people!" And this report concerning him spread through the whole of Judea and all the surrounding country (Luke 7:16-17).*

"God has visited his people!" is a favorite biblical exclamation for wonderful happenings, especially in times of joy. It came naturally now to the lips of those surrounding Jesus, the mother, the resurrected son, and doubtless, as was customary, it was taken up by the crowd and chanted aloud as an expression of thanksgiving and joy. They gave praise too to Jesus, as a great prophet and His fame spread abroad even more widely.

If only they had considered more deeply and recognized in Him their God-become-Man for them! How much praise is there in my own prayer-life? There are so many things to be grateful for: the beauty and panorama of so many places I have seen in the past or still see daily; so many special graces and favors...birth, baptism, parents, family, vocation, sacraments, perhaps cures (great and small), oh, so many wonderful things to be truly grateful for in my prayers! "God has visited his people!" Let me think on some of these things now, offer God due praise and resolve to live in a sense of special gratitude this day.

Sinner in Simon's House

One of the Pharisees asked him to eat with him, and he went into the Pharisee's house, and sat at table. And behold, a woman of the city, who was a sinner, when she learned that he was sitting at table in the Pharisee's house, brought an alabaster flask of ointment, and standing behind him at his feet, weeping, she began to wet his feet with her tears, and wiped them with the hair of her head, and kissed his feet, and anointed them with the ointment. Now when the Pharisee who had invited him saw it, he said to himself, "If this man were a prophet, he would have known who and what sort of woman this is who is touching him, for she is a sinner." And Jesus answering said to him, "Simon, I have something to say to you." And he answerd, "What is it, Teacher?" (Luke 7:36-40)

In view of the fact that the Pharisees were ever on the look-out for opportunities to trap Jesus and were aware that He knew it, it seems strange to find Him here actually invited to have a meal with one of them, who soon shows his own interior unfriendliness. According to the usage of those times the meal would have been held around a semicircular table in the middle of the room. The servants brought the dishes and served from the inside of this, while the guests reclined on divans leading away from the table on the other side. In view of what Simon, the host, really thinks of Jesus, it seems unlikely that there was a special feast put on in His honor. He was probably just invited casually in the hope of a slip-up, and it may even be that Simon provided intentionally the occasion that followed. We do not really know, but one immediate lesson comes out: the absolute necessity of sincerity in all our dealings with God and neighbor. To offer hospitality is a very kind act but look how it was spoiled here. Of course it is not always easy to arouse great feelings of kindness in ourselves when performing certain acts of external charity, simply because at times we are being caused great inconvenience. It is then easy enough perhaps to put on a mere external act of seeming to be kind and obliging, while interiorly grumbling or even fuming at the inconvenience. It is a pity to allow the better part, the intention, to be thus spoiled in the sight of God, just being content that the other person concerned is charmed by our seeming courtesy, kindness, etc. The main thing is that it doesn't ring true in the ears of God. How often this can happen. Therefore it is up to me on such occasions to make a very special effort to conquer unkind interior reactions, to offer up the mortification and inconvenience to God, humbly asking His help to make me kind and charitable not only exteriorly but especially interiorly.

Let me now examine my own sincerity of intention in my dealing with others. "Now therefore fear the Lord, and serve him in sincerity and in faithfulness" (Josh. 24:14). In all my relations with others, it is safest to look beyond the person before me in order to find and serve Christ in sincerity and faithfulness.

It is generally believed, but by no means certain, that the woman in this scene was Mary Magdalene, whose reputation as a public sinner was notorious, and the boldness of her entry into the dining-room seemed to accord with it. Simon's mind concentrated on this negative side, coupled with his contempt for the woman and for Jesus for allowing her action: If Jesus were really the great prophet He pretended to be, then obviously He would have repelled this disreputable sinner with horror, even harshness. How could He be the Holy One of God and allow such contact with a public sinner? To Simon came a certain sense of satisfaction no doubt that his own perspicacity had been proven by the distasteful incident. The idea of possible repentance, true sorrow, public penance, and the redemption of a soul even such as this, did not seem to find a place in Simon's mind.

Where uncharitable ways of thinking and judging are allowed to become the pattern of one's life, the sincerity of charity finds no place in the heart. How often we see things happen that seem worthy of instant condemnation—but is it wise to be precipitous in judging?

God alone can read into the innermost depths and judge truly any action. No matter how obvious things may appear, it is possible that God sees even one single motive that may throw the whole affair into an entirely different light. All the evidence before my eyes may urge me to condemn, but it is never wise to do so. God alone can see every detail, He alone can judge truly. Let me therefore leave all verdicts to Him. My job is not to appraise others, no matter what the evidence against them. I am simply to pray for God's saving mercy for them and for myself. Let me do so now, "for his mercy endures forever."

"Simon, I have something to say to you." And he answered: "What is it, Teacher?"

Notice the tact with which Jesus approached Simon in order to correct him. No harsh accusations, no severe telling off; even for Simon there is the chance of salvation. When things appear obviously bad, it may seem natural and justifiable to become upset and indulge in severity, but that is not the way of Jesus, for that is the very moment when the greatest charity and tact is needed. Harsh scoldings and bitter accusations often serve to harden our own heart as well as those we thus "correct"—they are useless, unpedagogical, unpsychological, futile.

Tact is the fruit of charity, of true love of neighbor: it will never be the outstanding quality of anyone who has the miserable habit of ever searching for faults, rash judging, harshly criticizing, proudly putting on, even mentally, the "better than thou" cloak of greater respectability. I should often pray for this real virtue of tact. Let me examine myself in practical fashion on it now, considering also the possibility that at this very moment, on this very subject, Jesus may be saying to me: "Simon, I have something to say to you." Let my reply, be truly humble and sincere and ready for anything when I ask: "What is it, Teacher?"

Parable in Simon's House

"A certain creditor had two debtors; one owed five hundred denarii, and the other fifty. When they could not pay, he forgave them both. Now which of them will love him more?" Simon answered, "The one, I suppose, to whom he forgave more." And he said to him, "You have judged rightly." Then turning toward the woman he said to Simon, "Do you see this woman? I entered your house, you gave me no water for my feet, but she has wet my feet with her tears and wiped them with her hair. You gave me no kiss, but from the time I came in she has not ceased to kiss my feet. You did not anoint my head with oil, but she has anointed my feet with ointment. Therefore I tell you, her sins, which are many, are forgiven, for she loved much; but he who is forgiven little, loves little." And he said to her, "Your sins are forgiven." Then those who were at table with him began to say among themselves, "Who is this, who even forgives sins?" And he said to the woman, "Your faith has saved you; go in peace" (Luke 7:41-50).

Simon, as the host, had committed great sins of uncharitableness toward Jesus and toward the public sinner, unaware of the fact that the God-Man could read his unkind thoughts. And now Jesus sets about correcting him tactfully by using an extremely short but very telling parable, with the most obvious answer, and still Simon can only say a precautionary "I suppose." Then tactfully Jesus lets Simon see that He knows just what has been going on in his mind. He contrasts the uncharitable mentality of a seemingly highly respectable man with the humble act of charity combined with deep sorrow for sin of an apparently open sinner who publicly made up for the host's lack of common courtesy toward Him.

Community life and our dealings with others call for quite a number of acts of common courtesy but these are expected by Christ to be not merely external formalism but the fruits of true charity and respect within. If this mentality is lacking, however, if our brethren, our neighbors are considered as people we just have to put up with, then it is easy enough for the common courtesies gradually to disappear or to become at least open travesties of true charity. How strange to find even souls specially dedicated to God and neighbor who no longer greet one another, are no longer considerate of the needs of others, no longer seek actual opportunities to be kind, helpful, polite to others! It happens—often! And it all goes back to that initial insincerity with God Himself, that holding back of even some part of the heart from Christ who owns it all. And even when we hear the same old truths about love of God and charity repeated over and over again, what spoils it all and prevents our own full response is the same over-precaution of Simon and we say: "I suppose it's all true in substance, but in *my* case...." Do I ever thus make myself an exception to the universal laws of charity, courtesy, kindness, especially to my nearest brethren? Any in particular? Why? In the future?...

The point that Jesus underlines very heavily when stating what the woman has done for Him is that of love and gratitude combined. In spite of all public appearances and her awful reputation, the woman had repented of her repentance, shown precisely by charity in action, mercy and goodness, that she felt obliged to show her sentiments in a public act of loving gratitude. Because of her repentance, shown precisely by charity in action, she was miles ahead of Simon in the eyes of God. If Simon thought his own sins were few or non-existent, he certainly had a lot of re-thinking to do, whereas the woman who apparently was weighed down with sin had wiped out her debt not so much with her perfume and hair but with her love and gratitude. For a man so proud it could not have been a very palatable lesson. Is there absolutely no danger of my being on the same level, with the same lesson to learn? Worth honest consideration! My love of Christ can be measured by my true gratitude as shown in sincere thoughts, acts, and words of charity. Where, when, with whom do I fail in this? Jesus,...

What tremendous consolation that woman must have received on hearing those words of Jesus: "Your sins are forgiven.... Your faith has saved you; go in peace." As St. Paul was to say later: "Since we are justified by faith, we have peace with God through our Lord Jesus Christ" (Rom. 5:1). Faith, love, sorrow, gratitude, charity in action: each followed in swift succession. We hear of no results in Simon, though. Was he converted, touched even? No indication, unless we are sadly to include him among "those who were at table with him" who murmured that Jesus dare forgive sins. It seems to have been the same old story of the hardening of the arteries of charity in these negative-minded Pharisees who missed one opportunity after another of recognizing the true light of Christ, of following it, of being converted, of becoming other zealous apostles of "the good news."

Pride could be the cause of our downfall too, especially through its outlets of uncharitableness and that unforgiving spirit which preserves a whole file of others' past offenses, all too forgetful of our own many past and even present sins contrary to the virtue of Christian love as exemplified at two extremes by the gentle, tactful Christ and the humbly repentant, grateful woman. Oh Jesus, help me to be truly charitable in thought, in word, in action, in love. Help me to abolish all unkindness from my life. Today....

Good Fruit

Either make the tree good, and its fruit good; or make the tree bad, and its fruit bad; for the tree is known by its fruit. You brood of vipers! How can you speak good, when you are evil? For out of the abundance of the heart the mouth speaks. The good man out of his good treasure brings forth good, and the evil man out of his evil treasure brings forth evil. I tell you, on the day of judgment men will render account for every careless word they utter; for by your words you will be justified, and by your words you will be condemned (Matthew 12:33-37).

These admonitions were addressed primarily in reproach to the Pharisees because of the perversity and obstinacy of their hearts that made them refuse, even when confronted with the irrefutable goodness of His life and deeds, to acknowledge any good in Jesus, still less His divine mission as the Messiah. He uses simple logic to refute them in the natural example of the tree and its fruits. They unfortunately, through that almost inexplicable twist in the workings of their minds, had the knack of making light into darkness and labeling the manifestly good and charitable actions of Jesus as works of the devil, so much so that the righteous indignation of Christ burst forth as He calls them "You brood of vipers!"

So strong are these words from the meekest person ever on earth that they sound frightening and should make us ponder deeply on the sin of those that called them forth: the persistent, obstinate refusal to listen to the voice of the Holy Spirit within. What is my own respect for the third Person of the Holy Trinity? Do I often revert to His presence within me? Am I grateful for so much that I owe to Him? In what ways can I improve?

Let me apply our Lord's simple words about trees to myself. The constant aim of my whole life should be persevering growth in the maturity of Christ, allowing Him to take ever greater possession and use of every single thing that goes to make up "me." The measure of this growth can be judged by the findings of the serious examinations of conscience I make before confession, on the occasion of my monthly, quarterly and annual retreats. Can I honestly say that my life actually shows an abundance of good fruits? Let me be specific about this. God, who is my Judge, will not be satisfied with any vague showing of moral rectitude. He wants to see the details in action! Let me not be afraid to admit that there are possible bad fruits. If there is some fault or habit that consistently shows up in my examination of conscience, should this not give me cause for worry lest I, in fact, be deliberately disregarding the voice of the Holy Spirit within?

What can I do about it this very day? Time is running out—perhaps faster than I realize! For a start, then, let me pray now very sincerely: O Holy Spirit, I beg the grace to melt the coldness and the thick ice that could be doing harm in this heart of mine which You should own fully....

"Out of the abundance of the heart the mouth speaks," says our Lord on this same frightening occasion, and He warns us of the danger lying in "every careless word." Can I really say that I have at least good control of my tongue? Does nothing ever slip out that I later regret? Very few seem able to say this honestly. In any case, here I should strive after perfect control, but in order to attain it I must rely very much on the daily cooperation I give to God's Holy Spirit with me.

How often it is sins of the tongue that worry Christians who do want to be good and to follow Christ. Isn't this my experience also? Let me pray, then, once more to the third Person of the Holy Trinity: O Holy Spirit, help me to avoid anything at all that is unkind, so that I may never offend You within me.

When Anyone Hears

Hear then the parable of the sower. When anyone hears the word of the kingdom and does not understand it, the evil one comes and snatches away what is sown in his heart; this is what was sown along the path. As for what was sown on rocky ground, this is he who hears the word and immediately receives it with joy; yet he has no root in himself, but endures for a while, and when tribulation or persecution arises on account of the word, immediately he falls away (Matthew 13:18-20).

We have to link this explanation of our Lord's with His previous description, "as he sowed, some seeds fell along the path, and the birds came and devoured them." The paths around the harvest fields were formed by the constant movement of the workers, the more the movement the harder the path. So too with the human heart and the process of hardening that comes about through the formation of habits. When a bad habit becomes solidly entrenched in the heart the surface in that area becomes so hard that the seed of the word of God fails to penetrate it, the whispering of conscience fails to be heard.

What bad habits have I allowed myself to contract? Am I inclined to brush aside any hints, whether of conscience, superiors or others, that concern these, refusing to correct myself? How dangerous this can be! The fact is that such a state of mind and heart is not inclined to remain inert. Well-worn paths have a tendency to spread outwards and in my heart they can only too easily, even if imperceptibly, become well-worn highways of the devil himself, gradually assuming full possession of what should be the kingdom of God within me. Our Lord uses the term "the evil one" but earlier He mentions "the birds," those little evil inclinations and attractions which we can so easily feed and encourage. "*Principiis obsta*"—the old Latin adage ("Stop the beginnings!") still holds good. It would be well for me now not only to take an honest look at habits already formed, to see what I can do about undermining them, but also at recent inclinations which threaten to become habits and lead me further away from God. Jesus, help me to do some serious thinking and praying now.

Again let us link the two relevant passages:

> *Other seeds fell on rocky ground, where they had not much soil, and immediately they sprang up, since they had no depth of soil, but when the sun rose they were scorched; and since they had no root they withered away (Matthew 13:5-6).*
>
> *As for what was sown on rocky ground, this is he who hears the word and immediately receives it with joy; yet he has no root in himself, but endures for a while, and when tribulation or persecution arises on account of the word, immediately he falls away (Matthew 13:20-21).*

Enthusiasm is a much-appreciated general characteristic of youth and youthful spirits and there are many attractive aspects about it, but it requires solid bulwarks to maintain it. Unless it is backed up by courage and endurance it can unfortunately resemble mere froth, lacking substance. Over and over again general experience has shown evidence of sometimes truly wonderful ideas and plans that have been enthusiastically expressed but have been still-born or short-lived through lack of will-power or perseverance. How often this occurs in the spiritual life also, the spark of fire that flashes forth as a result of a good inspiration, a fervent meditation, sermon, retreat, reading, advice,...but never to mature, never to create that lasting, wholesome blaze of the love of God that could make one a real apostle of Christ and His word. The cause?... Lack of depth, lack of maturity.... When the sun of opposition or trial of any kind comes, the first enthusiasm dies quickly and the ground lays strewn with withered resolutions.

Can I exempt myself from such a plight? Hell itself, they say, is paved with good resolutions. I need to do some serious examining here, don't I? How easy it is to overplay presumptuously the consoling tune of God's mercy as a mere excuse for continuing laziness and lack of true resolve to get down to solid and lasting effort. God of mercy and compassion....

Other seeds fell among thorns, and the thorns grew up and choked them (Matthew 13:7).

As for what was sown among thorns, this is he who hears the word, but the cares of the world and the delight in riches choke the word, and it proves unfruitful (Matthew 13:22).

The fruitful soil is there all right but too often we allow extraneous cares and preoccupations to take first place in the mind and soul. For so many people financial wealth becomes a leading obsession in life, for others it can be the richness of passion in one form or other that weakens our efforts in the things that really matter. The eternal truths, and the truth about our own soul in particular, can become choked, even to death, when we allow something other than God and His love to take predominance in our soul and mind. In this way even the best of resolutions never comes to fruition. Elsewhere our Lord tells us to abandon all cares and give our whole attention to the one thing that really matters, His love in our heart.

What are the things that seem to capture my thoughts mostly? What are my particular worries or preoccupations? Am I allowing mere material or temporal things to dominate my mind, sapping strength from my heart which should be devoted to God's love in far more important matters? O Jesus, help me to recognize in myself, to tackle bravely and to conquer whatever it is in me that continues to displease You as an obstacle to Your grace and love.

The Good Soil

Finishing His explanation of the parable of the sower and the seed, our Lord says:

> *As for what was sown on good soil, this is he who hears the word and understands it; he indeed bears fruit, and yields in one case a hundredfold, in another sixty, and in another thirty (Matthew 13:23).*

The word and inspiration of God is scattered widely throughout the world, throughout my life. Thanks be to God, not all of it is wasted, not all of it comes to nothing, even in my own case. Where the mind and heart is docile to every breath of the Holy Spirit there the word finds fruitful soil and helps the soul to mature consolingly through carrying out what God wants at all times and in all things. The greater the docility and readiness, the greater and more consoling the harvest. The holy cardinal, Merry del Val, constantly urged a spirit of complete trust and abandonment to God's loving care and he urged his listeners never to allow themselves to get preoccupied with worries about their future. How wise that advice!

The fact is that God is my loving Father; He is deeply interested in me; He cares for me. As long as I keep close to Him He will allow nothing evil to happen to me. As long as "my food is to do the will of him that sent me" (Jn. 5:40), I have every reason to be confident and secure. Jesus, You gave Yourself thus to Your loving Father; help me to....

The best and most receptive soil for seeds is the one that is rich in chemical matter, well-worked, well-drained, well-watered in season. So too with the soul. If the good chemicals are not already there we must infuse them; the various virtues must be practiced with diligence; humility must be frequently refreshed through the grace of the sacraments. I have all these opportunities. Do I use them? Diligently? Constantly? Perseveringly? Only then is my soul truly a receptive field for God's holy word; only then can He scatter in abundance, without fear of losing anything. In the Old Testament God called David a man according to His own heart because He was so anxious to do only God's will: "I have found in David, a man after my heart, who will do all my will" (Acts 13:22). David himself could declare sincerely and humbly: "My heart is steadfast, O God, my heart is steadfast!" (Ps. 56:8) All that he asked of the Lord was: "Teach me to do your will, for you are my God! Let your good Spirit lead me on a level path!" (Ps. 143:10)

If I give my will totally to God I give Him everything and He Himself asks precisely this when He says: "Son, give me your heart," for what I truly love in my heart, that is my will. St. Ignatius says: "Oh that men would abandon themselves to God! There are so few who understand what God would make of them if they permitted Him to do as He wills." Am I one of these? If not, why not? "Lord Jesus, without *if's*, without *but's*, without exception, may Your will be done in all things, in myself!" (St. Jane Frances de Chantal)

The better the qualities of the field, the more prudent the cultivation and care, the more proportionate the harvest. There can, after all, be degrees of care and degrees of faithfulness. How many spiritual fields unfortunately produce only a small percentage of their ultimate potential —limping saints, as it were! An example of the hundredfold mentioned by Jesus in the parable must surely be St. Thérèse of Lisieux, young but mature, weak and yet so wholehearted with God in everything. On her deathbed she could say with complete assurance: "In heaven the good God will do all I desire, because on earth I never did my own will."

There is no reason on earth why I too should not become a first-class saint, since I have exactly the same or very similar circumstances and opportunities in my spiritual and religious life. The little way of Thérèse was nothing else but the beautiful and childlike spirit of complete abandonment to God in all things and she never allowed any opportunity to pass her by of renewing her utter trust in her loving Father. By this simple means she attained great holiness. So too can I! Let me formulate now an act of holy abandonment.

Mustard Seed and Leaven

Another parable he put before them, saying, "The kingdom of heaven is like a grain of mustard seed which a man took and sowed in his field; it is the smallest of all seeds, but when it has grown it is the greatest of shrubs and becomes a tree, so that the birds of the air come and make nests in its branches" (Matthew 13:31-32).

In Galilee the mustard bush was quite a common sight and yet in itself quite a remarkable thing, springing as it did from the tiniest of seeds to become a huge bush or tree that sometimes reached up to ten feet. Its foliage was so plentiful that it could literally provide shelter and accommodation for many birds. The seed itself was used for condiment and medicine. Our Lord uses this illustration aptly for the kingdom of God, which began so humbly, confined at first to the limits of Galilee, then to spread all over the world, providing shelter, care, strength and medicine for souls. And what applies to the kingdom of God as a whole applies also to the kingdom of Christ within each individual soul: the tiny seed is planted at baptism but it is expected to grow and develop into the fullness of the maturity of Christ within. "Wherever they live, all Christians are bound to show forth, by the example of their lives and by the witness of their speech, that new man which they put on at baptism, and that power of the Holy Spirit by whom they were strengthened at confirmation" (*Ad Gentes,* 11).

It is only by carrying out my baptismal vocation to its fullest and utmost limit that I can ensure not only that I am doing all in my power to bring the kingdom of God within me to fruition, but also that I am taking my full share in spreading it upon earth. How much, in fact, do I value my Christian vocation and its splendid potentialities? "Those who believe in Christ, who are reborn not from a perishable but from an imperishable seed through the Word of the living God, not from flesh but from water and the Holy Spirit, are finally established as 'a chosen race, a royal priesthood, a holy nation, a purchased people'" *(Lumen Gentium,* 9). Let me meditate gratefully now on my privileges of being a baptized and confirmed Christian and a member of God's kingdom on earth, with firm promise of heaven also if I do all in my power to cooperate with God's abundant grace.

Inherent in my Christian vocation received at baptism is the missionary idea and ideal also. Through my membership in the Mystical Body of Christ I must do all in my power to cooperate in the extension of God's kingdom here on earth. In other words, I too must be essentially a missionary, even if I never set actual foot on so-called mission territory. I must be ready to give of myself totally for the spread of the Gospel and for the good of souls. What Vatican Council II says of the *de facto* missionary should apply to me also: "He who is sent enters upon the life and mission of Him who 'emptied himself, taking the nature of a slave.' Therefore he must be ready to stand by his vocation for a lifetime and to renounce himself... to become 'all things to all men.'" It goes on then to describe the qualities of a true missionary, which should be mine also: "Announcing the Gospel among the nations, he confidently makes known the mystery of Christ, whose ambassador he is. Thus in Christ he dares to speak as he ought, and is not ashamed of the scandal of the cross. Following in his Master's footsteps, meek and humble of heart, he shows that His yoke is easy and His burden light. By a truly evangelical life, in much patience, in long-suffering, in kindness, in unaffected love, he bears witness to his Lord, if need be, to the shedding of his blood.... Lest the heralds of the Gospel neglect the grace which is in them, they should be renewed day by day in spirit and in mind" (*Ad Gentes*, 24). Let me take each point of this in turn and examine it in the light of my own life so that I may see just how I am measuring up to my missionary vocation in the kingdom of God upon earth. Jesus....

He told them another parable. "The kingdom of heaven is like leaven which a woman took and hid in three measures of meal, till it was all leavened" (Matthew 13:33).

Our Lord gives yet further this other parable on the kingdom, bringing out once again the idea of growth and that the spirit of Christ has within it power to transform the whole earth. The work of yeast or leaven is silent and yet effective, penetrating and raising the whole mass of dough. The Jews of our Lord's time were expecting a tremendous splash for the establishment of the kingdom of God upon earth, but here instead Jesus tells them it is going to be a very quiet, almost unnoticed affair. History has proven this. I can do far more towards the establishing and spread of God's kingdom by my own quiet and unobtrusive good example than by the loudest and most impressive preaching. What I am will always shout far louder than what I say! One good example in action is worth more than a thousand precepts. "Let your light so shine before men, that they may see your good works, and give glory to your Father who is in heaven" (Mt. 5:16).

St. John Baptist de la Salle: "If you wish your pupils to do good, do it yourself; you will thus inspire them with the love and desire of virtue by your wise and well-ordered conduct more than by anything you can say to them." St. Paul to Timothy: "Let no one despise your youth, but set the believers an example in speech and conduct, in love, in faith, in purity...by so doing you will save both yourself and your hearers" ·(1 Tm. 12:16). "My Lord, teach me to be generous! Teach me to serve You as You deserve: to give and not to count the cost—to fight and not to heed the wounds—to toil and not to seek for rest—to labor and not ask for reward, save that of knowing that I am doing Your will" (St. Ignatius Loyola).

Storm at Sea

On that day, when evening had come, he said to them, "Let us go across to the other side." And leaving the crowd, they took him with them just as he was, in the boat. And other boats were with him. And a great storm of wind arose, and the waves beat into the boat, so that the boat was already filling. But he was in the stern, asleep on the cushion; and they woke him and said to him, "Teacher, do you not care if we perish?" (Mark 4:35-38)

A current of hot air rises constantly from the Jordan Valley and lingers especially over the Dead Sea. Sometimes, however, it is blown away by a cold wind that comes down from snow-clad Mount Hermon. At times this occurs unexpectedly and causes storms on Lake Tiberias that can become quite violent and cease almost as suddenly. On this occasion night had fallen and the danger became accentuated—and yet Jesus slept! St. Mark's account is far more detailed than those of Matthew and Luke: Jesus had come away just as He was, no particular preparations were made for this voyage, but He was given the special place of honor for a guest, a cushion in the stern of the ship and there He slept, tired out.

How often, even after we have "bravely" given up "all things" and followed Christ, we find things rather tough and complain loudly, bitterly. At times the storms that arise may seem so utterly unreasonable and unfair that we dare even to question the justice of Christ Himself who promised a hundredfold already in this life to all those who give up all things in order to follow Him. Is such an attitude really reasonable? To expect a perfectly quiet and calm life, its every detail a model of parquet patterning, is to contradict the whole range of human and physical experience. In the material world there is a plan behind every storm, earthquake, lightning and devastation. So too in the life of man. So too in the spiritual life. The reason for every single thing that occurs may well be beyond our limited intelligence to comprehend. Demanding it in the spiritual realm could prove both nearsightedness and pride combined. As long as Christ is in the ship with us—even if apparently asleep, we shall be safe, we shall overcome. Has there been perhaps at times a petulant, demanding, questioning spirit in my religious and spiritual life, especially when trials occurred? Let me think back on my last tempest and my reactions on that forlorn occasion. Have I nothing to reproach myself with, no need of a humble apology to Jesus here and now?

And he awoke and rebuked the wind, and said to the sea, "Peace! be still!" (Mark 4:39)

"And they woke him...." It is hard to imagine that the apostles, rough and rugged men mostly, in their excitement would have approached Jesus gently to awaken Him. Probably they were actually annoyed when in the hurry and flurry of trying to keep the boat upright they saw Him resting calmly, indifferently it seemed. No doubt one or more rushed up to Him then, shook Him roughly and shouted their reproach, possibly angrily, "Don't You even care!" Perhaps it is equally hard not to believe that Jesus would feel such treatment sensitively even though understanding the circumstances. It showed Him that these dearly beloved rough men of His, on whom the hopes of the kingdom depended so much, still considered Him too much of a man and not enough divine, and were not beyond treating Him roughly in moments of forgetfulness. Possibly this reflects my own attitude from time to time: an over-familiarity with things spiritual or sacred; taking things too much for granted; perfunctoriness about sacred ceremonies, prayers and actions; harsh treatment of Jesus within me shortly after Holy Communion. After all He has done for me, can I blame Jesus for being sensitive when I treat Him thus, even though He does not show it? Have I no regard for His human feelings as a Person, as my best Friend? O Jesus, in the past...but now and in the future....

And the wind ceased, and there was a great calm. He said to them, "Why are you afraid? Have you no faith?" And they were filled with awe, and said to one another, "Who then is this, that even wind and sea obey him?" (Mark 4:39-41)

With perfect tranquility Jesus awakes and at once pays heed to the plight of His frightened men, producing a calm that must by contrast have been as awe-inspiring as the tempest itself. No less impressive must have been His brief but firm reproach: after seeing Him perform so many miracles, should they not by now have far greater confidence in Him and His power to help and save them at all times? Moreover, were they not worrying too much about the safety and protection of their own bodies and possessions rather than being concerned about their souls? As long as He was in their midst and they obeyed His teachings and commands, all would turn out well.

The Scriptures have wonderful things to say of the soul and hence it should always be the primary object of my daily concern. No matter what storms may arise, my faith should meet the test if I have ensured that Jesus can rest tranquilly as its honored guest within it, at times apparently asleep but His heart beating constantly with anxious care for me until we both safely reach "the other side." O Jesus, I have such a lot to learn from this incident. Increase my faith, encourage my hope, fan my few small flames of charity.

Daughter of Jairus

And when Jesus had crossed again in the boat to the other side, a great crowd gathered about him; and he was beside the sea. Then came one of the rulers of the synagogue, Jairus by name, and seeing him, he fell at his feet, and besought him, saying, "My little daughter is at the point of death. Come and lay your hands on her, so that she may be made well, and live." And he went with him. And a great crowd followed him and thronged about him (Mark 5:21-24).

St. Luke tells us that when Jesus returned to that side of the lake from which He had set forth He found the crowd awaiting Him again. Among them however, one in particular was most anxious to see Him, Jairus, a ruler of the synagogue, one who led the prayers, organized the readings, etc. St. Mark gives very helpful details concerning the present incident but St. Luke at once tells us that the girl concerned was twelve years old and an only child. We can imagine then how anguished her father was to see her dying, and even though his faith seems to have been less than that of the centurion who believed Jesus could perform a miracle even at a distance, this man had sufficient reason to evoke the compassion of Jesus and make Him accede to his wishes. Naturally, the crowd accompanied them eagerly, looking forward to the miracle.

The sense of anticipation in this particular crowd must have been very great indeed and they were not to be disappointed. For us, however, the lesson might well be not to be demanding of God and even to expect disappointments. How often people pray, even desperately and perseveringly, for something they have very much at heart, and nothing, or the very opposite happens. How many then lose hope – and perhaps faith. Why? Because their love of God is not strong enough. If it were, it would seek only God's will not just their own. At times, however, we may feel that something must surely be God's will and still our prayers are not answered as we wish. This should tell us that we have been mistaken and that God's will is otherwise than we assumed and hoped. Consoling, too, the thought of St. Augustine: "What God refuses to our petitions, He grants to our salvation." What is my attitude in my prayers of petition? Do I expect God to work special miracles for me, regardless of His better judgment and will? Perhaps I need to be more mature about my prayers also.

While he was still speaking, there came from the ruler's house some who said, "Your daughter is dead. Why trouble the Teacher any further?" But ignoring what they said, Jesus said to the ruler of the synagogue, "Do not fear, only believe." And he allowed no one to follow him except Peter and James and John the brother of James. When they came to the house of the ruler of the synagogue, he saw a tumult, and people weeping and wailing loudly. And when he had entered, he said to them, "Why do you make a tumult and weep? The child is not dead but sleeping." And they laughed at him (Mark 5:35-40).

In this particular case Jesus saw the utility of going along with the man and his understandable desire of a miracle, and then suddenly it all seemed too late – the girl was already dead. Perhaps in the agonized look the father gave Jesus there was also just one last spark of hope that made Jesus encourage him to have faith still. By the time they arrived at the house, the traditional, rather rowdy mourning had already started and yet Jesus asks His astonishing question and says the girl is only asleep, not dead. "And they laughed at him" – what undertones one can read into those words on the part of the unbelievers, but Jesus is not put off and He "put them all outside," no doubt with quiet but firm authority. Only those who truly believed in Him, including the girl's parents now, were allowed to remain with Him inside the room.

In that moment surely the faith of all five must have increased tremendously. How often in the Gospels our Lord asks for faith, greater faith, and only when there is evidence of it does He perform any miracle, big or small. My prayers of petition depend so much on my spirit of faith and if at times I do not get what I pray for, instead of wailing against God, my most immediate reaction should be to examine honestly how much faith accompanied my prayers, how much readiness to accept whatever outcome God wished. Let me now consider my possible deficiencies in this respect and make sensible counter resolutions. O Jesus, You who have said, "Ask and you shall receive; seek and you shall find; knock and it shall be opened unto you...."

> *But he put them all outside, and took the child's father and mother and those who were with him, and went in where the child was. Taking her by the hand he said to her, "Talitha cumi"; which means, "Little girl, I say to you, arise." And immediately the girl got up and walked; for she was twelve years old. And immediately they were overcome with amazement. And he strictly charged them that no one should know this, and told them to give her something to eat (Mark 5:40-43).*

How simple, direct and tender are the action and words of Jesus as He brings the child back to life to continue her earthly pilgrimage yet longer: in the original Aramaic there are only two words: "*Talitha cumi!*" Imagine the overwhelming joy of the parents and the delight of the three chosen apostles when the child gets up at once and walks over to those she loves in order to embrace them where they stood petrified with amazement. Notice too the kindly common sense of Jesus as He smilingly brings them back to earth by telling them to give her something to eat—a proof that she was fully alive and well again. Nor did He wish any fuss to be made over the affair, although He must have known how difficult it would be since the crowd of people and the disappointed paid-mourners outside would know within minutes what had happened. The strange thing is that neither Mark nor Luke record the reactions that followed, although Matthew says, "And the report of this went through all that district" (9:26).

There are so many aspects one can meditate on in this touching incident: the kindness and condescension of Jesus. His spirit of sympathy and understanding, His graciousness in acceding to the father's desires, His tender love impressed so gently and firmly in the words of the actual miracle, His down-to-earth practicality regarding food for the child to eat, His sense of prudence in not wanting fuss and a lot of gossip. In each of these points I can find valuable material for my own improvement by bringing them down to practical application in my daily life with firm resolution, prayer and perseverance. Dear Jesus, my Master and Model,...

Issue of Blood

As he went, the people pressed round him. And a woman who had had a flow of blood for twelve years and had spent all her living upon physicians and could not be healed by any one, came up behind him, and touched the fringe of his garment; and immediately her flow of blood ceased (Luke 8:42-44).

On the way to the home of Jairus occurred this other miracle, tactfully narrated by Luke, doctor as well as evangelist, and, with possibly greater understanding of her frustrations, by the very observant Mark (5:25-29). The woman's sense of shame about her embarrassing illness was superseded by her powerful spirit of faith and humility. Neither did she wish to draw any attention to herself, nor did she want to distract Jesus momentarily. Her strong faith told her that all that was necessary was for her to stretch out her hand and touch even the very fringe of His garment. No one in such a crowd pressing about Him as He moved along would notice it; she didn't think that even He would. So holy did she consider Him that she was convinced that even His very garments were sanctified and hence she could safely touch them and be absolutely sure of a cure. This almost quiet little incident, occupying only a few lines in the Gospels, gives not merely an act of firm belief in vignette form but, to the discerning, a huge portrait of a noble woman full of the "sense of God." Especially in these questioning times there is such need of faith in the ever-continuing power and virtue of Christ. Vatican II said: "A change in attitudes and in human structures frequently call accepted values into question. This is especially true of young people, who have grown impatient on more than one occasion, and indeed become rebels in their distress. Aware of their own influence in the life of society, they want to assume a role in it sooner.... The institutions, laws, and modes of thinking and feeling as handed down from previous generations do not always seem to be well adapted to the contemporary state of affairs. Hence arises an upheaval in the manner and even the norms of behavior. Finally, these new conditions have their impact on religion" *(Gaudium et Spes,* 7).

It goes on then to point out the dismaying loss of faith in the modern world and underlines the vital need of "a more vivid sense of God," such as possessed by the humble woman in this meditation. How strong is my own sense of God during the day? Do I feel the need often to make conscious contact with Him by a glance, a thought, a prayer? What a pity if I should be leading a split life: one of work and one of prayer! Let me examine myself very strictly about this now, praying to my Master. Jesus,...

> *And Jesus said, "Who was it that touched me?" When all denied it, Peter said, "Master, the multitudes surround you and press upon you!" But Jesus said, "Some one touched me, for I perceive that power has gone forth from me" (Luke 8:45-46).*

The woman was mistaken in thinking that not even Jesus Himself would know she had touched His garment, for God is all-knowing and all-seeing. Even so He could have allowed the incident to pass unnoticed, but instead He asks the question, "Who was it that touched me?" It must have seemed a rather ridiculous question and the hasty Peter could not refrain from hinting as much—dozens were touching Him. Poor Peter! At this moment that poor woman scored much higher in faith than he did! By now he should have known Jesus better than to think He would ask anything without good reason, but he still had a lot to learn regarding hastiness and mature questioning! Perhaps I have, too.... Jesus knew instinctively that of all those who crowded about Him so enthusiastically just one single person had deliberately touched His garment with a true spirit of faith. To Him it was a case of the psalmist's "deep calling to deep": the depth of faith in that poor, suffering, humiliated and humble woman calling out to the abyss of His own love and power. At once He felt virtue within Him surging forth to cure that woman and in the process to confirm forever her own strong spirit of faith. "Faith can move mountains," Scripture tells us, and St. Augustine says: "Faith is to believe what we do not see, and the reward of this faith is to see what we believe."

How much confidence do I really have in the almighty power of Christ to help me—and the world—in all the difficulties and problems that arise? Can I foresee today anything likely to occur that will call upon my spirit of faith? Let me prepare for it prayerfully now.

> *And when the woman saw that she was not hidden, she came trembling, and falling down before him declared in the presence of all the people why she had touched him, and how she had been immediately healed. And he said to her, "Daughter, your faith has made you well; go in peace" (Luke 8:47-48).*

With the power of the miracle accomplished within her came also the grace of a vastly increased humility and unbounded gratitude. In spite of the fact that her ailment was a rather personal, humiliating one, through which she had suffered physically, mentally and financially, she now cast all human respect to the winds and, trembling (with excitement? surely no longer fear), she came forward, not only willing to make herself known (at risk of the crowd's scorn) but above all anxious to acknowledge the grace accorded her and to thank Jesus personally. Again this further act of faith received its reward by some of the kindest words in the Gospel: "Daughter, your faith has made you well; go in peace." What a lovely memory for all the years ahead; what a consolation at the hour of her death!

What wonderful memories I too could have if I trusted more in the power of the living Word of God, for faith is the only link that can bind my own nothingness to His almightiness. "He who believes in the Son of God has the testimony in himself.... And this is the testimony, that God gave us eternal life, and this life is in his Son. He who has the Son of God has life; he who has not the Son of God has not life" (1 Jn. 5:10-12). Lord, increase my faith....

They Told Him All

The apostles returned to Jesus, and told him all that they had done and taught (Mark 6:30).

If only I were to imitate the apostles constantly in this, how much happiness it would bring into my life, what greater understanding and maturity I would gain through this regular chat or conversation with Jesus—and, after all, that is precisely what prayer should be. The apostles came back from a very busy, perhaps even hectic, round of duties and at once felt the need and the joy of talking to Jesus about everything that had happened. Unfortunately one does find religious—who are supposed to be other apostles—who allow the very business of their lives to swamp their life of prayer and they may even plead duty as the excuse for neglect of truly intimate prayer. Yet we know from the Gospels that Jesus Himself, our Master and Model, made sure to *make* time for prayer even apart from work. There are indeed many very obvious indications that He impregnated even His business with prayer.

In my own case I may find I have also slipped up in this matter. Surely with a bit of ingenuity (and perhaps consultation) I could find at least five whole minutes per day, even at the end of the day, for quiet, private prayer, telling Jesus all I have "done and taught." Then, as to my actual duties themselves, the very things that make my day and life so busy, why must prayer be excluded from those? Look at our Lord again: before every miracle He prayed, a direct appeal to His heavenly Father to work with Him. There will be no miracles in my life, nothing really worthwhile or lasting, if I do not strive to punctuate my duties with trustful prayer. If I do not, then it becomes all too easy for the ego, the big capital

I, to push God out of my concerns. My deeds and activities and accomplishments may seem to shine, but without prayer it will be just a cheap gloss that is of no value at all in the eyes of God, no matter how well it may deceive those about me. Of what use is it if people say, "Oh, he's such a wonderful person, he's so...such a marvelous...!" if all that exterior splendor or attraction is a mere shell because interiorly I am not a person of prayer? Let me examine myself seriously on these considerations—and pray about them.

The apostles returning from their first mission must have realized just how much they had imitated Jesus in so many different ways. They would have had nothing worthwhile to tell Him if they had not put into practice during their apostolate the one big lesson they must have learned from Him—prayer. For not only before His miracles did Jesus pray, but He introduced prayer quite simply and naturally into the course of even the very ordinary doings of His daily life.

I too have probably already learned the necessity and importance of extra special and more intensive prayer in the major events of my own life. I should be consoled too and perfectly confident that whenever some big trial or event lies ahead of me I can always look to Christ for help and example. He Himself sweated blood in terrified anticipation in the Garden of Gethsemane and so I know I can rely utterly on His sympathy and assistance in whatever lies ahead of me. He understands my nervousness and natural fear of certain things, for He Himself pleaded for the removal of His own bitter chalice of sorrow and trial, though He still bowed His human will to the divine will of the Father, knowing He would supply all the courage and strength He needed as man. So too for me in the major climaxes and trials of my life. "If God be with me, who can be against me?" As long as I am safely on God's side in conscience and prayer, then it matters not one jot who is against me and, please God, I shall come through each trial glorious in merit in the sight of God. Perhaps in this light I shall see where I have failed in the past. I can at least apologize now and resolve sensibly to make my life more prayerful in the future. O Jesus,...

It is sad that not every religious seems to have learned the art of true, conversational prayer. So many rely too dependently on set formulas composed by others. Now, unless these forms express quite accurately what we really want to say, then we are not really being our own true selves with Christ. Prayer for me should be simply a conversation with my very best Friend, Jesus, or the Father or the Holy Spirit, or their special friends the saints, and it need not be on formal subjects only. It can be about anything at all and still be genuine prayer. Our prayers should never be a mere recital, a talking *at* God, instead of *to* God.

This, of course, does not automatically knock out all vocal prayers in common, for it was Jesus Himself in the first place who assured us of the tremendous value of such prayers uttered together by "two or more" in His name. It *is* possible, moreover, to make the sentiments of such communal prayers our own and that should prevent us from just reciting them. As with the apostles, my individual prayers should be generally about the things that interest me most. I am what I am, with my own very individual personality and character, temperament, likes and dislikes, faults and good qualities, talents and handicaps, my own particular interests, hobbies, etc. It is all these things that make me what I am and it is in these that Jesus is interested. Therefore He will understand and appreciate my praying about these things, because then my prayer becomes apostolic, real and living, down to earth and yet up to heaven, and quite to the point. Let me not forget, however, to pause now and then in order to *listen!* I mustn't be just a prayerful chatterbox! What about some practical practice right now! O Jesus,...

Rest a While

The apostles returned to Jesus, and told him all that they had done and taught. And he said to them, "Come away by yourselves to a lonely place, and rest a while." For many were coming and going, and they had no leisure even to eat. And they went away in the boat to a lonely place by themselves (Mark 6:30-32).

Again a lovely instance of the kind consideration of Jesus for others, and here especially for His weary apostles. When they had enthusiastically told Him of all their labor and experiences He urged them to rest a while, away from the crowds that continued to press about Him during their absence, making it well nigh impossible to find time or opportunity to eat. St. Matthew alleges also another motive, the increasing curiosity of King Herod who had recently put John the Baptist to death. Together with His beloved apostles then, Jesus sets off by boat in order to find a quiet place of rest for them. St. Luke says Bethsaida, at the north of Lake Tiberias, where Philip the Tetrarch was ruler, not Herod.

Let us take advantage of these few verses of the Gospel to consider the question of community life, especially as it concerns recreation and repose. In early Genesis we read that after the sublimely tremendous work of the creation God "rested on the seventh day from all his work which he had done" (2:2). St. Alphonsus Liguori says, "It is also the will of God that those who love Him should at certain times recreate themselves, for a bowstring should not be always stretched. David calls upon the just to rejoice and exult in the Lord in Psalm 31." There are at times religious who, out of mistaken zeal or an unbalanced love of work, will allow themselves little or no recreation at all. Others make the heavy pressure of work their excuse. All that is wrong reasoning, for as St. Alphonsus hints, if the bowstring is constantly taut it can snap—and then who has to do the work? Am I really sensible in this matter? Is there an area of my duties where I seem to be undergoing some undue strain? How can I quietly and lawfully remedy this? The advice of those in charge could help here. What I definitely gain from sensible recreation and lawful repose can help toward better fulfillment not only of my work and duties but, above all, of the will of Christ who gave this very advice to His disciples: "Rest a while...."

Recalling the very versicles of St. Mark we are meditating on, Vatican Council II exhorts priests not only to cultivate a fraternal spirit of hospitality and kindliness, but even "readily and joyfully to gather together for recreation" (*Presbyterorum Ordinis*, 8). Generally it is possible, if not actually prescribed, for religious to spend recreation time together, and here it should be the endeavor of each one not merely to enjoy himself but also to try to help the rest to do so, on as wide a scale as possible, avoiding cliques that seem to exclude others. Without any sense of lightheadedness, one can tactfully exercise the real apostolate of cheerfulness.

How much attention do I give to the community aspect of recreation? Do I try to dodge it, preferring rather to go off always on my own with a crony or cronies, regardless of the rest? If not, what efforts do I actually make to be a joy-bearer and a joy-giver? Here I can think too of Jesus as precisely that, to the world and to His apostles, and pray to Him accordingly. O Jesus,...

It seems a pity that the aspect of our Lord's cheerfulness is nowhere mentioned explicitly in the Gospels. Possibly it was taken for granted by the writers, who had become so accustomed to it and never thought to refer to it directly. Professor Elton Trueblood has expressed his amazement at the widespread failure in Christian writings to recognize and appreciate the actual sense of humor which Jesus must surely have had. In his interesting book, *The Humor of Christ*, he speaks at length on his belief that, in spite of the lack of any actual mention in the Gospels, Jesus must often have been cheerful, happy too when others were able to laugh. He singles out more than thirty passages in the Gospels which he maintains are open to humorous interpretation, and he concludes that we cannot avoid the logical conclusion that there is laughter and cheerfulness in the heart of God.

Surely this should encourage me in my own efforts to be cheerful and happy, especially at recreation time, and to help others also in this way. Cheerful, happy community life can be such a consolation in times of weariness or trouble. If I make sure to give my own generous contribution towards it, and particularly at times of community relaxation, I can be doing something very pleasing indeed to the heart of Christ, who is also there in the very midst of us enjoying Himself. A sensible resolution? An apt prayer now.

Multiplication of Loaves

On their return the apostles told him what they had done. And he took them and withdrew apart to a city called Bethsaida. When the crowds learned it, they followed him; and he welcomed them and spoke to them of the kingdom of God, and cured those who had need of healing. Now the day began to wear away; and the twelve came and said to him, "Send the crowd away, to go into the villages and country round about, to lodge and get provisions; for we are here in a lonely place" (Luke 9:10-12).

The weary apostles' chances of some quiet and rest, as desired for them by Jesus Himself, were destined not to materialize, for the people saw in which direction their little boat was heading, a rather deserted area beyond Bethsaida in the northwestern region of the lake or Sea of Tiberias. How often I too may find myself deprived of my lawful recreation and rest, but even though it is quite legitimate to try to prevent this happening, let me at least not put up a huge moan about it when it does occur. We read of no single complaint on the part of the very weary apostles in any one of the Gospel accounts of this incident. It has been suggested that their little boat met with contrary winds and so they could not make much headway on the sea. As a result, when they came to land, the crowd was already waiting for Jesus again, who welcomed them. Only when "the day began to wear away" did the apostles suggest that He send the crowd away. Here again there is no mention of their own convenience but rather the very common sense point of lack of provisions and the need for the people to find shelter for the night. This last factor leads us to believe that many of the crowd were not local dwellers but came from some considerable distance, possibly pilgrims on the way to celebrate the coming paschal feast at Jerusalem. Their eagerness touched the hearts of Jesus and His apostles. Jesus welcomed them, spoke of the kingdom, cured many.

What can I find here for my own imitation in the conduct of Jesus and His apostles? One point has already been mentioned; another could be that of kind consideration for others first, before seeing to my own personal comfort and needs. The lack of considerateness can make community life at times unnecessarily irksome, e.g., such mundane but not negligible points as the use of things and places, leaving them as we ourselves would like to find them, not causing inconvenience for others by misplacing articles used, e.g., library books; trying to foresee and as far as possible provide for the needs of others, e.g., at table. In hundreds of simple but apostolic ways I can show the Christ-like example of considerate and kindly spirit. Am I already noted for this in my community? How can I lawfully improve my image in these matters—A.M.D.G.?

> *But he said to them, "You give them something to eat." They said, "We have no more than five loaves and two fish—unless we are to go and buy food for all these people." For there were about five thousand men. And he said to his disciples, "Make them sit down in companies, about fifty each." And they did so, and made them all sit down (Luke 9:13-15).*

Our Lord's reply to the suggestion of the apostles was quite astonishing to them. They could have thought He was trying to be funny but because of His very considerateness towards themselves they knew this could not be so. Nevertheless they were greatly perplexed, even though they suggested they could go and try to buy food for the huge crowd, their faith strained to the utmost. To us obviously Jesus was deliberately testing that faith of theirs in all He then said and did, His inquiries about the number of loaves and fishes (St. Mark), making them organize the crowd into sitting parties of hundreds and fifties (Mark)—why these particular numbers? One wonders too how those weary apostles ever managed to sort them all out as ordered in the swiftly approaching dusk of that summer evening. Their patience must have been well taxed, but again no mention of complaint in any of the Gospel accounts.

What lessons here for me? There could be many, perhaps, e.g., trying sensibly to eliminate resentments about the orders or suggestions of superiors that I don't fully understand, presuming always on their greater knowledge or at least their good will and desire to do the right thing. Superiors, true, are not infallible—neither am I. Do I sometimes or often fail here? The point of orderliness could also arise. Are my personal affairs, my belongings, my room, my desk, etc., well organized and tidy? Any weaknesses here or there? Remedies? What is the measure of my spirit of faith? Can it bear but little strain? Here surely I can pray now and resolve....

> *And taking the five loaves and the two fish he looked up to heaven, and blessed and broke them, and gave them to the disciples to set before the crowd. And all ate and were satisfied. And they took up what was left over, twelve baskets of broken pieces (Luke 9:16-17).*

First the test of faith, then the tremendous miracle of love that foreshadowed the even greater one to come—the Eucharistic multiplication. It is well to notice Jesus' whole attitude throughout this remarkable happening: His tender solicitude for the crowd (St. Mark says: "He had compassion on them, because they were like sheep without a shepherd"—6:34); His orderly mind that insisted they be grouped so as to ensure that all would be fed; His following out of the traditional manner of praying before a meal; Himself presiding as father and breaking the bread as was the custom; His care that even the fragments be gathered. At the Sermon on the Mount He had exhorted extreme confidence in God's kindly Providence without worrying overmuch about food and drink, etc. Here He Himself gave an extreme proof of it because these people were hungry not only in body but in soul, seeking the kingdom of God and His justice, and so they were rewarded physically and spiritually. Unfortunately, however, so fired with enthusiasm did the crowd become that their minds diverted once more to the earthly, political kingdom of Christ for which they hoped. Sadly, therefore, as St. John tells us (6:15), seeing they wanted to make a king of Him, Jesus left them and even His apostles, who were possibly fired by the same vain desire.

For myself, let me reflect on the compassion of Jesus, His orderliness, His fatherliness, His devout manner of praying, His love in the Holy Eucharist and Communion, His sadness when I spoil His plans for me by my wayward desires and obstinacies, and especially when, through my own fault, the Blessed Sacrament cannot benefit me and my life as it should. I have a lot to pray about directly to Jesus here, with a sound resolution attached.

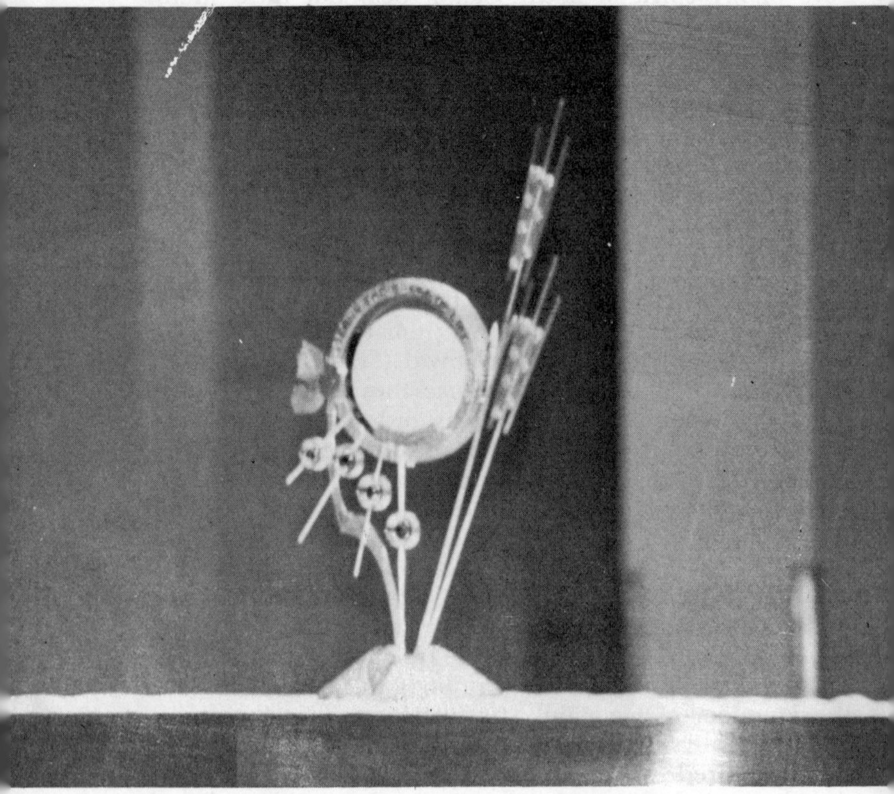

Another Storm at Sea

Then he made the disciples get into the boat and go before him to the other side, while he dismissed the crowds. And after he had dismissed the crowds he went up into the hills by himself to pray. When evening came he was there alone (Matthew 14:22-23).

A tremendous sadness must have filled the heart of Jesus on seeing the misinterpretation of the wonderful miracle of the multiplication of the loaves and fishes. Instead of firing the crowd with spiritual ardor, as intended, it had finally aroused a mere political ferment, in which possibly His apostles also were caught up. He felt constrained therefore to dismiss them all, while He Himself went off quietly into the darkness of the mountainside to pray. I must expect this kind of thing to happen in my life also, and probably it has already. Sometimes, when one has worked at some project with the very best of intentions and tried to keep one's motives pure, the results can be quite disappointing, even shattering: totally unexpected effects, misinterpretations, mistrust, jealousies, abuses.... This can indeed be one of the hardest trials of a follower of Christ anxious only to imitate Him. When it occurs, as undoubtedly it will (why should the disciple expect better than the Master?), then it is time to imitate Jesus even more closely. Notice, He does not dismiss the erring crowd with harshness. We read of no loud protestations or lengthy explanations. No, He dismisses them quietly and goes further up the mountain in the darkness to pray alone to His Father.

That too must be my resort: lifting myself to the higher sphere of prayer, albeit in darkness as to the whys and wherefores of what has gone wrong, praying simply for God's will to be done, for *His* plans to be realized, abandoning myself anew to His loving, all-seeing, all-powerful Providence, praying also for those who have harmed or betrayed me, harboring no resentment, judging or scorning no one. I shall then gather great strength up there on the mountainside with Jesus, and be able to come down with renewed courage, as He did, to perform even greater things out of love for Him and for His glory alone.

The boat by this time was many furlongs distant from the land, beaten by the waves; for the wind was against them (Matthew 14:24).

Especially in the late spring, after a strangely calm, hot day, a sudden cold and violent wind can work up in the Jordan Valley blowing in a southerly direction causing great storms on the lake. This happened now and the already over-weary apostles feared for their lives, unable to make headway towards the port of Capernaum for their boat was violently buffeted about. Quite possibly the apostles had already set sail in a mood of disappointment and frustration. Jesus had promised them a rest and they were still unable to take it, and now, to their amazement, He had turned down the chance of being proclaimed a king and brought to political power. On top of all that, He had ordered them back to sea on a night such as this, Himself safely on land! It would have been quite human and understandable at that stage to think along such lines of annoyance and, now, terror. How often Jesus allows this kind of thing to happen to those whom He loves most. He knows that while a tremendous love fills their hearts, there remain at the bottom human dregs that must somehow be purged before they can truly conform to His likeness and love. First He tries gentle persuasion in many simple ways (reminders in reading, advice given, examen of conscience) that certain faults or habits are not pleasing to Him, but since little solid effort is made to improve, He is constrained to use violence in the form of severe trials. Instead of realizing that our own faults are the cause and that we have forced God to shake us thus violently, how often perhaps we are inclined to resent it deeply, blaming not ourselves but God.

Let me examine any past experiences I have had in this line and my reactions at the time. Was I not too hurt in my pride, too assertive of my utter innocence, excusing myself too easily, blaming others, allowing bitterness to enter my soul, passing harsh judgments even on God Himself, convinced He had unfairly left me alone on a violent sea of storm and darkness? Surely now I must acknowledge how utterly good He was to have allowed me such nerve-racking trials for my ultimate good and greater maturity and sensibility. Let me thank Him now for bringing me safely through it all in spite of myself and resolve not to act so foolishly again in times of trial.

> *And in the fourth watch of the night he came to them, walking on the sea. But when the disciples saw him walking on the sea, they were terrified, saying, "It is a ghost!" And they cried out for fear. But immediately he spoke to them, saying, "Take heart, it is I; have no fear" (Matthew 14:25-27).*

At about three in the morning, when they were just about at their wit's end, first one and then the other apostles made out something strange in the morning mist that was gradually replacing the darkness of night: the seeming figure of a man walking upon the water. Terror upon terrors, as if the dreadful storm had not been enough! To make matters worse, it was approaching them, causing them to cry out in alarm. In reply comes the strong but gentle voice of the Master Himself, reassuring, comforting, "Take heart, it is I; fear not!"

Here again I have probably had a similar experience. When, in times of dreadful trial, things have seemed at their lowest possible ebb and I could so easily have given myself up to despair, delusion or fatal decision or action, has not God sent me some extraordinary sign to fan the almost extinct sparks of faith and hope and charity bright again, helping me rise and recover and struggle on because of His strength and presence beside and in me? Coming out chastened from such frightening experiences I should now be a much wiser, more mature, more prudent and far holier person that I was before. Have I remembered and benefited by such hard lessons, recalling the words of the poet, "Is my gloom, after all, but a shade of His hand, outstretched caressingly?" Let me now gratefully thank, praise and resolve.

Walking on Water

And Peter answered him, "Lord, if it is you, bid me come to you on the water." He said, "Come." So Peter got out of the boat and walked on the water and came to Jesus; but when he saw the wind, he was afraid, and beginning to sink he cried out, "Lord, save me" (Matthew 14:28-30).

After the terrifying storm at sea and the further frightening appearance of what they at first took to be a ghost, the apostles must have been deeply relieved to hear the voice of Jesus assuring them it was He. But they were still not sure—at least Peter wasn't! Here in this incident we see evidence again of the ardent character of this great but very human apostle and at the same time of his deep love of Jesus. His faith, too, though not perfect, was great indeed and prompted him impetuously to challenge Jesus to allow him to go to Him upon the waters. Surely Jesus smiled at this impulsiveness of His rough Prince of Apostles and, taking up the challenge, He said simply, "Come!" Without further ado Peter eagerly clambered overboard and began walking across the waters as though on heaving glass that was firm beneath his feet. It was certainly at first a wonderful act of complete and confident abandonment. What, then, upset him? It seems almost laughable after such a miracle: a gust of wind! Poor Peter!

How often we, too, may allow similar disproportions to enter into our lives and unreasonably upset us. We have done the hard things for Jesus by giving up the physical presence and proximity of our families and many friends, sacrificing many pleasures we could lawfully have, as well as possibly splendid opportunities regarding a professional career. Our Lord appreciates all that greatly and will reward us accordingly. He even allows us, on the strength of our generosity, to walk upon the undulating waters of our continuing weaknesses in order to do great things for Him and for souls. What a great pity, then, if we allow unimportant or petty things to upset us unduly, making us pause during our progress toward Jesus, or even sink beneath the waves of despondency or fear! Doesn't that kind of thing sometimes happen to me? Do I hear the voice of Jesus: "O you of little faith! Why do you doubt?"

> *"Lord, save me." Jesus immediately reached out his hand and caught him, saying to him, "O man of little faith, why did you doubt?" (Matthew 14:30-31)*

Strangely enough, it does not seem to have been the heaving water upon which he was walking that upset Peter for the Gospel says: "When he saw the wind he was afraid," and then only, with that sudden lessening of a remarkable spirit of faith, did he begin to sink. Here perhaps we can draw out a likeness in ourselves. At times we can become too cocksure of our own selves, our capabilities, bodily strength, and even virtues, especially wisdom. We stride forth, secretly hopeful or confident of a blaze of glory, too easily forgetting that without God we would have none of these gifts and capabilities, and even our meager virtues would be sterile. How forgiving the Master is to allow us to get away with so much! How fortunate that He realizes the inherent good will deep down in those at times over-enthusiastic hearts and ways of ours!

Overconfident in myself in many ways, haven't I at times allowed myself to get overly upset by other things of far less weight than my own dangerous self-esteem? Forgetting that it is Jesus who holds me up and keeps me going, do I begin to doubt Him on some other score, or get afraid or angry, or lose faith, and so I begin to sink? Peter, fortunately, did have great faith and so, even in his moment of weakness, he was still able to call out confidently, "Lord, save me!" Immediately Jesus "reached out his hand and caught him." Do I resort to prayer automatically and confidently in times of doubt, panic, worry? By now surely this should be my instinctive habit. Only then can I hope for help from such a loving Master, who is ever close at hand, ever ready to assist me, only waiting for my humble cry for help to break through and sound above the loud howling of the winds of pride that threaten to destroy me, no less than the weakness of my body and state of virtue. Let me now in prayer make up for my past overconfidence in self and my lack of sufficient trust in God and His ever superabundant help.

> *And when they got into the boat, the wind ceased. And those in the boat worshiped him, saying, "Truly you are the Son of God" (Matthew 14:32-33).*

Only when Jesus kindly reproaches Peter does the apostle suddenly realize just how much he depends on Him; and the others, watching the scene, learn the same much-needed lesson, worshiping Him as the Son of God. How often can Jesus reproach me in the same way and with the same title: "O man of little faith, why did you doubt?" Yes, indeed, often enough I have given Jesus occasion for saying that to me. Nevertheless, His invitation remains to walk upon the waters of my very nothingness toward Him, disregarding all unwarranted fears, relying not on my own strength but solely on the power of His word and grace. Perhaps I feel that only a miracle can bring me finally to Him, but why should I doubt the possibility of even that? By myself I shall certainly fail, but not when I rely on Him and do my humble best to fulfill His holy will, taking one step at a time, confidently, toward Him. Jesus, bid me walk upon the waters to You. I rely on You, I trust You completely, I know that You will never let me down!

Bread of Life

When they found him on the other side of the sea, they said to him, "Rabbi, when did you come here?" Jesus answered them, "Truly, truly, I say to you, you seek me, not because you saw signs but because you ate your fill of the loaves. Do not labor for the food which perishes, but for the food which endures to eternal life, which the Son of God will give you; for on him has God the Father set his seal." Then they said to him, "What must we do, to be doing the works of God?" (John 6:25-28)

It would seem that Jesus deliberately told the apostles to head the ship away from Capernaum so as to avoid the crowds He would probably find there, possibly still anxious to force political power upon Him. At any rate it would seem that a little time elapsed before He did go to Capernaum and in the meantime the apostles probably had their well-earned rest. Immediately on landing, His work began at once with the same intensity. He adroitly avoids explanation of how He came to be with His apostles again (Am I not myself inclined to give grand explanations of my achievements and perhaps embroidered exploits?) and proceeds to raise the minds of His audience to higher matters. Their minds, however, seemed to run essentially on materialistic lines and they were thus unable to appreciate the true value of His words foretelling the forthcoming miracle of bread which was to be outstandingly greater than the multiplication of loaves that had so excited them—the Holy Eucharist.

Do I myself appreciate this constant and daily miracle at its true worth? St. John Chrysostom says: "How many nowadays say, 'Would that we could gaze upon His form, His figure, His raiment, His shoes!' Lo! you see Him, touch Him, eat Him. And you desire to see even His clothing, but He gives Himself to you, not to look upon only, but even to touch and eat and receive within you...." Scope for much personal examination here: let me pursue it honestly.

> *Jesus said to them, "Truly, truly, I say to you... my Father gives you the true bread from heaven...which gives life to the world." They said to him, "Lord, give us this bread always." Jesus said to them, "I am the bread of life; he who comes to me shall not hunger and he who believes in me shall never thirst. But I said to you that you have seen me and yet do not believe. All that the Father gives me will come to me; and him who comes to me I will not cast out" (John 6:32-37).*

The saints and many great spiritual writers have spoken beautifully about Holy Communion and its effects upon the devout soul. Of this I should be already long convinced. However, it is up to myself to ensure that for me it does not remain mere written theory. Each time I receive Holy Communion there should be a definite increase in my personal intimacy and relationship with Christ, my divine Guest, the very possessor of my soul and body. That, after all, is what Jesus Himself tried to get across to His listeners that day at Capernaum.

Do too many material considerations and the dullness of daily routine deaden my own convinced acceptance of the literal meaning of His words which today He addresses to me? Do I really believe that Holy Communion has the power not only to sustain but also to strengthen the life of my soul, that the most wonderful blessing coming from it is that tremendous increase of sanctifying grace which is the very life of my soul? I also thereby receive actual grace which enables my mind to recognize God's light and inspirations and strengthens my will to do what God wishes and nothing else, thus completely avoiding my great enemy, sin. What steps can I take to remind myself of these facts more frequently in order to strengthen my faith in and longing for the true Bread of Life? O Jesus,...

> *Truly, truly, I say to you, he who believes has eternal life. I am the bread of life. Your fathers ate the manna in the wilderness, and they died. This is the bread which comes down from heaven, that a man may eat of it and not die. I am the living bread which*

came down from heaven; if any one eats of this bread he will live for ever; and the bread which I shall give for the life of the world is my flesh" (John 6:47-51).

Talking of the great spiritual consolation and strength Christians can derive from the continued presence of Jesus in the Holy Eucharist, Pope Pius XII said, "He is their counselor, their consoler, their strength, their refuge, their hope, in life and in death." In the quotation from St. John, Jesus Himself tells us with even greater precision how all this can be so. He says in effect that anyone receiving Him bodily with the right dispositions will not die a spiritual death but will receive instead the germ of immortality. The coming sacrifice of the cross and the sacrament of the Eucharist, He implies, are intimately connected. Jesus, mystically sacrificed in the Eucharist, is the Bread of Life, for He gives Himself to us under the form of food and drink in order to infuse into us the life of grace merited for us by His sacrifice on the cross.

What does all this mean to me in practical effect? In what sensible way during this very day can I try to show my deep appreciation of all that my Eucharistic Savior means to me? Jesus, how often You have come to me in Holy Communion....

A Hard Saying

He who eats my flesh and drinks my blood abides in me, and I in him. As the living Father sent me, and I live because of the Father, so he who eats me will live because of me (John 6:56-57).

Even though He sensed the shock, almost horror, produced in a great many of His hearers by what He had been saying about the coming Eucharist, Jesus withdraws no single word. His flesh, He says, is true food and His blood is true refreshment because they are able to produce, in a soul rightly disposed, effects that are analogous to those produced in a body by the ordinary material foods; they will, in fact, maintain and augment the life of grace and unite the soul most intimately with Jesus so that it may live indeed with the very life of Christ Himself, who will then be for us the inexhaustible source of true life and the mainspring of our sanctification.

Pope Paul VI says: "The Eucharist is, above all, communion with Christ, God from God, Light from Light, Love from Love, living, true, substantially and sacramentally present; the Lamb immolated for our salvation, the manna which restores us for everlasting life; the friend, brother, spouse, mysteriously hidden and humbled under simple appearances, but glorious in His resurrected life and giving us life by means of the fruits of the Paschal mystery. We can never meditate enough on the riches which this communion of faith, love, will, thoughts and sentiments with the Eucharistic Christ makes available to us. The mind is bewildered, because it has difficulty in understanding; the senses are doubtful, because they are in the presence of ordinary and well-known realities—bread and wine, two very simple elements of our daily food. Yet the very 'sign' with which this divine presence is offered to us tells us how we should think about it.

The bread and wine, these species with which we are all familiar, act as symbols, as signs of something else. They are signs of the greatness of Christ's power, because He hides His immense reality under the most ordinary forms—just as He did at Bethlehem, Nazareth and Calvary. In this way He made it possible for all to approach Him." How truly grateful I should be for all this tremendous goodness of Jesus to the world and to myself in particular. In this attitude let me meditate prayerfully on what I have just read.

> *"He who eats this bread will live for ever." This he said in the synagogue, as he taught at Capernaum. Many of his disciples, when they heard it, said, "This is a hard saying; who can listen to it?" But Jesus, knowing in himself that his disciples murmured at it, said to them, "Do you take offense at this?" (John 6:58-61)*

The doctrine being propounded by Jesus sounded so strange to His hearers, and even to His disciples, that many of them at once angrily rejected it and went off indignantly, especially when, at the end of the long discourse He recapitulated all He had already said and then declared that the gift of His own flesh and blood as food and drink was infinitely superior to the manna enjoyed by their forefathers in the desert. So important did St. John reckon this discourse that he mentions exactly where it took place, at the synagogue of Capernaum (probably during a liturgical service on the sabbath).

Paul VI admits that "the Eucharist is a great mystery which our minds cannot comprehend" but he goes on to say: "Yet we can at least understand the love that shines there with a hidden and consuming flame. We can think about the friendship which Christ wants to have with each of us. That is His promise.... He is the Bread of everlasting life for us pilgrims in this world; by this means we have already been taken across the swift flowing river of time and have reached the shores of eternity."

Let me accept all this in a spirit of faith and love, trying to show my appreciation now by prayers of gratitude and resolve to strengthen my daily devotion to the Blessed Sacrament in practical ways. In this way I shall not be one of those who, weak in faith, reject our Lord. Jesus,...

After this many of his disciples drew back and no longer went about with him. Jesus said to the twelve, "Will you also go away?" Simon Peter answered him, "Lord, to whom shall we go? You have the words of eternal life; and we have believed, and have come to know, that you are the Holy One of God" (John 6:66-69).

Those who, in their pride or ignorance, could not bring themselves to submit their minds to the impressive teaching of Jesus hardened their hearts against Him, deserting Him for easier ways of life and thought, rejecting the precious gift of faith. So highly, however, does Jesus respect man's free will and the gift of faith that He even gives the twelve specially chosen apostles the chance of leaving Him too if they cannot accept His doctrine. Peter's ardent confession of faith on behalf of all bursts forth so humbly and sincerely that it must have deeply consoled the heart of Jesus, so saddened at seeing many others deserting Him.

The union of minds and hearts among Christ and His apostles at that moment must have been deeply moving to them all and a fine reflection of another wonderful effect of Holy Communion, for as Paul VI says, "The Eucharist is communion with Christ, as sacrament and sacrifice. But it is also communion among us, who are brothers; it is communion with the community, with the Church. Revelation tells us so, in St. Paul's words: 'Because there is one bread, we who are many are one body, for we all partake of the one bread.' The Second Vatican Ecumenical Council threw profound light on this reality when it called the Eucharist 'the supper of fraternal communion,' and when it said that 'refreshed at the holy gathering by the Body of Christ, they then manifest concretely the unity of the People of God, which is fittingly signified and wondrously brought about by this most holy sacrament.' The Eucharist is truly intended to fuse us believers into one, to unite us with all our brothers in the world. This is another kind of charity, which also comes from Christ but has to be practiced by us. Celebration of the Eucharist is always a beginning of union, of charity, not only in feeling but in practice: 'Love one another as I have loved you.'"

Let me, with all the faith and humility of Peter, say now to Jesus: You have the words of eternal life, Lord; I have believed and I have come to know that You are the Holy One of God. Because of You, I shall try my utmost to love my brethren as You love them and unite myself to them and to You in a very special manner at Holy Communion.

Miracle at the Pool

After this there was a feast of the Jews and Jesus went up to Jerusalem. Now there is in Jerusalem by the Sheep Gate a pool, in Hebrew called "Bethzatha," which has five porticoes. In these lay a multitude of invalids, blind, lame, paralyzed. One man was there who had been ill for thirty-eight years. When Jesus saw him and knew that he had been lying there a long time, he said to him: "Do you want to be healed?" The sick man answered him, "Sir, I have no man to put me into the pool when the water is troubled, and while I am going another steps down before me." Jesus said to him, "Rise, take up your pallet and walk." And at once the man was healed, and he took up his pallet and walked (John 5:1-9).

According to Scripture experts, this incident, although in an earlier chapter of St. John's Gospel, must have taken place after the multiplication of the loaves up at Capernaum. At any rate we find Jesus now in Jerusalem for some unspecified public feastday. The Sheep Gate was at the northeastern angle of the temple, getting its name because of the sacrificial sheep that entered here. The pool, in which they were probably washed, was toward the north of the temple and at certain times miracles were attributed to it, the popular belief being that an angel sometimes moved the waters and the first to enter would be cured. St. John is the only evangelist who mentions this incident but neither he nor Jesus commits himself to any statement about the place, though one wonders indeed why Jesus chose to go there. However, seeing there this man who had been paralyzed for thirty-eight years (He must have asked about him), His heart is filled with compassion towards him as He asks: "Do you want to be healed?" Perhaps in thus questioning him Jesus wanted to arouse in him first of all, not only faith but also the necessary virtue of hope.

With great compassion, then, on seeing his miserable plight and recognizing the merit of his long perseverance, Jesus thereupon cures him outright, thus rewarding, even canonizing, the virtue of hope. Perhaps not enough attention is paid by Christians to this virtue, whereas even the ancient pagan writers spoke highly of it, e.g., "While there's life, there's hope" (Cicero, *Epistolae ad Atticum);* "My hopes are not always realized, but I always hope" (Ovid, *Heroides).* How often hope leads on to greater faith. Let me, like my Master, be ever on the alert to stimulate this virtue in others.

Let me think prayerfully about what I could do along this line today. "Rise, take up your pallet, and walk."

Can you imagine our kind Master speaking with an expressionless face to that poor man? Surely not. He whose heart was so full of kindness must have let it overflow on that occasion and surely as He sparked up once more the glimmer of hope in the man's heart, there must have been a kindly smile on that gloriously handsome face of His. The Salesian Bishop of Krishnagar (India), Msgr. Louis Laravoire Morrow, in founding the Catechist Sisters of Mary Immaculate Help of Christians, wrote this in the Introduction to their Constitutions: "Just a little *smile* on your lips cheers your heart, beautifies your face, promotes your health, inspires kindly deeds, induces kindly thoughts, keeps you in good humor, preserves peace in your soul. *Smile to yourself,* until you have warmed your own heart with the sunshine of your most cheery countenance. Then go out and *radiate* your smile. It has work to do—for *God.* You are an apostle now, and your smile is your instrument for winning souls. Sanctifying grace will give your smile special charm for doing good. Smile on the timid, the lonely, the sorrowful, the wrinkled, the familiar faces! Let *all* enjoy the beauty and cheer of your smiling face. Your smile can promote contentment, encouragement, joy and confidence in the heart of others. The influence of your smile can inspire unselfish, even noble deeds, unknown to you. Your smile can awaken a religious vocation. It can bring about a *metanoia,* bring a sinner back to God. It will certainly win for you many devoted friends."

No picture of our dear Master can be complete if we do not see Him smiling. Let me try to imitate Him in this according to the above quotation, so that even in this I may become more Christlike. Jesus,...

To complete our previous thoughts, and still bearing in mind the lovable picture of Jesus smiling kindly on the poor paralytic at the side of the pool, let us quote further from Bishop Morrow: "Smile, too, at God, in loving acceptance of whatever He sends into your life. Then you will merit having the radiantly smiling Christ look upon you with love throughout eternity!... We must become Christlike! That is the purpose for which we have consecrated ourselves entirely to God. Many others who, like us, embraced the religious life have become truly Christlike, also many others who have not embraced the religious life. Why and how did they become Christlike? Because they were cheerful when it was difficult to be cheerful; patient when it was difficult to be patient. They pushed on when they wanted to stand still. They kept silent when they wanted to talk. They were agreeable when they wanted to be disagreeable."

Possibly all this may sound like a very difficult program, and indeed it often can be. Relying, however, on the constant help of our kind Master, it becomes much more simple to act according to such a program. How often indeed it can start off with the mere habit of smiling, enkindling our smile at the sight of Jesus standing alongside a man who had been full of misery for thirty-eight long years, reviving his spirit of hope, smiling at him, setting him on his feet soundly again, bidding him take up his bed and walk—and surely he did so smiling, his heart overflowing with love for the kindly, smiling Man who had healed him. Prayer. Resolution.

"Without Me...Nothing!"

I can do nothing on my own authority; as I hear, I judge; and my judgment is just, because I seek not my own will but the will of him who sent me (John 5:30).

Following the cure of the paralytic at the poolside and its consequence among the ranting scribes and pharisees, Jesus felt constrained to make a long discourse in defense of His divine mission (Jn. 5:19-47). He defends His open declaration of equality with the Father and the duties arising from it as the dispenser of life and the universal judge. Unfortunately the effect on His learned critics was merely a further hardening of heart and mind. At any rate, let me draw from the discourse three points that I can apply to myself, the first one being the above quotation. "I can do nothing on my own authority." What Jesus admits in all humility and truth applies infinitely more to myself, who depend from breath to breath upon the power, mercy and kindness of my Creator. Let me never make a decision unless in the presence of Jesus. Doing that should make me realize my utter dependence on God for all my powers, including that of deciding. Then let me use that power to decide as objectively as I possibly can, praying with confidence for the help of the Holy Spirit in coming to the right decision and trusting utterly that Jesus, my Master, will help me carry through bravely whatever I sincerely feel is His holy will: "I can do all things in Him who strengthens me."

All things—it needs tremendous confidence at times to make that statement to myself, but that is precisely what Jesus expects of me: total trust, courageous action and then absolute abandonment of the outcome according to His all-seeing plans. Like Him I must "seek not my own will but the will of him who sent me." It is so easy to allow the human element or angle to get into the picture and assume undue proportions that interfere with the perfect fulfillment of what God wills. I must constantly be on the lookout for this. It can be tricky, since God does indeed wish me to use my own human knowledge, experience, common sense, and the advice, wisdom and experience of others, but the ultimate criterion must always be: What does God want in this particular case, regardless of my own whims, comfort,... I need to be a person of deep prayer in the radiant presence of God to live up to the message inherent in our Lord's words for my own self. But is there any really sound reason why I should not be such!

> *But the testimony which I have is greater than that of John; for the works which the Father has granted me to accomplish, these very works which I am doing, bear me witness that the Father has sent me. And the Father who sent me has himself borne witness to me. His voice you have never heard, his form you have never seen (John 5:36-37).*

If one had all the faith and confidence implied in the previous point (and again, why not!), then one would not worry so much about ways and means—and results! If I am trying my honest best to do well "the works which the Father has granted me to accomplish," then all will be well. So evident should be my sincere confidence in God and His all-powerful guidance and help that "these very works which I am doing, bear me witness that the Father has sent me."

How deep indeed is my confidence in Jesus, my Master and Exemplar? How often do I pray to His Holy Spirit for the help I need? If only I permit Him (What audacity in that very phrase!), God could do such marvelous things through even someone like myself. Don't I need to inject a lot of this optimism, this supreme trust in God and His power, into my various undertakings? Let me now concentrate prayerfully on those where the need seems greatest.

> *How can you believe, who receive glory from one another and do not seek the glory that comes from the only God? (John 5:44)*

In twining the heavy steel cable that must bind all my apostolic endeavors to and about God's holy will, there is unfortunately always the danger of the weak strand of vanity slipping in to weaken the link. How frighteningly easy for hope of self-glory to come sneaking into even those affairs we honestly set out to do solely for the greater honor and glory of God! How extremely important it is always to have a pure intention before God in all that we do. Pride can so easily slip in! A little bit of praise can so readily deflect us. Because of all this, how wise and important it is to renew frequently our purity of intention. It is a matter of striving toward complete conviction on this point, constantly reminding myself, perseveringly getting back to God, aiming always for His not my own glory. Let me now pray with deep humility about all this to my all-seeing God who loves me. Jesus, You see me through and through....

Deaf-mute

Then he returned from the region of Tyre, and went through Sidon to the Sea of Galilee, through the region of the Decapolis. And they brought to him a man who was deaf and had an impediment in his speech; and they besought him to lay his hand upon him (Mark 7:31-32).

Instead of returning to Palestine by the shortest route from Tyre, Jesus makes a much longer journey, northward to Sidon in Phoenicia then south-eastward, passing through Lebanon and along the eastern bank of the River Jordan until He arrives at Genesareth Lake once more in the territory of the Decapolis—the famous League of ten original Greek cities of *Coele Syria* founded by Pompey in 63 B.C. as a continuous block of political territory bounding Palestine on the East.

Let me stop here a while with Jesus at the lakeside to see what application I can make for myself from the cure of the deaf-mute. How often there is deafness and muteness even at prayer! Prayer can become so mechanical and routine that at times we are not even aware we are actually supposed to be *praying* then, not just rattling off formulas; rather, listening to the voice of God make itself heard. This, of course, is more particularly prevalent perhaps when it is a question of prayers in common with others. How unpleasant and saddening it must be to God the Father to hear His beloved Son's rich prayer, the *Our Father*, uttered as though an unmeaning nursery rhyme! How discordant in the ears of Jesus the tones of a *Hail Mary* rattled off carelessly and yet supposedly in honor of the Mother He loved so deeply and manfully—worse still when He has to listen to fifty such in what can and should always be a truly devout and well-said repetition of meditated prayer, the rosary. If we merely *recite* prayers then indeed God might well block His ears, not granting what we ostensibly pray for, since we ourselves obviously haven't the matter very much at heart if such be the manner of our praying! Better to be mute on such occasions rather than slight God or His holy Mother or the saints in public. But the same dull monotony that deadens vocal prayer can occur even privately. Then indeed I am deaf to the sound of God's voice, mute in spite of my utterings. Does this occur at my prayers? Surely I should be quite concerned about this important matter—Jesus is!

> *And taking him aside from the multitude privately, he put his fingers into his ears, and he spat and touched his tongue; and looking up to heaven he sighed, and said to him, "Ephphatha," that is, "Be opened." And his ears were opened, his tongue was released, and he spoke plainly. And he charged them to tell no one; but the more he charged them, the more zealously they proclaimed it (Mark 7:33-36).*

There has been much speculation as to why Jesus actually took the man aside in order to perform the cure and why He employed the particular ritual mentioned. Ricciotti suggests that it might have been to ensure that the man actually saw what was going on, thus enlivening his faith, and then he would be able to hear clearly the voice of Jesus aside from the clamoring crowd. The Abbot of Solesmes, Dom Paul Delatte, says that Jesus worked with the weak material He found, the imperfect faith of the man, making use of a ritual that probably corresponded to it as the way a cure should be performed according to simple minds *(L'Evangelo).*

From the reasons adduced I can draw something useful for myself. Let me look at each in turn again and see when Jesus has acted similarly with me at various times.

> *And they were astonished beyond measure, saying, "He has done all things well; he even makes the deaf hear and the dumb speak" (Mark 7:37).*

It is essential to the very nature of my religious vocation to be trying constantly to be Christlike in every possible way: "The religious life is intended above all else to lead those who embrace it to an imitation of Christ and to union with God" *(Perfectae Caritatis,* 2). At the end of my life there should therefore be no hesitation on the part of those who have shared my life in saying sincerely, "He has done all things well." Jesus has indeed taken me apart from the crowd to be healed by the conversion of my life toward Him; He put His finger into my ears to grant me good spiritual hearing; He loosened the roots of my tongue, not for idle chatter and gossip or mere vain eloquence but so that it could at all times praise God in word and prayer, proclaiming His holy truths and exhorting others also to follow His teachings courageously.

How often, in spite of all that, I may have failed to do all things well through forgetfulness of the one and only source of my strength and abilities, disregard of the need of sanctifying grace, lack of cooperation with the many actual graces so lavishly offered me by Jesus in my religious and Christian life. The height of perfection to which my Christian vocation calls me could be frightening were it not for the fact that all Jesus needs from me really is my faithful, prayerful cooperation each day to be what I should be in all sincerity and to try to do all things well. Given that cooperation, He does the rest! Let me now consult Him on where I am still lacking and prayerfully beg Him to continue being patient with me until I do indeed, even if only on my deathbed, reach the level He wishes. Jesus,...

The Light of Christ

No one after lighting a lamp puts it in a cellar or under a bushel, but on a stand, that those who enter may see the light. Your eye is the lamp of your body; when your eye is sound, your whole body is full of light; but when it is not sound, your body is full of darkness (Luke 11:33-34).

This passage reverts to similar expressions elsewhere in the Gospels, pointing to Jesus as the light of the world. It can be interpreted personally in the sense that if Christ is that to me, then indeed, as He Himself says in the above passage, I must not hide that glorious Light but let it shine forth for others as well. I myself must be a radiating center of light, in my own community as well as to outsiders. The world of today is so very much in need of spiritual illumination because of the prevalent confusion that has come about rather rapidly through profoundly changed conditions of a social, psychological, moral and even religious order. "A change in attitudes and in human structure frequently calls accepted values into question. This is especially true of young people, who have grown impatient on more than one occasion, and indeed become rebels in their distress.... The institutions, laws, and modes of thinking and feeling as handed down from previous generations do not always seem to be well adapted to the contemporary state of affairs. Hence arises an upheaval in the manner and even the norms of behavior.... Growing numbers of people are abandoning religion in practice" *(Gaudium et Spes,* 7).

How easy even for us religious to fall victim to so much imbalance existing in the modern world. Perhaps for us too there is a danger of falling into the modern temptation of evaluating things too much from the angle of productivity rather than genuine quality. Mass production and worldwide competition have definitely led to a deterioration in things material as well as spiritual. Even in the intellectual world, how much useless cramming has to be done in order to obtain a job-securing diploma, regardless of how much real learning has actually sunk in. The newspapers, radio, television, movies, and advertising world pour forth a vast amount of untruths uncannily mixed in with at least a semblance of truth. Plausibility reigns supreme. How easy, therefore, to be deceived; how vitally, therefore, we need the light of Christ in our lives in order to help us to sift the true from the false. It is that light, deep and full within, and radiating outside, that alone can give me that true discernment which I need. Perhaps within myself, too, there are still patches of darkness that need to be illumined by the light of Christ? Let me pray about this to Him now. Jesus, You are the light of the world; I need Your light in order to....

Therefore be careful lest the light in you be darkness (Luke 11:35).

It is worth considering further Vatican II's excellent Pastoral Constitution on the Church in the Modern World, in the light of the words of Jesus Himself. "The truth is that the imbalances under which the modern world labors are linked with that more basic imbalance rooted in the heart of man. For in man himself many elements wrestle with one another. Thus, on the one hand, as a creature he experiences his limitations in a multitude of ways. On the other, he feels himself to be boundless in his desires and summoned to a higher life. Pulled by manifold attractions, he is constantly forced to choose among them and to renounce some. Indeed, as a weak and sinful being, he often does what he would not, and fails to do what he would.... The Church believes that Christ, who died and was raised up for all, can through His Spirit offer man the light and the strength to measure up to his supreme destiny.... She likewise holds that in her most benign Lord and Master can be found the key, the focal point, and the goal of all human history. The Church also maintains that beneath all changes there are many realities which do not change and which have their ultimate foundation in Christ, who is the same yesterday and today, yes and forever. Hence in the light of Christ, the image of the unseen God, the firstborn of every creature, the Council wishes to speak to all men in order to illuminate the mystery of man and to cooperate in finding the solution to the outstanding problems of our time" *(Gaudium et Spes,* 10).

I must therefore guard carefully against failing in my sense of responsibility toward God, the Church, toward mankind, especially those with whom I come into frequent contact, for they look to me for the light of Christ and do not expect to find in me the darkness of sham and insincerity, so easily detectable. Let me pray now on this point.

> *If then your whole body is full of light, having no part dark, it will be wholly bright, as when a lamp with its rays gives you light (Luke 11:36).*

The greater one's inner purity of mind and heart, through the light of Christ allowed full play therein, so much the greater will be one's power as an apostle radiating Christ. Uncontrolled passions and bad habits can cause enlarging areas of darkness. "Faith throws a new light on everything, manifests God's design for man's total vocation, and thus directs the mind to solutions which are fully human.... In the depths of his conscience, man detects a law which he does not impose upon himself, but which holds him to obedience. Always summoning him to love good and avoid evil, the voice of conscience can when necessary speak to his heart more specifically: do this, shun that. For man has in his heart a law written by God. To obey it is the very dignity of man; according to it he will be judged. Conscience is the most secret core and sanctuary of a man. There he is alone with God, whose voice echoes in his depths. In a wonderful manner conscience reveals that law which is fulfilled by love of God and neighbor. By fidelity to conscience, Christians are joined with the rest of men in the search for truth, and for the genuine solution to the numerous problems which arise in the life of individuals and from social relationships. Hence the more a correct conscience holds sway, the more persons and groups turn aside from blind choice and strive to be guided by objective norms of morality. Conscience frequently errs from invincible ignorance without losing its dignity. The same cannot be said of a man who cares but little for truth and goodness, or of a conscience which by degrees grows practically sightless as a result of habitual sin" *(Gaudium et Spes,* 11, 16).

Conscience, then, must be the lamp that holds the light of Christ, so that my whole being may be filled with His grace in order that I in turn may be for others an instrument of Christ, a lamp that is "wholly bright." Is there any fear of my having a dull, numbed or even blind conscience? In that case this very meditation could be the ray of Christ's light seeking entrance into my mind and heart so as to bring about my total conversion and resurrection. At any rate I have much cause for prayer and sensible resolution, haven't I? Dear Jesus,...

Touch of a Kind Hand

And they came to Bethsaida. And some people brought to him a blind man, and begged him to touch him. And he took the blind man by the hand, and led him out of the village; and when he had spit on his eyes and laid his hands upon him, he asked him, "Do you see anything?" And he looked up and said, "I see men; but they look like trees, walking." Then again he laid his hands upon his eyes; and he looked intently and was restored, and saw everything clearly. And he sent him away to his home, saying, "Do not even enter the village" (Mark 8:22-26).

Jesus and His apostles land now at Bethsaida Julia on the northern side of the Lake of Tiberias, close to where the Jordan flows. Again Jesus is approached for a cure and again He wishes to avoid all fuss and clamor. He actually takes the blind man by the hand and leads him out of the village. What an honor indeed for that poor man, what a wonderful memory for the rest of his life: the warm, kind touch of that manly hand! Again Jesus chooses to use saliva to effect the cure, bowing to the common belief in the merits of "fasting-spittle," even though here it was His own divine power at work. The man had not been born blind, for he already had some idea of what trees looked like. Only after a little ritual does Jesus completely heal him, sending him off to his own home away from the village. And, for once, He seemed to be obeyed for nothing further is said about the event.

Abbé C. Fouard suggests that Jesus performed this particular miracle in the way He did (by stages) in order to stimulate the faith of the blind man. It has also been proposed that He further did so in order to increase the light of faith and understanding in His own apostles, since only they saw Him perform the cure. They too had once been completely blind to Him and even at this stage they understood Him only vaguely. A master of pedagogy, He used this audio-visual aid as a further impressive step in their education. How great indeed was the apostles' need of faith—how great my own! St. John of the Cross says: "Faith is the sole proximate and proportionate means of the soul's union with God, seeing that there is no other alternative but that God is either seen or believed in. For as God is infinite, so faith proposes Him as infinite, and as He is Three and One, so faith proposes Him to us as Three and One. And thus by this means alone that is faith, God manifests Himself to the soul in the divine light which surpasses all understanding, and therefore the greater the faith of the soul the more is that soul united to God.... For in this darkness God unites Himself to the understanding, being Himself hidden in it" *(Ascent of Mt. Carmel).*

The faith of the apostles had to measure up to that standard eventually—so must mine. At what stage do I feel I am now? Let me pray for an increase of faith.

How great indeed is my need of faith as a modern apostle in the building up of the kingdom of Christ! There is the matter too of co-responsibility with all the rest who labor similarly in the Church.

The whole aim of this set of meditations is precisely to make me a person of faith, basing my whole life on Christ and His Gospel—not in vague or sentimental abstractions but in detail in daily life. Where the written word fails to make the applications practical enough, then I myself must use my faith and ingenuity to make it so in my own case.

St. Paul says that "faith comes from what is heard, and what is heard comes by the preaching of Christ" (Rom. 10:17). What the evangelists heard of the preaching of Christ they have transcribed in the four Gospels and hence by these meditations on the Gospels I have the excellent opportunity each day of bringing Christ intimately (at times courageously) into my life. I should subject even my time and method of meditation to the microscope of honest examination to look for possible flaws. If I find any—and even if I don't—let me still accept "the heavy price to pay for following the logic of the Gospel." Lord, increase my faith!

St. Paul says of Abraham: "He did not weaken in faith.... No distrust made him waver concerning the promise of God, but he grew strong in his faith as he gave glory to God, fully convinced that God was able to do what He had promised. That is why his faith was 'reckoned to him as righteousness.' But the words 'it was reckoned to him' were written not for his sake alone, but for ours also" (Rom. 4:19-23). It is so easy to get one's vision of the plan and workings of God out of focus.

Faith, then, is not just the intellectual acceptance of whatever Jesus Christ has revealed; it means far more than that. Faith is that whole-hearted trust in God and His Providence, quite confident that in Him alone lie all the right answers, in Him alone lies our hope for fulfillment, peace and happiness in this life and the next. Does my own faith measure up to all this? Do people see me as a person of very obvious faith? This should certainly be so if I am the apostle of Christ I should be. "He who through faith is righteous shall live" (Rom. 1:17). Jesus,...

Two or More in My Name

Where two or more are gathered in my name, there am I in the midst of them (Matthew 18:20).

In recent times the Union of Superiors General in Rome made a wide survey concerning defections in the priesthood and religious life, and sadly it was revealed that a large majority of those who left admitted as root-cause the fact that they had become careless about prayer or had given it up altogether. This fact should give emphasis to the question of renewal in the Church, among the clergy and in religious congregations, for this matter of prayer, personal and community, lies at the very core of the whole idea. Individuals and communities, therefore, must try their utmost to reinvigorate their spirit of prayer in all its various forms—and we can be thankful that nowadays in this matter our prayer-life and style have been made more attractive and helpful in form and content. In other meditations we have dwelt on so many personal difficulties about prayer and praying; in this one let us concentrate more on the matter of community prayer and our own responsibility toward it.

The Apostolic Constitution *Laudis Canticum* urges us to look upon our duty of prayer not as "a mere law to be observed" but as something whose intrinsic importance, as well as its pastoral and ascetical utility, we fully recognize. If in fact we do realize that, then we shall also admit that the two aspects of apostolic prayer (personal and community) are really inseparable, that we cannot eliminate one or the other from our lives as apostolic religious. We should therefore strive to integrate both into our daily program in a way that will enrich our whole being personally and add tremendous strength to our community. The power before God of a prayerful community is beyond telling.

However, when we use the term "prayerful community" and link it up with our Lord's own words in the Gospel quotation above, we must surely recognize that this title implies far more than the mere formal act of a group of people uttering prayers aloud together or even assisting at the liturgy in common. The title "praying community" implies that we are all sensible, serious-minded people who do want to pray well, mature enough to make the effort needed to recite prayers together reverently, to withdraw our minds for a while from work and distractions in order to establish a more direct personal and community contact with the God we love and worship in our hearts and minds. Is this my own attitude toward community prayer? What efforts do I really make to avoid distractions and to enter fully into the spirit of community prayer? Lord Jesus, You said, "Where two or more are gathered in my name...."

My physical presence at community prayer is already something meritorious; so too could be the mere mechanical but respectful uttering of the various formulas together with my fellow-religious, and especially when I am in a state of dryness, but in general much more generosity is required. No matter how dry I may feel, no matter how fervent, there should be a real anxiety to use my community prayer to establish direct contact with God in union with my brethren and in my own mind and heart. The effort required sets a golden seal upon my mere presence with the community.

It should be my definite desire and aim to accustom myself to insert my own humble effort at prayer into that of the whole community which is striving in turn to insert the community prayer into that of Christ Himself "ever interceding for us with the Father." In this way, no matter how dry I may feel, no matter how hard the effort is, I can feel sure that community prayer is tremendously enriched and precious before the throne of God. And from this personal and community participation in the living prayer of Jesus countless blessings will flow into the personal lives of each, upon the community as such and onto all the bustle of our daily work and apostolate.

If I and my community are really trying to pray in this manner, in union with the constantly prayerful Christ, then our prayer becomes so enmeshed with that of Jesus that the results of all that we are trying to do for God and souls must inevitably be far more wonderful than we can ever anticipate. Why? Simply from the fact that whatever we are trying to do then is no longer merely *my* or my community's work, prayer, or interest but—far more importantly—the direct work and prayer and personal interest of the Master Himself who is able to bring all things to good issue in spite of all our weaknesses and limitations.

Let me pray about this now and consider how I can improve in my efforts not merely to unite myself in prayer with my community but, above all, with the prayerful Christ. O Jesus....

In another Apostolic Exhortation, *Evangelica Testificatio* (1971), Pope Paul VI stated: "Whatever their size, communities large or small will not succeed in helping their members unless they are constantly animated by the Gospel spirit, nourished by prayers...." And he goes on to stress the importance and helpfulness of the liturgical life: "There is surely no need to remind you of the special place occupied in your community life by the Church's liturgy, the center of which is the Eucharistic sacrifice, in which interior prayer is linked to external worship...." It is here above all, surely, when we celebrate the Eucharist together, that community prayer should reach its highest peak each day, but again it is my own personal efforts that are also of such great importance in helping attain it.

How grateful we should be that the revised liturgy approved by the Church has given us such splendid opportunities for making our own personal and community prayer richer and more meaningful. What a wonderful thought that I and my community can be there together with the living, praying Christ, offering up our sacrifice to the Father, praying with Him, inserting our prayer into His. Community prayer at this level, therefore, is surely sublime and when I try to enter into it fully, with all my mind and heart, then already I and my community are enjoying something of the very glory of Christ's own resurrection. This thought should surely spur me on to an ever greater generosity in contributing my full share toward making my community a prayerful one through, with and in the prayerful Christ Himself. Let me now ask the help of Jesus and Mary....

His Face Shone

And after six days Jesus took with him Peter and James and John his brother, and led them up a high mountain apart. And he was transfigured before them, and his face shone like the sun, and his garments became white as light. And behold, there appeared to them Moses and Elijah, talking with them. And Peter said to Jesus, "Lord, it is well that we are here; if you wish, I will make three booths here, one for you and one for Moses and one for Elijah" (Matthew 17:1-4).

According to an extremely ancient and constant tradition, the scene of the transfiguration was Mount Tabor, a very distinctively shaped solitary eminence to the east of Nazareth and not many hours journey from it. From its summit the panorama, extending from the Mediterranean on the one hand to the Lake of Genesareth on the other, is quite magnificent. It would have taken the six days mentioned in order to come from Caesarea Philippi and to climb it. As to the choice of those present at the event, Peter was obvious as the head of the apostles and, after his recent outburst against the coming passion of Christ, Jesus probably felt that this scene would strengthen him in faith and hearten him in the sad days to come. James was to be the first apostle to die for Christ, John the last. These three all had good reasons for being selected, therefore, for this special privilege.

Here we find them, then, with Jesus on this high mountain, their weak faith being bolstered up by the extraordinary vision they would never be able to forget, their ecstatic eyes lit up by the rays of Christ's pure white majesty and glory in the very presence of Moses and Elijah who betokened for the Jews the Law and the Prophets and who thus confirmed the divine mission of Jesus. Peter is so overcome with joy that he gives one of his usual impetuous outbursts, this time of enthusiasm, anxious to stay up there for as long as possible, even to the extent of building rough shelters. But such was not the will of God: hard work and suffering lay ahead for the apostles also and the vision was intended to sustain them bravely through it all until they too could enjoy it in full in heaven.

For myself? As a true follower of Christ endeavoring to become actually Christlike, I also should be transfigured before others by the perfect honesty, sincerity and simplicity that people can read in my face and in my words, by the outstanding purity and decency of my life as a Christian, as a holy religious. Is this really the case with me? What evidence have I? What is lacking? What needs improvement or reform? Something to pray about now.

> *He was still speaking, when lo, a bright cloud overshadowed them, and a voice from the cloud said, "This is my beloved Son, with whom I am well pleased; listen to him." When the disciples heard this, they fell on their faces and were filled with awe (Matthew 17:5-6).*

It is probable that the transfiguration took place at night since in his account of it St. Luke says they descended the mountain the next day (9:31), and we know that Jesus was often accustomed to spend the night in prayer on a mountainside. The bright cloud mentioned is frequently found in the Old Testament as a sign of the actual presence of God and now the actual voice of the Father is heard acknowledging His Son, praising Him and urging obedience to Him. This again the privileged apostles would never be able to forget. Nor must I, for I too in so many different ways hear the voice of the Father saying to me of His Son, "Listen to him." In what ways? Through the Gospel, through these very meditations, through the voice of lawful authority, through the frequent inspirations of His Holy Spirit. Do I really stand in respectful awe of my Christian vocation and of the voice of Christ? How much attention do I give each day to listening for His voice and messages? How prompt am I in obeying them? Is my faith still very weak in this matter? Can the Father say of me too: "This is my beloved son, with whom I am well pleased"? Prayer.

But Jesus came and touched them, saying, "Rise, and have no fear." And when they lifted up their eyes, they saw no one but Jesus only (Matthew 17:7-8).

How often I can lose sight of my Master and His teachings, lying flat on my face until He Himself comes and touches me, raising me up with gentle hand and saying: "Rise and have no fear." If only my faith were stronger in the presence and help of Jesus, each time I too raise my eyes I should see "no one but Jesus only." It is up to me throughout the day to keep raising my eyes from mere material occupations and preoccupations to Him, through whom alone I can achieve anything, materially, spiritually, apostolically: "Without me you can do *nothing*"—"I can do *all things* in Him who strengthens me." How often do I recall these phrases? They too could be not only a source of tremendous consolation and confidence but help also to transfigure my life and personality, making me a much holier and much more effective and practical apostle of Christ. Let me pray now for this great grace.

Not To Give Offense

When they came to Capernaum, the collectors of the half-shekel tax went up to Peter and said, "Does not your teacher pay the tax?" He said, "Yes." And when he came home, Jesus spoke to him first, saying, "What do you think, Simon? From whom do kings of the earth take toll of tribute? From their sons or from others?" And when he said, "From others," Jesus said to him, "Then the sons are free. However, not to give offense to them, go to the sea and cast a hook, and take the first fish that comes up, and when you open its mouth you will find a shekel; take that and give it to them for me and for yourself" (Matthew 17:24-26).

This tax of half a shekel (a silver coin) is spoken of as early as the Book of Exodus: "Every one who is numbered in the census, from twenty years old and upward, shall give the Lord's offering. The rich shall not give more, the poor shall not give less than the half-shekel, when you give the Lord's offering to make atonement for yourselves" (30:14-15). Jesus could have claimed exemption but He did not. Note His courtesy once again: "not to give offense to them." Notice, too, that Jesus stayed in Peter's house "when he came home." The apostle had given up all for Christ but Jesus did not forbid him ever to visit his family and former home again. He availed Himself of its hospitality. At the same time He does not exempt Himself from the payment of taxes.

Possibly here I can learn very practical lessons for myself concerning my family and home, my visits there (Do I do good as Jesus did?). I must not be dependent financially on those who perhaps are less well-situated than I am myself. On such occasions I should use even more prudence and tact than usual, being careful not to appear as either a mere do-gooder on the one hand or a sponger on the other. Nor should I in any way act as though

I am a superior sort of being because of my religious status, but at the same time there should be no false humility either. Perhaps I can do most good and give more happiness to others as well as myself by being perfectly natural and sincere, without any affectation or bluff. Is that my way in my dealings with others? Jesus, I have before me the example of Your sincerity at all times; help me, please, to....

To this day in the Lake of Tiberias fishermen still haul in a species of fish called *chromis Simonis* (locally, "the dog-fish"), which has a rather large mouth and gullet because there its young are incubated. The fish has to swallow a stone or other hard object in order eventually to eject them in birth. Hence there was nothing really extraordinary in this particular fish having a coin in its mouth. The marvel is: how did Jesus know all the details, that the first fish Peter caught would have a whole shekel in it, enough to pay the tax for both of them? Notice the extent to which Jesus goes in order to avoid giving any scandal, not so much to the hardened tax-gatherers but rather to the people with whom He was staying.

Another practical lesson for myself. There must never be any question of scandal when I am staying with others, no seeking after cheap popularity, no loud talking or monopolization of conversation, seeking attention, boasting, exaggerations, still less lies or even detraction. To live outside one's own community circle demands a great amount of prudence, tact, considerateness, and that supreme courtesy that is born of true humility within, that sees Christ Himself in others and is always attentive to their needs and interests rather than one's own. How has my past conduct shown up in the light of all this? Resolutions to make for the future? Jesus,...

The harm done by the bad example or carelessness (to say nothing of scandal) of a religious among outsiders can be great indeed because so unexpected from one publicly dedicated by profession to a virtuous service of God and neighbor. When it occurs, it is very often through one or other of the above causes. How often, too, disloyalty comes in when speaking of the faults of one's brethren, superiors, the episcopate, the Church. Surely on this point there should be a united front of loyalty on the part of all, such as exists in families outside, for they do not go blathering out their faults to others. These things are taken for granted, because of human nature's weaknesses, but not gossiped about! What a poor and unapostolic show, then, is put up by a religious indulging in such immaturity and disloyalty! Yet it happens, it happens....

Rather let me raise my sights and include Christ in the picture to get it into better perspective. Just as Jesus so intimately included Peter in seeing that the tax was paid, let me also consider myself as privileged always to share all things with my Master, who sees to all my needs and those of my brethren, who so mercifully has patience with my faults as well as theirs, who possibly forgives them more easily because they have and show more true love for Him. My loyalty, then, to even the weakest of my brethren is intimately bound up with my loyalty to Christ. Let me remember this in all my inside and outside relationships. Prayer (if necessary, of reparation) and resolution.

Who Is the Greatest?

At that time the disciples came to Jesus, saying, "who is the greatest in the kingdom of heaven?" And calling to him a child, he put him in the midst of them, and said, "Truly, I say to you, unless you turn and become like children, you will never enter the kingdom of heaven. Whoever humbles himself like this child, he is the greatest in the kingdom of heaven" (Matthew 18:1-4).

St. Luke puts it more boldly, saying "an argument arose among them as to which of them was the greatest" (9:46). Possibly it was caused (as suggested by many writers) by Jesus giving continual preference to Peter. Jealousy may well have been present, for Peter certainly had outstanding faults. At any rate, whatever the cause, they ask Jesus directly for an answer. Instead He uses the audio-visual aid again in order to impress the lesson all the more. He uses a mere child, perhaps to put them to shame also for their own childishness. What Jesus wants from His apostles and from me, is not the immaturity and lightheadness of a growing child but the confident docility, holy abandonment and tranquil simplicity of a child that is innocent and loving.

St. Francis de Sales had all the humility of the little child that Jesus so lovingly took in His arms and placed among His apostles as an example. We are told of him that "it was not his habit to use expressions of humility in speaking of himself; he avoided such language, as one of the gulfs in which that virtue is apt to suffer shipwreck. He so strictly adhered to this practice that nothing but stringent necessity ever led him to say good or evil of himself, even in the most indifferent matters. He sometimes said that it was as difficult a feat to speak of one's self as to walk along a tightrope, and that a strong balance as well as wonderful circumspection was requisite to avoid a fall. He did not like to hear people talking very humbly of themselves, unless their words proceeded from a thoroughly sincere inward feeling. He said that such words were the quintessence, the cream, the elixir, of the most subtle pride. The truly humble man did not desire to *appear* humble, but to *be* humble." How do I fit into such a picture, as God sees me?

Let me continue further with the highly intellectual and accomplished Bishop of Geneva, so greatly esteemed by all who knew him, and yet who remained always the simple and humble St. Francis de Sales. "Humility is so fragile that she fears her own shadow, and cannot hear her own name mentioned without running the risk of perishing. He who blames himself may be indirectly aiming at praise, like the rower who turns his back on the quarter which all his strength is employed to reach. He would be very sorry were we to believe all the evil he says of himself; and it is his pride which makes him desire to be reckoned humble."

Let us add some useful considerations of his great follower, St. John Bosco: "One who has but mediocre ability but is virtuous and humble, does far more good and accomplishes far greater things than a learned man who is proud" *(M.B.,* VIII); "Let no one boast of what he knows or does; when it comes to the test, let each one do what he can, without ostentation" *(M.B.,* XI); "Do what you can. God will do what we cannot accomplish. Confide everything to Jesus in the Blessed Sacrament and to Mary, Help of Christians, and you will see what miracles are" *(M.B.,* XI); "Do what good you can, without any fuss. A violet is hidden but it is recognized and found because of its perfume" *(M.B.,* XVIII). Consideration. Prayer. Resolution.

In the endeavor to acquire and practice true humility, St. Francis de Sales placed great store on the gracious acceptance of humiliations that come to us unexpectedly. He said, however, that this is unfortunately rare—because there is much more abjection in suffering, loving, embracing, and receiving with joy, the humiliations which come to us unsought, than those which are of our own choosing; for in things of our own choice we are much more exposed to the assaults of self-love, unless our intention is very single and pure; and also because where there is less of our own will, there is more of the will of God. "The crosses we carve for ourselves are always more delicate than the others!" He set more value on an ounce of suffering than on several pounds of action, good as it might be, which proceeded from our own will.

Again for myself, more matter for thought, examination, prayer. "But as for me, my prayer is to you, O Lord. At an acceptable time, O God, in the abundance of your steadfast love answer me. With your faithful help, rescue me from sinking in the mire; let me be delivered from my enemies and from the deep waters [of pride]. Let not the flood sweep over me, or the deep swallow me up, or the pit close its mouth over me" (Ps. 69:13-15).

Religious Formation

And if your hand causes you to sin, cut it off; it is better for you to enter life maimed than with two hands to go to hell, to the unquenchable fire. And if your foot causes you to sin, cut it off; it is better for you to enter life lame than with two feet to be thrown into hell. And if your eye causes you to sin, pluck it out; it is better for you to enter the kingdom of God with one eye than with two eyes to be thrown into hell (Mark 9:43-47).

Although strictly speaking, our Lord was referring here to scandal given to others, nevertheless, this particular message may well find application to ourselves also. Is it possible to give scandal to oneself? To one's own conscience, certainly. St. Francis de Sales speaks of the two selves that exist in us, the better self striving towards God, the lower self tending downwards, ever giving scandal to the other. For practical application let us consider the matter of religious formation and training. This, after all, should not be something that takes place merely at the beginning of our religious lives—it is something that should endure to the very end, a process of cooperation with the Holy Spirit so that God the Father may find us constantly malleable and thus be able to shape us into the image of His Son, our Lord Jesus Christ.

What Vatican II said of seminary training should apply to all religious: "The norms of Christian education are to be religiously maintained, and should be properly complemented by the latest findings in sound psychology and pedagogy. By wisely planned training there should also be developed a due degree of human maturity, attested to chiefly by a certain emotional stability, by an ability to make considered decisions, and by a right manner of passing judgment on events and people. They should be practiced in an intelligent organization of their proper talents; they should be trained in what strengthens character; and, in general, they should learn to prize those qualities which are highly regarded among men and speak well of a minister of Christ. Such are sincerity of heart, a constant concern for justice, fidelity to one's word, courtesy of manner, restraint, and kindliness in speech" (*Optatam Totius*, 11). It may appear as though, in the above quotation, nearly all the emphasis is given to human formation but it is, of course, only one section. Nevertheless it is a very important part of Christian and religious formation and I would do well now to consider each point in turn to see how I am measuring up to it in my own life, as Christ desires.

A very sad story is told about the aftermath of World War II in Europe. By various means a poor peasant in Italy had managed to collect what was then considered a large amount of money, the sum of four thousand *lire*. When things were getting normal again he went along to a bank in order to deposit all his savings, looking upon it as a golden nest-egg for the future. Imagine his dismay and indignation when the bank cashier took the money, examined it carefully, and then deliberately got a scissors and destroyed the notes, saying angrily: "These notes are false and I should report you at once!" Seeing the absolute astonishment on the poor peasant's face, he said: "I can see that you did not know, and so I shall not report the matter. You may go now." Dumbfounded, the man went back home, threw himself into a well and drowned. Obviously he was not culpable about collecting all those spurious bank-notes, he had probably sold much of his farm produce for them and been cruelly cheated.

What a terrible thing it would be if a religious were to go through life hoarding false credit notes because of a lack of pure intention in the many exteriorly good actions performed in his apostolate! Such a person could hardly escape culpability, for he is constantly given every possible help to avoid such a disaster. How pathetic that any religious could fall into such a miserable trap of the devil! If whatever my hand does is not really for the greater glory of God, then I should at once boldly cut off my own miserable vanity. If where I am going is not because of love for God but simply for my own pleasure, I should rather cripple or even cut off my lack of good intention. Let me now examine my intentions in the various duties I perform, praying to my all-seeing God about every single thing....

The religious vocation in its actual daily fulfillment is a constant challenge to become Christlike, not just vaguely, not just by the end of life, but Christlike this very day. In other words this call to perfection that is the Christian and religious vocation is a very practical matter of a day to day courageous effort to live as perfectly as possible, to live it as Jesus would.

Every walk of life needs its own corresponding amount of courage, when it comes to following in the footsteps of a man scourged and cruelly tormented as He carries His heavy cross. Our own much smaller burdens do require courage too. However, the very sight of Jesus, right there before us, should help us endure patiently the trials He allows to come our way. How sanctifying our crosses can be! Let me pray now to my suffering Savior for all the help I need. Jesus,...

Kindly Tolerance

> *John said to him, "Teacher, we saw a man casting out demons in your name, and we forbade him, because he was not following us." But Jesus said, "Do not forbid him; for no one who does a mighty work in my name will be able soon after to speak evil of me. For he that is not against us is for us" (Mark 9:38-40).*

This is the first time we see young John, the future evangelist, coming out as the "son of thunder," as he and his brother James were jokingly called by the rest. His impetuosity and youthful zeal needed to be channelled in the right direction towards apostolic maturity, and in this he serves as an example to us in our own dealings with the youth of today. But the lesson Jesus teaches him, that of tolerance, is one that is badly needed on both sides of the border-line of youth. Too often people point out the faults of others in order to distract attention from their own. How much scope there is for Christlike kindness and tolerance when we see the weaknesses of others. Even to Magdalene Jesus said: "Nor do I condemn you."

Christ, my Master, would have me learn from all angles the lessons He Himself inculcates in the Gospel. In his *Imitation of Christ*, Thomas à Kempis says: "Endeavor to be always patient of the faults and imperfections of others; for you have many faults and imperfections of your own that require forbearance. If you are not able to make yourself what you wish, how can you expect to mold another in conformity to your will?" How tolerant am I really, in general and in particular? Is there any group or individual towards whom I fail to practice this Christlike virtue? What can I do about remedying matters, apart from praying now about it?

In order to practice the tolerance urged by Jesus on His apostles, one needs also to be patient. St. Francis de Sales teaches that the quiet, constant effort to control look and tone, word and manner, in our everyday life, will in time effectually sweep away every real hindrance to Christian perfection. In his epistle to the Romans (2:1-4), St. Paul warns that unless we learn the lesson of tolerance, patient kindness towards others, we can expect a hard judgment from God, having then no right to "presume upon the riches of his kindness and forbearance and patience. Do you not know that God's kindness is meant to lead you to repentance?" The great St. Teresa of Avila said: "Let us remember well that we can acquire through the sufferings that God sends us and those that come from our neighbor, greater merit in one day than we can gain in ten years through mortifications and other exercises of our own choice." How much self-control do I exercise and actually show in my dealings with others? Am I noted in my community and sphere of work for my spirit of forbearance and patience? Prayer and resolution.

Antipathies and prejudices often lie at the root of intolerance, as was the case in young John when he objected to someone else doing what he himself considered the monopoly of his own circle. The wise and gentle Francis de Sales says: "It is perfectly natural that we should love some people and not others by a kind of instinct.... Now, we must not dwell too much upon these instinctive antipathies or attractions, provided all are kept in reasonable subjection.... What remedy is there for these antipathies, since no one, however perfect, can be exempt from them? The only remedy, as indeed for all other kinds of temptation, is simply to turn away from it, and think no more about it. When, however, you find that it is going too far, beyond the bounds of reason, you must fight against it and overcome it, for reason will never permit us to foster antipathies and evil inclinations, for fear of offending God."

Perhaps one of the best and most disciplinary means of overcoming antipathies and lack of patience and tolerance with others is by creating definite acts of kindness towards them on every possible occasion, until they no longer upset us. It is not enough to be able to say at the examen, "I have committed no faults against charity today." Far more important is it to be able to say: "Today, for the love of God in my neighbor, I did such and such a positive act of kindness towards him." Intolerance, impatience, antipathy are worn away by constant positive acts of love. Let me think, pray, resolve about this.

How Often?

Then Peter came up to him and said to him, "Lord, how often shall my brother sin against me, and I forgive him? As many as seven times?" Jesus said to him, "I do not say to you seven times, but seventy times seven" (Matthew 18:21-22).

Peter seems to have considered himself quite magnanimous in his "high" standard of forgiveness, but Jesus soon disillusions him, letting him see clearly that Christian charity knows no limits, based as it is on the infinite mercy of God our Father. Since each of us stands so greatly in need of God's mercy, surely each should be ready in turn to show that same spirit of forgiveness towards others, without any calculation of times. "As a father pities his children, so the Lord pities those who fear him. For he knows our frame; he remembers that we are dust" (Ps. 103:13-14). Jesus had already given mercy as one of the great beatitudes in His Sermon on the Mount and yet how slow the apostles and other Christians down to our own day have been to learn it.

How often and easily we quote Shakespeare's famous lines: "The quality of mercy is not strain'd, it droppeth as the gentle rain from heaven upon the place beneath. It is twice bless'd: it blesseth him that gives and him that takes.... It is an attribute to God Himself" (*Merchant of Venice*).

Surely then, since I hope with the psalmist that "goodness and mercy shall follow me all the days of my life" (Ps. 23:6), then I too must exercise mercy towards others, thus imitating Christ my own merciful Master. The Psalms are full of the praises of God's mercy and compassion and this theme should be forever in my own mind and heart, looking on the one hand with confidence towards God, glancing ever with compassion towards my neighbor on the other.

The rabbinic principle behind St. Peter's self-esteemed "magnanimity" was that one should forgive three times only, and this they tried to base on Scripture itself, wrongly interpreted. Jesus takes up Peter's question by telling the parable of the man who owed his master ten thousand talents, could not pay up and was condemned to punishment; he begs mercy, is immediately forgiven but then promptly goes out and gives harsh treatment to another man who owes him the tiny sum of one hundred denarii; the master finds this out and duly punishes severely the unforgiving heavy debtor (cf. Mt. 18:23-35). In the parable Jesus purposely mentions two vastly different sums of money in order to underline the tremendous mercy of God on the one hand and the often miserably petty lack of it among human beings in forgiveness.

Let me directly apply this to myself: on the one side God's extremely compassionate forgiveness of me on innumerable occasions during my life; on the other my own perhaps frequent meanness and pettiness of spirit in regard to the faults and failings of others. How dreadful if Jesus should say to me: "You wicked servant! I forgave you all that debt because you besought me; and should not you have had mercy on your fellow servant, as I had mercy on you?" Let me examine my past conduct fearfully, prayerfully.

The whole of St. Matthew's eighteenth chapter deals with charity in one form or another and we should recall that all this was special instruction being given by Jesus to His apostles—this was their leadership formation course and He pulled no punches in trying to get so many important points across. This last one, then, is almost a final supplement, but one of tremendous value in its details for application in Christian and religious daily life. Since each of us has such great need of God's mercy because of our own many faults, let us in turn practice mercy towards our brethren in Christ first of all and then towards all others, whoever and wherever they may be. It is so easy instead, for some characters at any rate, to pick out the faults of others, hold them up to scorn, and then perhaps say harsh or bitter things, perhaps with various forms of petty vindictiveness attached. It seems unthinkable that this could occur among religious. Have I ever indulged in such unchristian conduct?

Yet perhaps I do put on a show of forgiveness but never actually forget. Of what use is it merely to bury the hatchet if I make sure to mark the spot well? Is this Christian forgiveness at all? Perhaps past conduct now examined will reveal much reparation still to be made to my merciful Savior and my prayer should be then: "Have patience with me and I will pay you everything." Let me not, however, strain the patience of God and presume on His mercy without being merciful myself.

Come to Me!

Come to me, all who labor and are heavy laden, and I will give you rest. Take my yoke upon you, and learn from me; for I am gentle and lowly in heart, and you will find rest for your souls. For my yoke is easy, and my burden is light (Matthew 11:28-30).

The greatest and happiest fulfillment of these words of Jesus we religious should find in prayer and above all in Eucharistic union with Him as the source of our strength and rest. At the Holy Mass each day we offer ourselves with Jesus and through Him to the Father, trying to conform ourselves to the holy dispositions of His own soul: adoration, gratitude, reparation, resignation to the divine will. It is up to me, however, for the rest of the day to ensure that there is no inconsistency between my behavior and thoughts then and my sentiments at Holy Mass.

To live the Mass means to repeat or continue the symbolism of it all in actual practice in the big or small sacrifices I am called upon to make during the day, sacrifices that touch upon or even deeply affect my desires, my time, my God-given talents, my strength and health, my leisure, or even my own ideas about things. Giving of these things will not always prove easy, but in virtue of the Sacrifice of the Mass, I must try to offer them up gladly, freely, completely, never denying in word, thought or action the truth of my daily Mass. After all, how can I offer myself symbolically to the Father with the host and wine and then grudgingly withdraw the offering later in the day!

Naturally, the various acts of sacrifice during the day are going to cost me something, but the more costly the price the closer I come to imitating the total sacrifice of Christ. I am asked to plunge the knife of death into any number of things concerning myself day after day: dying to self over and over again in this or that, perhaps death to my own cherished ideas, hopes, plans because of some greater good; death to my own comforts and convenience—death to self inch by inch. A heavy burden? A hard yoke to bear day after day, year after year? But Jesus reassures me it is all going to prove worthwhile if I persevere at it, generously, cheerfully: "Come to me, all who labor and are heavy laden, and I will give you rest."

At the Offertory in the Holy Mass we ask God the Father to accept our sacrifice which we make in a spirit of humility and with a contrite heart. In that plea we have the two essential dispositions for offering ourselves in sacrifice to God with the divine Victim Himself, Jesus: humility, because we are creatures, poor, lowly, helpless; contrition, because we are sinners. The deeper I allow these two qualities to enter into my heart, the more God will be able to effect in my soul through the Holy Mass. The more I grow in humility, the greater will become my dependence and reliance on the Mass for all my strength and courage in carrying out my life of sacrifice each day cheerfully and gladly, thus finding Christ's yoke easy and my cross light. In uniting myself with Jesus as the Victim of the Mass I unite myself with Him also in His humiliations that led to Calvary. It may even happen at times that awful humiliations come my way, and it is then particularly that I must recall all this, grateful for the chance of becoming more like Him, especially after having been made one with Him in Holy Communion.

It was not merely the humiliating circumstances of His passion and death that constituted the real humility of Jesus, but rather the actual dispositions of His own will in accepting all these things readily, in spite of human repugnance to them. My humility must be something internal, a similar tendency of soul that makes me ready to accept whatever sufferings may occur during the day. If I tell Jesus this at Holy Mass when I unite myself with Him, then I am bringing real humility to my sacrifice, becoming more and more like Him, putting on His mind and characteristics. In religious and community life, in my apostolate, in all my dealings with others, I do need humility badly, the humility of Jesus Himself. Let me beg it of Him especially at Holy Communion when we are made one in soul and mind and heart. Jesus,...

With an ever-deepening sense of humility in my life, I shall indeed find the yoke of the religious life easy, and its many burdens light, for I shall find all the rest and consolation I need in the gentle and lowly heart of my Master. To learn this humility I can find tremendous help in the Holy Mass, because throughout the Holy Sacrifice we are reminded of this virtue in many ways, starting with the initial examen of conscience and confession of sins. The Mass can remind me too that Jesus, as St. Paul says, "emptied himself, taking the form of a servant," humbling Himself, becoming obedient not only to His Father but even to the vilest of men and right unto the humiliating and painful death on the cross.

In the Holy Mass He humbles Himself anew, to the lowest possible point of humility, taking the form not merely of a servant but of an inanimate thing such as bread and wine, realizing well that careless men can treat Him just as such, increasing His suffering, intensifying His sacrifice. I must take care then at Holy Mass not to be standing with Christ's tormentors on Calvary! Perhaps by my carelessness and negligence in the past I have all too often unwittingly caused Jesus further sufferings in this way. He inspires me now to make reparation, not only in prayer, but in strong resolution to realize more deeply what the Holy Sacrifice of the Mass means, my own intimate part in it, for it is there especially Jesus says to me: "Come to me.... I will give you rest.... Take my yoke upon you.... Learn from me." Jesus,...

With All

And behold, a lawyer stood up to put him to the test, saying, "Teacher, what shall I do to inherit eternal life?" He said to him, "What is written in the law? How do you read?" And he answered, "You shall love the Lord your God with all your heart, and with all your soul, and with all your strength, and with all your mind: and your neighbor as yourself." And he said to him, "You have answered right; do this, and you will live" (Luke 10:25-28).

The question as put to Jesus seems simple and straightforward and the lawyer's own answer when Jesus tactfully made him give it, was excellent. Only in a later verse are we led to suspect that this man nevertheless lacked the true virtue of simplicity, merely trying to push Jesus on to verbal indiscretion. However, let us take his first question and his own answer as thought for meditation, for they are both precise and understandable. The lawyer quoted directly from Deuteronomy words that each Jew was supposed to recall twice a day—smartly adding in as fuel for his next question, a part of Leviticus referring to love of neighbor. He certainly knew the answers—but did he himself practice them? It is one thing to know the laws and rules by heart, quite another to practice them, yet still another to do so with one's whole heart. This too I must remember. To be practical straight away, let me consider that valid answer of his in its three first sections, leaving the last to the following meditation on the parable Jesus based upon it.

First: "You shall love the Lord God with all your heart and with all your soul." Considered in itself, the human heart is just a thing of flesh, a double muscular pump lying within the thorax, resting upon the diaphragm, between and partly covered by the lungs. Each side of it has two chambers, the atrium for receiving blood, the ventricle for expelling it. Nowadays the most intricate and daring operations have been performed on the human heart because of its immensely important function in the life of man.

Has any really adequate answer been given yet for making the name of this important organ signify the whole ensemble of man's affection and aspirations? Without the vital activity of the heart man cannot live and so when the Bible says I must love God with all my heart and soul it means with everything that keeps me alive and going, that the love of God within me should be the very life-blood that is pumped in and out of that heart of mine. This involves the whole dedication of my soul also, for once the heart ceases to function altogether the soul divides itself from the body. If my physical heart functions poorly, my life is endangered. If my spiritual heart is weak, so too is my soul in peril. Let me examine this last statement carefully to see what exactly my spiritual health is like just now.

With all your strength.

The human body is truly one of God's great masterpieces which, in good health, is a mysterious living organism made up of many parts, some quite remote from one another, and yet whose functions and activities cause it to survive in a wonderful coordination. Just think for a moment of the marvel of the circulatory system, which carries materials from regions where they are in large supply to other regions where they are to be either immediately utilized, or stored, or else eliminated. Eminently coordinated in itself, the healthy body adjusts its activities in such a way as to take into account the nature of and changes in whatever environment it finds itself. God expects me to do my best to preserve my body in the best health possible for His greater glory and for the sake of my apostolic work.

Ecclesiasticus says too: "Better off is a poor man who is well and strong in constitution than a rich man who is severely afflicted in body. Health and soundness are better than all gold, and a robust body than countless riches. There is no wealth better than health of body, and there is no gladness above joy of heart" (Sir. 30:14-16). Vatican II says religious "should take advantage of those natural helps which favor mental and bodily health" (*Perfectae*

Caritatis, 12). St. John Bosco used to quote Pythagoras' dictum giving as remedies for every sort of physical inconvenience three things: sensible food, fresh air and activity *(M.B.*, VI). St. Ignatius took pleasure in seeing the signs of health and youthful vigor among his followers and one day, seeing a novice heartily enjoying his meal, he encouraged him, saying: "Continue to nourish yourself well, and grow strong in order to serve God and the Society."

And there we have it, going right back to the early Bible and confirmed by our Lord Himself: "You shall love the Lord your God...with all your strength." Am I thus careful, in a sensible way, in preserving my health for such high motives? Let me pray about that now.

With all your mind.

In our complete dedication to the love of God, it is wise to consider also the question of mental health. This, of course, cannot be defined with precision, since it is closely related to the varying customs and requirements of society, with a multiplicity of factors. In its broader sense, however, perhaps we can say that true mental health suggests a degree of happiness and satisfaction, under conditions that warrant such a state of mind, and a capacity for making satisfactory personal, social and supernatural relationships. "A sound mind in a healthy body" has always been a desirable criterion in life and for me as a religious dedicated to love of God and neighbor it is a very sensible standard to aim at and maintain.

I must constantly strive to develop the faculties of my mind to their utmost capacity, using my intellectual talents as fully as possible and yet with humility and gratitude, striving always after an ever greater knowledge, understanding and appreciation of God Himself that will bring ever greater happiness and satisfaction in my relationship with Him. I must strive also to echo all this in my dealings with my fellowmen and above all with those with whom I live or come into contact more frequently. I must learn to find peace of mind with myself also through my love of God and neighbor. In these ways, by these endeavors, I gradually eliminate intellectual pride and come more and more into line with the wish of Christ that I should love God also with my whole mind. Let me humbly pray now on these lines.

Good Friends

Now as they went on their way, he entered a village; and a woman named Martha received him into her house. And she had a sister called Mary, who sat at the Lord's feet and listened to his teaching. But Martha was distracted with much serving; and she went to him and said, "Lord, do you not care that my sister has left me to serve alone? Tell her then to help me." But the Lord answered her, "Martha, Martha, you are anxious and troubled about many things; one thing is needful. Mary has chosen the good portion, which shall not be taken away from her" (Luke 10:38-42).

It is from such a pleasant domestic scene as this that one can infer so much more about the life and social activities of Jesus than the evangelists mention. It is a good thing for us poor humans to see Jesus relaxed, enjoying the pleasant company of friends, taking pleasure in their kind attention and generous hospitality. St. Luke makes no mention of the third member of this family, Lazarus, but St. John does, telling us also the name of the village, Bethany, just outside Jerusalem, on the eastern foot of the Mount of Olives along the Jericho road. In the light of Jesus' example it is good for me to consider the subject of friendship, about which the Bible and wise men have said many fine things, e.g., "A faithful friend is a sturdy shelter: he that has found one has found a treasure. There is nothing so precious as a faithful friend, and no scales can measure his excellence. A faithful friend is an elixer of life and those who fear the Lord will find him. Whoever fears the Lord directs his friendship aright" (Sir. 6:14-17). "Friendship is nothing else than accord in all things, human and divine, conjoined with mutual goodwill and affection" (Cicero, *De Amicitia);* "The perfect friendship is that between good men, alike in their virtue" (Aristotle).

St. Jane Frances de Chantal, great friend of St. Francis de Sales, that close imitator of Jesus, gives a fine picture of what true friendship should be like when she says of him: "He received everyone with a serene and gracious countenance, never sending away anyone, whoever it might be. He listened quietly to everyone for as long a time as each one desired. You would have thought he had nothing else to do, so patient and attentive was he. Everyone left him so cheerful and satisfied that people were very glad to have something to say to him, in order to enjoy the extreme kindness and serenity which he diffused in the hearts of all who spoke to him. By this means he drew people on to perfect confidence. The saint's manner and way of speaking were most dignified and serious, but at the same time most humble, kind and simple; he was always entirely free from affectation, mannerisms or stiffness. He was never heard to utter an ill-timed word or to make an unkind remark. He spoke quietly, gently and prudently, and though he never used fine words, all that he said had the greatest effect. He spoke neither too much nor too little, but always said just what was necessary and he expressed himself so well that nothing further remained to be added to his words. He sometimes related amusing little anecdotes, but always so modestly that those who heard them were edified as well as entertained by them" (St. Jane Frances de Chantal). Is my conduct similar with my friends? Who exactly are my best friends? Are they really good for me, helping me, I helping them? How often do I pray for them? What about now!

Mary of Bethany shows great devotion to Jesus as a friend, sitting at His feet, listening to Him, perhaps consulting Him. "In our friend Jesus," wrote Contardo Ferrini, "we shall find ourselves steeped in friendship, since we hope through His merits and by His love to be transformed into Him and to be joined to Him with the strongest love."

It would be a sad thing indeed if at this stage of my life I could not say that I honestly consider Jesus as a friend, my best friend. But how deep is our friendship? What a wonderful thing it would be if the intimacy between us and Christ were so great that we would never think of doing a single thing without first consulting

Him in quiet prayer. He, after all, is the constant partner in our life, far closer than any other human being could ever be. Moreover, He is Wisdom itself and at the same time so understanding and sympathetic, so patient that we need never fear any irritation on His part no matter how often we consult Him. Many of the saints, canonized and uncanonized, achieved this complete intimacy and trust. There is no reason whatsoever why I should not do so also. What is keeping me from it? Am I improving in any way at this? Is my friendship with Jesus a really personal thing, the most meaningful thing in my life? If it were, how much better a friend I would be to others also! Jesus, I have a lot to think about here. You know my needs even better than I do, so please help me to....

Just as Martha allowed herself to get so taken up by the importance of her own activities as to unbalance her standard of values somewhat, so can the same thing happen to me. Mind you, she did not forget Jesus during them but she still had to learn to sublimate them to prayer-level. Nor should she have criticized her sister, misjudging her attitude, underestimating her. Probably smiling affectionately, Jesus corrects Martha gently, telling her to keep cool and calm, and not to forget the main thing necessary, union with Him, and then all things will turn out well.

The whole aim of Christian life should be constant union with Christ, so that even when I am exteriorly extremely busy and my mind has to concentrate on important matters, my heart should be ever at the feet of Jesus, in a position of submission, ready to accept with docility every inspiration His Holy Spirit will give me. In this way I shall never have to neglect my work just for the sake of formal prayer, but all my duties, no matter how intense, will become true prayer because of my docility. This way of combining the active and contemplative lives is not an unattainable ideal—it can be made extremely practical. Let me examine now as to how far it has taken hold of my apostolic life and in what manner I can improve it. Jesus,...

Persistent Prayer

And he said to them, "Which of you who has a friend will go to him at midnight and say to him, 'Friend, lend me three loaves; for a friend of mine has arrived on a journey, and I have nothing to set before him'; and he will answer from within, 'Do not bother me; the door is now shut, and my children are with me in bed; I cannot get up and give you anything'? I tell you, though he will not get up and give him anything because he is his friend, yet because of his importunity he will rise and give him whatever he needs. And I tell you, ask and it will be given to you; seek, and you will find; knock, and it will be opened to you. For every one who asks receives, and he who seeks finds, and to him who knocks it will be opened. What father among you, if his son asks for a fish, will instead of a fish give him a serpent; or if he asks for an egg, will give him a scorpion? If you then, who are evil, know how to give good gifts to your children, how much more will the heavenly Father give the Holy Spirit to those who ask him!" (Luke 11:5-13)

After giving the apostles an easy model of prayer in the *Our Father,* Jesus now proceeds to tell them in parables that our prayers should be persistent and trustful. As in many hot countries, so in Palestine people often traveled by night in order to avoid the heat of the day. Here we find such a man, unable to complete his journey, tired out and hungry, asking hospitality from a friend, who finds himself unable to feed him properly. The host feels he can safely inconvenience someone else on the grounds of friendship, even at midnight. The friend's reply seems curt enough but it is understandable at that unearthly hour, hence the other takes no offense, sure of winning him around at length. And so it happens—a very human incident that must have occurred frequently.

The lesson for me is that God, my Father, wants no superficial, unmeaning prayers from me. He wants my sincerity, my maturity, my confidence, even my persistence when He seems not to bother. If He seems not to hear, it is because whatever is worth having is worth paying for, even at the price of continued knocking—but let that knocking be respectful even if persistent, never impatient, never resentful: "Be still before the Lord, and wait patiently for him" (Ps. 37:7). Hence St. Gregory says: "True prayer is not in the voice but in the heart. It is not our words, it is our desires that make, in the mysterious ears of God, the strength of our cries. If with our mouth we ask for eternal life without desiring it from the bottom of our hearts, our silence cries out" *(Moralia).*

If God seems deaf to our prayers, there must be a wise reason for it. At times it may be His purpose merely to strengthen our spirit of perseverance in praying, to increase our faith and hope. It may even be that He sees quite clearly that what we ask for is not going to be good for us, and so in His love He does not grant it. Whatever the situation, let me never doubt God's wisdom or love. Jesus, help me to have at all times a right attitude toward prayer.

Any lack of concentrating on the holy will of God, any weakness of faith could be the cause of so many of my own prayers going apparently unanswered. It is up to me, then, to make sure that each time I pray for an intention, I seriously consider first whether it can possibly fit in with God's will, then whether I am prepared to let Him take His own time about answering it—thus making the necessary act of faith and confidence in His all-holy wisdom and fatherliness. "I waited patiently for the Lord; he inclined to me and heard my cry" (Ps. 40:1). "Trust in him at all times, O people; pour out your heart before him; God is a refuge for us" (Ps. 62:8).

The prophet Jeremiah says: "Blessed is the man who trusts in the Lord, whose trust is the Lord. He is like a tree planted by water, that sends out its roots by the stream, and does not fear when heat comes, for its leaves remain green, and is not anxious in the year of drought, for it does not cease to bear fruit" (17:7-8).

That should be the picture of my spirit of prayer, never fearing that God will let me down, only anxious to accomplish His holy will in all things, ready to wait patiently for His own good time. "To trust God though ways be dark, though the pain stuns and the burden crushes; to know in one's soul that His love is there behind the cross He sends; to trust Him absolutely, this is prayer at a white heat; from this does God receive honor, and His dying on the cross becomes fruitful and worthwhile. Is not all growth and development of the soul really growth in prayer? Not to grow in prayer is as if a grown man were stunted in the intellect and underdeveloped in his highest faculties. It is to be deaf and blind and dumb in the presence of the wonders of God—His glory, His mercy, His love. Prayer means letting the light into the soul, without which it lies half-living and stunted, like a plant in a sunless room. The soul needs the light and the warmth of its God; it needs the reassurance of His loving presence for its full growth as much as a child needs the comfort of a mother's arms" (Anon.).

Perhaps at times when, in frustration at "unanswered" prayer, I think God is deaf or dumb or blind, it is myself who suffer from these very things: deaf to the voice of God speaking in so many ways; dumb when I should speak to Him about the things that really matter in my life; blind in not noticing His loving presence and not seeing His finger pointing in the direction I should go if I really do want to fulfill His holy will. It is I who so often fail in generosity, never God. Let me get my personal and community prayer life resolutely in order and I will find my life so very much happier. Let me pray now to Jesus that this may soon come about.

Knowing Christ

Jesus said to him: "Have I been with you so long, and yet you do not know me, Philip?" (John 14:9)

How often the great ideal is placed before us of striving to become more and more Christlike. It is a good thing from time to time, however, to stop and ask ourselves just exactly how much we know about the Christ whom we are supposedly trying to imitate. So much, of course, depends on our Christian education, our knowledge of the Scriptures, our spirit of prayer and understanding. Certainly we should never be satisfied with our limitations in any of these respects but endeavor constantly to widen our knowledge and love of the Master whom we wish to follow closely. St. Paul, in his own personal efforts, was able to say eventually: "It is no longer I who live, but Christ who lives in me."

What a happy thought that is, that the more closely I imitate Christ, the more I am becoming myself as God wants me to be! Naturally, much of my endeavor will look automatically to the human example of Jesus as portrayed in the Gospels but I must never forget the spiritual. Romano Guardini has written a book called *The Humanity of Christ* which is well worth reading in full because of its many revealing insights. In this meditation we have time to consider just some aspects that can serve to make our imitation of the Master really practical. Guardini underlines the fact of the utter sincerity of Jesus at all times, His complete lack of any show of cleverness or tactics. There was in Him no deception or exaggeration, none of the maneuvers which politicians so often use in order to achieve their ends. For Jesus one thing only was necessary, the glory of His Father involved in the redemption of mankind.

In all these thoughts I have plenty of matter for meditation, personal examination and application. Does my own conduct in any way contrast with that of Jesus? Am I always oriented toward the one thing He considered necessary? Jesus....

Emotions play a great part in the life of mankind, and in this too we look to Jesus for example. Guardini points out various emotional reactions we can recognize in the actions and words of Jesus, showing that He was by no means cold and aloof but full of human warmth and fellow-feeling (cf. Mk. 9:36), able to look on someone and love him (cf. Mk. 10:21), irritated by hypocrisy (cf. Mk. 3:5), rejoicing with His apostles on their return from the apostolate (cf. Lk. 10:21). Nevertheless His essential calm and peacefulness of spirit is pointed out: "Peace I leave with you; my peace I give to you; not as the world gives do I give to you. Let not your hearts be troubled, neither let them be afraid" (Jn. 14:27). Tranquility of spirit is indeed a great grace, a grace that can come suddenly as an extraordinary kind of gift of God or else be gained by those constant efforts after self-control that are so often necessary. How do I stand in this regard? Am I too excitable, too easily upset, too quick to lose my emotional balance? Let me pray about this now, asking my Master to help me to achieve the calmness of spirit that comes from His peace deep within me. Jesus,...

Vatican Council II rightly emphasized the respect due to human dignity and individual personality, saying among other things: "By no human law can the personal dignity and liberty of man be so aptly safeguarded as by the Gospel of Christ which has been entrusted to the Church. For this Gospel announces and proclaims the freedom of the sons of God and repudiates all the bondage which ultimately results from sin. The Gospel has a sacred reverence for the dignity of conscience and its freedom of choice, constantly advises that human talents be employed in God's service and men's, and, finally, commends all to the charity of the brethren. All this corresponds with the basic law of the Christian dispensation" (*Gaudium et Spes*, 41).

None of this is meant in any way to clash with sound religious ideas about obedience, though some would foolishly have it so. Although I can never hope to become as perfect as Jesus, to become as free as Jesus in His divine liberty, nevertheless I can make His example in obedience my objective. For me too obedience should not mean the relationship between stronger and weaker, power and submission, but simply a question of the holy will of God which—even in its more difficult forms at times—I am not only anxious but even happy to fulfill. Obeying with the spirit of Jesus I shall never want to complain about orders given. If they are the will of God, that for me is sufficient—as it was for Jesus. When I can obey always as Jesus did, then indeed I shall have found my own true self, my own true dignity and personality. Let me speak to Him now about this. Jesus,...

Without a Hearing

The officers then went back to the chief priests and Pharisees, who said to them, "Why did you not bring him?" The officers answered, "No man ever spoke like this man!" The Pharisees answered them, "Are you led astray, you also? Have any of the authorities or of the Pharisees believed in him? But this crowd, who do not know the law, are accursed." Nicodemus, who had gone to him before, and who was one of them, said to them, "Does our law judge a man without first giving him a hearing and learning what he does?" They replied, "Are you from Galilee too? Search and you will see that no prophet is to rise from Galilee." They went each to his own house (John 7:45-53).

Then, as now, Jesus was the subject of contention and the cause of division. In fact there were three parties: those who believed in Him, those who violently opposed Him, those who were merely indifferent. Amid all this contention, "No man ever spoke like this man!" coming from the lips of the very officers sent to compromise and apprehend Jesus, was a splendid eulogy indeed. In the endeavor to catch Him, to find cause for His arrest, they must have followed Him about frequently, listening attentively for treasonable words, watching Him closely all the time. But in the end they realize the futility of their charge and return to their scheming employers disillusioned, full of praise for Jesus. The courage to say what they did might have meant conversion for the officers; to the chief priests and Pharisees who had employed them it meant an increase in obduracy, an increase in sin, for they were not only failing in justice but further indulged their anger and uncharitableness. With sarcasm the Pharisees jibed at the officers for their seeming weakness and openly expressed their contempt for the simple people whom they called "accursed," they themselves being the only righteous ones! The implication was obviously again the neon-lighted advertisement in the prevalent darkness of ignorance that they alone possessed the monopoly of truth and infallibility! For the others even to express their honest opinions was repulsive. What frightful injustice and uncharitableness this shows in men who, because of their undoubted learning, should have been the very ones to recognize the Christ, to persuade others to follow them humbly to the very feet of Jesus. On the contrary we see what we read. As in all these instances, however, there is always the danger of ourselves falling into a like fault instead of learning from their negative example to avoid the same sins of injustice, pride and uncharitableness. Think of the contrary example of Jesus Himself, of whom Isaiah said: "He shall not judge by what his eyes see, or decide by what his ears hear; but with righteousness he shall judge the poor, and decide with equity for the meek of the earth" (Is. 11:3-4).

Am I inclined to be self-righteous and obstinate about things? If I feel even in the least way inclined towards this grave fault, I shall have to work really extra hard on the virtue of humility, basing my efforts on the words of Jesus: "Learn of me, for I am meek and humble of heart." Let me scrutinize my general conduct in order to track down any self-righteousness or obstinacy. When was the last occasion I noticed it? How did I behave then and afterwards? Did I ever apologize? What shall I do in the future? A good start will be to pray now about it. O Jesus....

Vatican Council II has said: "Mindful of the Lord's saying: 'By this will all men know that you are my disciples, if you have love for one another,' Christians cannot yearn for anything more ardently than to serve the men of the modern world even more generously and effectively. Therefore, holding faithfully to the Gospel, benefiting from its resources, and united with every man who loves and practices justice, Christians have shouldered a gigantic task demanding fulfillment in this world. Concerning this task they must give a reckoning to Him who will judge every man on the last day" (*Gaudium et Spes*, 93).

There is so much call for true justice in the world of today that we should do all we can to promote it in whatever way possible, starting deep within ourselves at our own judgments of others. The Book of Wisdom says of God: "You are righteous and rule all things righteously, deeming it alien to your power to condemn him who does not deserve to be punished.... You who are sovereign in strength judge with mildness, and with great forbearance govern us.... Through such works you have taught your people that the righteous man must be kind" (12:15-16, 18). How applicable all this is to the Son of God, my Master and Model.

Let me examine now my own sense of justice in general, then more closely as to how I myself actually exercise it in practice and in my judgments on others.

In our meditation Gospel extract we see the secret disciple of Jesus, Nicodemus, having the courage to speak up on His behalf even if somewhat indirectly, quoting every man's right to a hearing in order to obtain justice. This merely makes the others more angry, more uncharitable. How often those two vices are connected, in fact always, because any form of unkindness has its source in some sort of even hidden anger against another. The Bible has so many fierce things to say about unjust anger, its hatefulness, grievousness and effects. "Anger and wrath, these also are abominations, and the sinful man will possess them" (Sir. 27:30); "Let all bitterness and wrath and anger and clamor and slander be put away from you, with all malice, and be kind to one another, tenderhearted, forgiving one another, as God in Christ forgave you" (Eph. 4:31).

Losing one's temper is never worthwhile. I upset not only myself and others, but above all I offend Jesus. I also offend my neighbor, no matter how many his faults. Even if I feel that my indignation is righteous because of some very obvious fault committed by someone, it is wiser to try to keep very calm and wait a while before saying anything about it, and then only after praying about it. There are so many things in human life liable to upset any one of us, so that we all need a spirit of Christlike compassion one toward the other. What particular people do I find awkward or upsetting at times? Let me pray now for each of them in turn in a very positive way, asking our kind Jesus to bless them greatly and to help me to see only the good qualities they undoubtedly possess. Jesus, You have given us the most wonderful example of loving forgiveness; I don't always find it easy, but....

Not My Glory

I do not seek my own glory; there is One who seeks it and he will be the judge. Truly, truly, I say to you, if any one keeps my word, he will never see death (John 8:50-51).

These words are but one small extract from a long wrangle Jesus had with His adversaries. He had tried by every argument to convince them of their waywardness, but to no avail, for their prejudice and obstinacy was granite-hard. Here now He contrasts His own God-seeking with their self-seeking. They had just insulted Him personally, again accusing Him of having a demon, but even this He passes by, recognizing it as but part of the shadow of the cross looming ahead. He merely points out that it is the Father's glory that is His supreme concern; it is the Father who will vindicate and glorify His Son and all those who follow the Son's example and teachings will have eternal life.

Here let me pause to consider once more how much I am concerned with God's glory rather than my own. All through the years I have been urged to make A.M.D.G. one of my mottoes, to do all for the greater honor and glory of God, trying to forget self, seeking to do everything with absolute purity of intention. How far have I come in the actual practice of this grand principle? Surely experience has already often shown me the advantage of following it.

St. John Bosco said: "I always keep to this principle in all my enterprises. I seek first to ensure that it will redound to the greater glory of God and the advantage of souls and only then do I go ahead, quite sure that God will not fail to assist me" (*M.B.*, VI). Jesus, help me to squeeze out pride and self-seeking from all my undertakings, so that only Your name may be enhanced, not mine; grant me deep humility....

In the same argument with His opponents Jesus says, "If I glorify myself, my glory is nothing; it is my Father who glorifies me, of whom you say that he is your God" (8:54). Instead, then, of seeking my own glory in the things God allows me to do and which so often I may think are just the outcome of my own personally created cleverness, I must constantly do things gratefully for my Creator's glory, leaving to Him any rewards He may choose to allow to come my way. "Do all to the glory of God," exhorts St. Paul (1 Cor. 10:31).

Fr. D. Tomaselli, S.D.B., writes: "In the Gospel we read: 'The eye is the light of your whole body, so that if your eye is clear the whole of the body will be lit up.' The Sacred writers signify the word 'eye,' of which Jesus speaks, the intention with which an action is done. By 'body' they mean the action which is vivified by the intention in the same way as the body follows the eye. If we examine the Gospels we see what importance Jesus gives to good actions performed by men. What did He think of the prayers, fasts and almsgiving of the Pharisees? For all these good actions He reproved and condemned them, because their intention was not the right one. Our Divine Master took occasion to teach His disciples and all mankind what should be the purpose of their good works, in order that they might not lose their merit. 'Be sure you do not perform your acts of piety before men for them to watch; if you do that, you have no title to a reward from your Father who is in heaven'" *(Purity of Intention).*

In my early spiritual training so much stress was placed on this fundamental lesson. By now it should be of the very fiber of my being, but is it? Let me pray for light now, asking Jesus to help me put aright what is still amiss. Jesus,...

Our Lord says further: "I do know him and I keep his word." This can only be true of me if I can prove to both Christ and myself that in all things "I live because of the Father" (Jn. 6:57), desiring only to love and please Him. St. Alphonsus gives several signs by which I can recognize how pure my intention is in all things: "The first mark is if, when your undertaking has not been successful, you are not disturbed but remain as tranquil as if you had attained your object. This will certainly be the case when you have acted only for God; because when you see that He has not wished your efforts to be crowned with success, neither will you wish it; for you know that He demands an account, not of the success or failure of your undertaking, but of the purity of your intention. The second mark is to rejoice at the good done by others as if it had been done by yourself. He who seeks nothing but the divine glory cares not whether it is promoted by others or by himself. The third mark is not to desire one office more than another, one occupation more than another, but to be content with whatever is prescribed by obedience; because in everything you seek nothing but the pleasure of God. The fourth sign is not to desire approbation or thanks for your good works, but to remain in the same tranquillity of mind even when censured and maltreated, satisfied at having succeeded in pleasing God, which was your sole object."

A careful examination of each of those signs should give me a fair indication of how much I do really know the mind of Christ and how far I imitate Him in my own life. Let me now pray to my Master, asking His necessary help to improve greatly.

Light to the Blind

As he passed by, he saw a man blind from his birth. And his disciples asked him, "Rabbi, who sinned, this man or his parents, that he was born blind?" Jesus answered, "It was not that this man sinned, or his parents, but that the works of God might be made manifest in him. We must work the works of him who sent me, while it is day; night comes, when no one can work. As long as I am in the world, I am the light of the world." As he said this, he spat on the ground and made clay of the spittle and anointed the man's eyes with the clay, saying to him, "Go, wash in the pool of Siloam" (which means "sent"). So he went and washed and came back seeing (John 9:1-7).

After the previous long and fruitless argument Jesus was almost stoned by His foes but He "hid himself and went out of the temple" (8:59). St. Augustine remarks that He fled more from their stone-like hearts than from the stones they picked up to throw at Him. So much of what He had said concerned spiritual light and darkness and now He proceeds to perform a miracle of light, giving sight to a blind man. It is obvious from the simplicity and naturalness with which St. John describes the event and its dialogue not only that he himself witnessed it but that it made a deep impression on him. Jesus emphasizes again the idea of light, of Himself as the Light of the world, of treating His life as a period of light when He must work hard before the darkness of death comes upon Him, and just as light purifies the darkness so Jesus sends the man to the Pool of Siloe outside the city to test his faith and get across to his simple mind the idea also of spiritual purification.

The disciples too had a lot to learn from this incident for they were still steeped in the rather morbid, ancient belief that all physical deformities were obviously caused by sin, personal or hereditary. Jesus answers their curiosity on this point very briefly, as though telling them to have more sense. What He says in effect is simply that we are all in the hands of our Creator who can permit or send trials even to any of us for some good purpose. Here in the blind man before Him, Jesus was the Father's instrument of bringing light to him and many others, for the man was a symbol also of those spiritually blind. He did not cure the man on the actual spot, and the miracle took place only after his obedience and the faith underlying it took him to the waters of Siloe to bathe his eyes.

My first lesson here can perhaps be the one that so often I do not see the light in so many things because I am lacking in the fundamentals of firm faith and a readiness to obey God's will whatever it may be. So often I need just to take God's word blindly, on sheer faith, to keep stumbling on until I find the Pool of Siloe, ready to obey Him fully and then to set about doing so, even when I don't understand why it should be so. Only then can He lift the scales from my eyes to make me see and understand things His way. Where in my life are there signs of the need for all this?

> *So he went and washed and came back seeing. The neighbors and those who had seen him before as a beggar, said, "Is not this the man who used to sit and beg?" Some said, "It is he"; others said, "No, but he is like him." He said, "I am the man." They said to him, "Then how were your eyes opened?" He answered, "The man called Jesus made clay and anointed my eyes and said to me, 'Go to Siloam and wash'; so I went and washed and received my sight." They said to him, "Where is he?" He said, "I do not know." They brought to the Pharisees the man who had formerly been blind (John 9:7-13).*

The miracle performed in such a strange way by Jesus caused quite a lot of excitement, especially among the man's friends and acquaintances who could hardly believe their eyes on seeing him now restored to sight; they even doubted his identity at first. As a beggar outside the temple he was well known and we can imagine his own joyful and bright-eyed excitement as he described everything that had happened. Perhaps the majority of the

Jews in those days were very much under the negative influence of the scribes or the Pharisees or Sadducees, accepting their dicta without much reasoning or inquiry. Now the cured man's neighbors find it the obvious thing to go along and report the whole affair to the Pharisees and one can only hope there was no malice in their doing so.

At any rate I can draw for myself the useful reflection about consulting the right people in life. Too often those who have a gripe in life go almost automatically to those who will "sympathetically" agree with them, and as a result there are two people grumbling instead of one. Evil has an insidious way of spreading like this, like an oil slick that eventually extends to many shores, spoiling their beauty and ruining the pleasure of those who have a right to it. The ex-blind man narrated the facts correctly; how often the grumbler does not, and as they go the rounds they become more and more twisted, the harm increasing in inverse proportion. Sometimes one cannot help feeling upset about something that has occurred and at times it is a good psychological thing to get it off one's chest. However, let it be with someone who rather than too readily agree with me will listen calmly and impartially and then help me put things in right perspective, if necessary courageously pointing out where I may be wrong. This should always be the case with one's confessor or spiritual director, but one is fortunate indeed if one can find another also who can prove a true, God-approved friend and consultor in this way. With the correct people one need never fear that when one asks, "Where is He (Jesus)?" they will reply, "I do not know." The Bible says: "As much as you can, aim to know your neighbors, and consult with the wise. Let your conversation be with men of understanding" (Sir. 9:14-15). Something here for me still to learn? Jesus,...

Now it was a sabbath day when Jesus made the clay and opened his eyes. The Pharisees again asked him how he had received his sight. And he said to them, "He put clay on my eyes, and I washed, and I see." Some of the Pharisees said, "This man is not from God, for he does not keep the sabbath." But others said, "How can a man who is a sinner do such things?" There

> *was a division among them. So they again said to the blind man, "What do you say about him, since he has opened your eyes?" He said, "He is a prophet" (John 9:14-17).*

The grumbling Pharisees were only too happy to find a further handle against Jesus but even among themselves there was division. Under the mask of greater wisdom these blinded men were forever attacking Jesus, discussing everything He did or said, giving credit not even to His many philanthropic actions. So it is with all inveterate grumblers. The talents, actions and words of individuals, whether subjects or superiors (but especially these!), all commands, the management of affairs, the whole organization—all without exception seems to come under the microscope of the grumbler so that he can dissect or even roughly tear apart practically everything. There is hardly a thing in the world that can satisfy his bile-filled spiritual digestive system, for his jaundiced eyes can see nothing but defects and failings.

No wonder then that grumbling has been called "one of the most terrible scourges of society, one of the most grievous wounds of the human race." It is seriously up to me to avoid any intimate association with such people, still less consult them about my own troubles and moans. But, even more, ensure by frequent and honest self-examination that I am not of their number. It has been said that one of the finest resolutions one could make is "I will never complain." St. Paul says: "I consider that the sufferings of this present time are not worth comparing with the glory that is to be revealed to us.... If we hope for what we do not see, we wait for it with patience" (Rom. 8:18, 25). Let me now renew in myself this hope and patience in Christ, my Light of life, apologizing humbly for any grumbling transgressions of the past. Jesus, my Master and Model, help me....

Hear His Voice

It was the feast of the Dedication at Jerusalem; it was winter, and Jesus was walking in the temple, in the portico of Solomon. So the Jews gathered round him and said to him, "How long will you keep us in suspense? If you are the Christ, tell us plainly" (John 10:22-24).

In 164 B.C. the pious leader Judas Maccabeus instituted the feast of the Dedication of the Temple to commemorate its re-consecration after it had been profaned by Antiochus the Illustrious, the King of Syria whom II Maccabees describes as "that godless man...a murderer and blasphemer." Antiochus was not only responsible for forty thousand people's deaths by violence and as many sold into slavery, but "not satisfied with this, he had the audacity to enter the holiest Temple in the entire world.... With his unclean hands he seized the sacred vessels, and his impious hands swept away what other kings had presented for the advancement, the glory and the honor of the place" (2 Mac. 5).

The feast commemorating the re-consecration was a national one lasting for eight days. It was popularly called "the feast of lights," for not only were there many public illuminations but each household had to keep a light burning throughout those holy days. Although not obligatory, it was a very popular feast and even though it occurred in the depth of winter it attracted huge crowds to Jerusalem. Jesus Himself came to celebrate the feast. Here we find Him walking (meditating?) in the Temple's Portico of Solomon, dating back to the time of that king himself who, in his good days, fulfilled the great desire of his father, King David, to build the temple at Jerusalem. The Chaldeans had destroyed practically all his work except this portico which jutted out over the valley of Cedron. The scene from there must have been very beautiful and, knowing

Jesus' quick eye for the details of nature, one can imagine how much He appreciated it. But such thoughts and contemplation are interrupted now on His being recognized and surrounded by a group of Jews. They dare to question Him sharply on something which should already have been well known to them through so many supernatural signs and wonders performed by Jesus to prove that He was indeed the Christ, the Messiah. How often in life we too miss the obvious signs of God's existence, His loving kindness and solicitude for all mankind and for each individual. The beauties and marvels of nature itself cannot be explained away as simply as agnostics or so-called atheists would have us believe. The worst accomplishments of the worst tyrants have passed and nature and mankind still endure through the loving care of God's all-seeing Providence. I myself have survived so many wintry trials and mistakes simply because the grace of God has taken hold of my hand, lifted me up and helped me to continue onward toward the full possession of God in heaven. How thankful I should be, letting nothing whatsoever draw me from the right track. Am I?

> *Jesus answered them, "I told you, and you do not believe. The works that I do in my Father's name, they bear witness to me; but you do not believe, because you do not belong to my sheep. My sheep hear my voice, and I know them, and they follow me" (John 10:25-27).*

Jesus is forced to reproach His questioners with their own hypocrisy and incredulity, for though they pretended to be anxious to find out the truth, the fact was that they obstinately refused to believe in either His words or deeds. This proved, He maintained, that they did not belong to His flock, for they lacked the docility, humility and simplicity that would make their minds and hearts open to receive the word of God. Instead of these, instead of love, they were filled with envy and hatred, deliberately blinding themselves to the obvious truth. "My sheep hear my voice," He says, "and I know them and they follow me."

How consoling to think that God loves me in a very special way as an individual, that He understands me through and through and has such a tremendous interest in me! No matter what my faults or moods, He is constant and consistent in His loving care, only anxious for me to tell Him everything and then listen to Him as a little child does.

How infinitely good my Father is to me! Let me now thank Him sincerely as I think upon these facts.

> *And I give them eternal life, and they shall never perish, and no one shall snatch them out of my hand. My Father, who has given them to me, is greater than all, and no one is able to snatch them out of the Father's hand. I and the Father are one (John 10:28-30).*

Although Jesus says "no one shall snatch them out of my hand," there remains of course the fact of man's free will which can negate even this strong will of His because of His equally strong desire to have us love Him freely and not as servile slaves. How awesome, how awful this necessary gift of free will! St. Augustine says: "If the flock is tranquil under the care of a shepherd, who is, after all, merely a man, how great should be our tranquillity under the care of God who not only feeds us but has even made us!"

If I am fully convinced of this I need have no fear that Satan will ever snatch me from the hands of Christ. O Jesus,...

Blessed Mother

As he said this, a woman in the crowd raised her voice and said to him, "Blessed is the womb that bore you, and the breasts that you sucked!" But he said, "Blessed rather are those who hear the word of God and keep it!" (Luke 11:27-28)

The first recorded verification of the young Virgin of Nazareth's Magnificat prophecy that all generations would call her blessed is found precisely in these later verses of Luke. Carried away with admiration for Jesus and His teachings, a woman shouts out public praise of His Mother for being so blessed as to have such a son. The reply of Jesus must not be misinterpreted, for implicitly He acknowledges the truth of what she says but hints that it was not enough just that Mary should have been chosen for such an honor; what really mattered more was that she had not only heard the word of God but kept it faithfully all her life—the constant echo of those early words: "Behold, I am the handmaid of the Lord; let it be to me according to your word" (Lk. 1:38).

Let us see what Vatican II has written on this matter. It says: "In the public life of Jesus, Mary made significant appearances. This was so even at the very beginning, when she was moved by pity at the marriage feast of Cana, and her intercession brought about the beginning of miracles by Jesus the Messiah. In the course of her Son's preaching she received His praise when, in extolling a kingdom beyond the calculation and bonds of flesh and blood, He declared blessed those who heard and kept the Word of God, as she was faithfully doing. Thus the Blessed Virgin advanced in her pilgrimage of faith, and loyally persevered in her union with her Son unto the cross.... By her maternal charity Mary cares for the brethren of her Son who still journey on earth surrounded by dangers and difficulties, until they are led to their happy fatherland. Therefore the Blessed Virgin is invoked by the Church under the titles of Advocate, Auxiliatrix, Adjutrix, and Mediatrix. These, however, are to be so understood that they neither take away from nor add anything to the dignity and efficacy of Christ the one Mediator. For no creature could ever be classed with the Incarnate Word and Redeemer.... The Church does not hesitate to profess this subordinate role of Mary. She experiences it continuously and commends it to the hearts of the faithful, so that encouraged by this maternal help they may more closely adhere to the Mediator and Redeemer" *(Lumen Gentium*, 58, 62).

Blessed indeed, then, is the Mother of Jesus and blessed am I to have such a wonderful Mother also, one who is so interested in me as an individual and anxious to do all she possibly can to help me become the fulfilled and happy personality God wants me to be, the zealous, practical and prudent apostle-follower of Jesus her Son. Mary, dear Mother,...

Lumen Gentium says that Mary "stands out among the poor and humble of the Lord" (55). How true this is, for she was just a humble maiden in the poor village of Nazareth and yet singled out to become "blessed" to all generations.

From the humble poverty of Mary, with her as its channel, flowed the superabundant richness that is Christ, for that indeed was and is her mission in the world and in the Church, to give Jesus to souls. If Mary had been selfish she could have merely treasured all her life the blessed memory of being chosen by the Father as mother of His Son and of having nurtured and educated that wonderful Son through so many cherished years, content to die happily with just such glorious memories. But as Jesus hinted in our text today, Mary not only heard the word of God but practiced it, fulfilling her unselfish and difficult mission not only to Calvary's heights but beyond, not only until her own precious death but further, a mission she will always faithfully fulfill until the end of time, the commission of giving Jesus to others and to as many as possible, repeating always: "Do whatever he tells you"

(Jn. 2:5). Let me consider how she has fulfilled her task toward myself and the response I have made to her and to her words. Mary,...

How beautifully Pope Paul VI wrote of Mary in his apostolic exhortation entitled *Marialis Cultus,* saying among other things: "Mary is also the Virgin in prayer. She appears as such in the visit to the Mother of the Precursor, when she pours out her soul in expressions glorifying God, and expressions of humility, faith and hope. This prayer is the Magnificat, Mary's prayer par excellence, the song of the messianic times in which there mingles the joy of the ancient and the new Israel. As St. Irenaeus seems to suggest, it is in Mary's canticle that there was heard once more the rejoicing of Abraham who foresaw the Messiah, and there rang out in prophetic anticipation the voice of the Church: In her exultation Mary prophetically declared in the name of the Church: 'My soul proclaims the glory of the Lord....' And in fact Mary's hymn has spread far and wide and has become the prayer of the whole Church in all ages.... The title Virgin in prayer also fits the Church which, day by day, presents to the Father the needs of her children, 'praises the Lord unceasingly and intercedes for the salvation of the world....'"

Blessed indeed is Mary for all God's wondrous goodness to her; blessed indeed are we for having been given such a wondrous Mother by Jesus Himself. Let me pray to Him now that I may imitate His own sincere devotion to that lovely Mother. Jesus,...

Nothing Covered Up

In the meantime, when so many thousands of the multitude had gathered together that they trod upon one another, he began to say to his disciples first, "Beware of the leaven of the Pharisees, which is hypocrisy. Nothing is covered up that will not be revealed, or hidden that will not be known. Whatever you have said in the dark shall be heard in the light, and what you have whispered in private rooms shall be proclaimed upon the housetops" (Luke 12:1-3).

At the outset of our religious training, emphasis was given to the essential point of purity of intention in all things because God not only knows and sees all things, even our most secret thoughts, but longs for us to do everything with love. Here again in the Gospel Jesus warns us against every slightest form of hypocrisy, bluff or false pretense.

Let us glance at the New Testament for some standards: "Each one of you has received a special grace, so, like good stewards responsible for all these different graces of God, put yourselves at the service of others. If you are a speaker, speak in words which seem to come from God; if you are a helper, help as though every action was done at God's orders; so that in everything God may receive the glory, through Jesus Christ, since to him alone belong all glory and power for ever and ever" (1 Pt. 4:16); "So whether you eat or drink, or whatever you do, do all to the glory of God" (1 Cor. 10:31); "He who does what is true comes to the light, that it may be clearly seen that his deeds have been wrought in God" (Jn. 3:21); "Beware of practicing your piety before men in order to be seen by them; for then you will have no reward from your Father who is in heaven" (Mt. 6:1).

How easy it is to start off a project feeling almost completely sure that we are doing this solely A.M.D.G., but how often that one iota of doubt takes over the mastery and the slightest whiff of praise will soon reveal how the big ego has eaten away our so-called purity of intention. As St. John Bosco put it: "If we work for our own honor, then our thoughts, findings, inventions and works are valueless. Woe to him who works expecting praise from the world, for the world is a poor payer and always pays with ingratitude" *(M.B.,* X).

It is safer then, surely, to work only for God, really for God, trying to cleanse my motives of even the slightest sign of dross. If my heart is really sound then I can calmly concentrate on this, for "it is only with the heart that one sees rightly; what is essential is invisible to the eye" (St. Exupery). Is my heart all that sound? Is my eye really pure?

In our meditation quotation our Lord tells us that nothing is more powerful than the light of the searching eyes of God. How often those beautiful eyes see the lack of beauty in our own works through absence of true purity of intention. How often, too, we can lack a sense of proportion, of values, allowing small and unimportant things to upset us unduly. If someone seems to neglect us, we can resent it; if a greeting is not returned, we may take it as a snub; if we seem to be excluded from something, how easily we take offense. How much there is of this!

If the love of God truly gripped my heart, all this kind of pettiness within me would be eliminated. If I were truly trying to be and to do all things in and for God I would have none of these upsets. I must really work against this kind of thing. Not only should I start off each day well with a sincere Morning Offering that gives every single thought, word and action of the day to God for His glory alone, but frequently during the course of the day let me specifically renew that intention. How grand it would be if as I commenced each new action or duty I could give a swift mental glance at Jesus, my Master, and say: "All for You, Lord really for You this time!" What great happiness and blessings that could bring into my daily life! Have I such a good habit? If not, why not? O Jesus, my Master and Lord, from now on....

Marcus Aurelius of old said: "The happiness of your life depends upon the character of your thoughts."

If I am really and truly doing everything, all my actions and duties, solely out of love for God and in a sincere endeavor to imitate Jesus as my Model, then I should be a very happy person indeed. True, now and again circumstances will arise that may momentarily upset my equilibrium, but as the old Chinese saying goes: "Broken and broken again on the sea, the moon so easily mends."

Largely it is a matter of training in self-control, mind and heart control for the highest intentions. O Jesus,...

Holy Abandonment

Are not five sparrows sold for two pennies? And not one of them is forgotten before God. Why, even the hairs of your head are all numbered. Fear not; you are of more value than many sparrows (Luke 12:6-7).

In talking to "his disciples first" our Lord here reminds them again of the confidence they should have in divine Providence—and on this subject one can never meditate enough. In a recent meditation we recalled the words of Jesus' Mother at the wedding feast at Cana: "Do whatever he tells you." That sentence really sums up in excellent Marian form the whole of abandonment to God's Providence. In other words it is based entirely on the holy will of God, whether that will be directive (God's actual arrangements as He Himself plans them) or merely permissive (what He allows to happen).

But how am I to attune myself to this constant readiness to accept the will of God at all times whatever it may be, fully confident that, as Jesus says, I need never fear about God's constant solicitude for me? In actual fact the method could not be simpler.

First of all, am I fully convinced that I am God's child? Of course. Then let me act in His ever-constant, loving presence with the true simplicity of a child, for Jesus says: "I tell you solemnly, unless you change and become like little children you will never enter the kingdom of heaven" (Mt. 18:2). Just before He said that, the disciples had asked Him who would be the greatest in the kingdom and our Lord had taken up into His arms a little child and placed it before them and said: "The one who makes himself as little as this little child is the greatest in the kingdom of heaven" (v. 4). Where did He get that little child? We can imagine Him asking this favor from its mother, one of those good women who listened so eagerly to Jesus. How glad she must have been to hand over her little one into His kind arms. Here I can picture myself as God's little child being handed over to Him by Mary my Mother. Picture that loving Mother, her eyes brimming over with tenderness and love as she stands before God, my most kind and loving Father, whose love is infinitely greater even than Mary's. She realizes this fully, for is she not, by her own admission, the humble handmaid of the Lord? And realizing this, she knows that the very best place for me to be is not in her own arms but in those of God Himself, and there she wishes always to place me so safely and so confidently. My best efforts at holy abandonment, then, can always be safely made through Mary. Do I, in fact, bring her into the picture at all? It would help me tremendously if I did.

Little children are at times petulant or irritable and then, foolishly, they struggle when their mother wishes to hand them over to their father, and that, of course, only adds to their discomfort. Do I at times act like that, unwilling to resign myself to God's holy will, reluctant to face up to facts, realities, corrections...? A good-natured child does not act like that. No, it allows its mother to do as she knows best—and why? Simply because in its own short but very intense experience that little child knows that its mother has never yet betrayed or neglected it: "Never was it known that anyone who implored your help or sought your intercession was left unaided" (*Memorare*).

I should be most eager, then, to abandon myself to my Father through the loving hands of Mary, confiding to her all my troubles and trials, my worries and perplexities, my sorrows and even my joys, so that she may place them and me into the arms of God. Let my own attitude then be one of complete abandonment and of total relaxation in the surrounding love and care of Mary my Mother and God my Father. Let there be no struggling therefore against what they know is best for me. A child realizes its own littleness and its father's greatness and so it rests there in his arms, humbly we might say. So I too must rest *humbly* in the powerful arms of God. That child cannot help but love that gentle father whose love it has experienced in so many ways, and hence the love of his eyes reflects back in its own and it stays in his arms *lovingly*—so too must I in God's loving arms. A normal child is at ease when it gives itself over completely to its father, not content just to cling half-heartedly. It wants to feel that it belongs to its father, whose loving protective arms surround and support it firmly. So, too, I, as God's little child, must abandon myself *completely* to His ever loving and protective Providence: "Fear not; you are of more value...." How do my efforts compare with all this? Heavenly Father,...

Completing the picture of true abandonment to God, let me envision again the ideal little child. If it did not really trust its father, it would not stay in his arms, it would wriggle out of them, showing its discontent. But a normal, healthy child stays there quite confidently—so, too, I in the arms of God: *confidently!* God's Providence governs the whole world and if Jesus could tell us that He has a solicitous eye for the grass of the field and the poor little sparrows, then how much more should I, so dear and precious to Him, be willing to abandon myself humbly, lovingly, completely and confidently into the loving arms of that same divine and all-seeing Providence, now and always, and in all things. Am I still a struggling, awkward, unhealthy little baby? Am I still so proud and obstinate in my opinions, my likes and dislikes, my methods and manners? Do I still resent corrections and take them badly? Am I still over-sensitive? Am I still greedy, sensual, lazy, unmortified? If so, all the more cause for hurling myself with confident abandonment into God's arms, for "when I am weak, then I am strong." Our Lord says to me as to Paul, "My grace is sufficient for you, for my power is made perfect in weakness" (2 Cor. 12:10, 9).

Let me now ponder prayerfully on and make my own the profound meaning and sentiments of the following prayer: O most holy Trinity—Father, Son and Holy Spirit—

through the immaculate heart and most pure hands of my dear Mother Mary, Help of Christians, I *abandon* myself *humbly, lovingly, completely and confidently*, into the loving arms of Your divine Providence, that You may do with me, Your child, as You please, *now*, and always, and in all things. Amen. If I say this prayer *often*—but *slowly* trying to mean it, emphasizing the main words, I shall surely find greater peace of mind and joy of heart through holy abandonment to my Father's loving Providence. Resolution: I will do precisely this!

The Holy Spirit in My Life

And when they bring you before the synagogues and the rulers and the authorities, do not be anxious how or what you are to answer or what you are to say; for the Holy Spirit will teach you in that very hour what you ought to say (Luke 12:11-12).

Our Lord's words to His disciples give me now the wholesome opportunity of meditating on devotion to the Holy Spirit, a devotion so necessary for perfection and yet so often largely misunderstood. Perhaps people do not appreciate enough the full significance of the Third Person in the Blessed Trinity.

St. Paul tells us: "Hope does not disappoint us, because God's love has been poured into our hearts through the Holy Spirit who has been given to us" (Rom. 5:5). I am trying in these meditations to put on the mind of Christ, to become Christlike by imitating His example and fulfilling His words, but let me recall that the energy for all this comes through the Holy Spirit who wishes to glorify Jesus in me also. He is the one who supplies all the gifts and graces which spur me on to a closer imitation of Christ in my thoughts, words and behavior. Let me never neglect Him. Holy Spirit within me, keep me....

With true devotion to the Holy Spirit, what Isaiah of old prophesied of the Messiah can become true for me too as a diligent follower of Christ: "The Spirit of the Lord shall rest upon him, the spirit of wisdom and understanding, the spirit of counsel and might, the spirit of knowledge and the fear of the Lord. And his delight shall be in the fear of the Lord. He shall not judge by what his eyes see, or decide by what his ears hear, but with righteousness he shall judge and decide with equity" (11:2-4). Then indeed as our Lord says in our meditation quotation, I shall never need to be anxious, for I shall possess the gifts of the Holy Spirit which St. Thomas Aquinas says are necessary in order to secure salvation (cf. *Summa*, 1, 11, Q. 68, a 2).

How more highly privileged we are than the contemporaries of Jesus. They indeed saw Him, many of them stayed close to Him as He moved about, and rightly we consider them extremely blessed. But whenever we receive the sacraments with faith we enter into a much closer relationship with His very existence than ever they were able to, and all this through the Holy Spirit whom He and the Father sent to us so that He might retell us all about Jesus and show us how to enter into constant communion with Him.

I personally owe so much to the Holy Spirit who first inspired me with thoughts of a vocation to follow Christ more closely. I should show that gratitude to Him daily in prayer and by consciously following His inspirations. Holy Spirit of God, how much indeed I owe to You....

St. Paul has an excellent thing to say about the Holy Spirit and His gifts which I should ponder seriously, making applications to myself: "We teach what Scripture calls 'the things that no eye has seen and no ear has heard, things beyond the mind of man, all that God has prepared for those who love him.' These are the very things that God has revealed to us through the Spirit, for the Spirit reaches the depths of everything, even the depths of God. After all, the depths of a man can only be known by his own spirit, not by any other man, and in the same way the depths of God can only be known by the Spirit of God. Now instead of the spirit of the world, we have received the Spirit that comes from God, to teach us to understand the gifts he has given us. Therefore we teach, not in the way in which philosophy is taught, but in the way that the Spirit teaches us: we teach spiritual things spiritually. An unspiritual person is one who does not accept anything of the Spirit of God: he sees it all as nonsense; it is beyond his understanding because it can only be understood by means of the Spirit. A supernatural man, on the other hand, is able to judge the value of everything, and his own value is not to be judged by other men. As Scripture says: 'Who can know the mind of the Lord, so who can teach him?' But we are those who have the mind of Christ" (1 Cor. 2:9-16).

Am I still much lacking in the things of the Spirit through my own fault and neglect? I might well make my own now this prayer of the psalmist, addressing it specifically to the Holy Spirit: "Incline your ear, O Lord, and answer me, for I am poor and needy.... Gladden the soul of your servant, for to you, O Lord, do I lift up my soul. For you, O Lord, are good and forgiving, abounding in steadfast love to all who call on you.... Teach me your way, O Lord, that I may walk in your truth.... Turn to me and take pity on me; give your strength to your servant, and save the son of your handmaid. Show me a sign of your favor" (Ps. 86).

Ready for His Coming

"Be like men who are waiting for their master to come home from the marriage feast, so that they may open to him at once when he comes and knocks" (Luke 12:36).

Although the Master wanted His followers to live very much in the present, fulfilling the Father's holy will from moment to moment, He desired them to keep an eye on the future also, to be always ready for death and judgment. After all, we live the present not just for the sake of the present but for the sake of the future, and the future for us represents the happy possession of the kingdom of God for which we are now working steadily. This was always an important theme in the mind of Christ.

Jesus was well aware that it is very easy for us to get so absorbed in the present, especially in a busy life, that we do not give enough attention to eternity ahead.

Even if we allow ourselves to get lost in the present, the fact remains that the God of eternity is constantly approaching us. It would be wise, therefore, to be ever ready for His coming. Here our Lord makes use of another parable with an interesting background concerning the clothing of His times. People then used to be robed in a long garment which was gathered about the waist by a wide cincture that could also have pockets for storing things and especially one's money. When working or running or even walking fast one could ease matters by tucking the ends of the garment into this or simply pull it up. Jesus says that, spiritually, we should always be like that, our garment tucked up for working in the present and ready at any moment for the journey into eternity, ready to run and meet the Lord at His coming.

Our Lord's mention of "lamps burning" implies that one should be always prepared, even at night, for whenever the call comes. Constant vigilance is a must, even though busy with present affairs. Jewish marriages usually took place in the late evening without any specific termination time and Jesus uses this idea to underline again the point of being ever-ready for His second coming. Death can come so suddenly and unexpectedly—even for me! If it were to come for me this very day would our Lord find me perfectly ready in soul and with all my material affairs neatly in order? Let me not only pray about this but really prepare for possible death today.

> *"Blessed are those servants whom the master finds awake when he comes; truly, I say to you, he will gird himself and have them sit at table, and he will come and serve them" (Luke 12:37).*

Here again the same idea is repeated for further emphasis on something Jesus considered most important. Am I really of the same mind—not just in theory but in practice? Here, however, Jesus goes on to hint at the magnificent reward for those found ready and waiting for the Lord: He Himself will serve them with the glorious joys of heaven for all eternity. In other words, if we do all we can in our earthly lives to serve God as He wishes, then in eternity He will reverse that service almost as though our servant. To drive home this point even further, soon afterwards at the Last Supper we see Jesus in fact girding Himself with an apron and acting as though the servant of His apostles. If our Lord seems to use a bit of hyperbole in all this it is surely only to drive home the two important points of vigilance while working lovingly for Him and the glorious reward He will give for it in eternity. Nor need there be, nor should there be any morbidity about our vigilance.

"Heaven beyond," we might say, was one of the favorite themes of St. Augustine's sermons exhorting his audience to prepare well for it by present vigilance. One sermon ended thus: "Brethren, I implore you, love God with me! Hasten on the road with me by your faith! Let us all yearn for that glorious fatherland, yes, yearn for it, ever realizing that we are but pilgrims here" (*Tract* 33). So infectious was his enthusiasm that more than once the people burst into applause at the very thought of all the joys beyond. Hence for me also, no morbidity in my vigilance concerning death, but calm and joyful, generous service at all times, confident in heaven beyond! Jesus, my eternal reward, help me....

> *"If he comes in the second watch, or in the third, and finds them so, blessed are those servants! You also must be ready; for the Son of man is coming at an hour you do not expect" (Luke 12:38, 40).*

Our Lord here refers to the prevalent system of timing, with the same message. What Thomas Jefferson said of earthly warfare applies even more to the spiritual battle of life on earth: "Eternal vigilance is the price of victory." The idea of perpetual vigilance regarding both human and spiritual affairs was a common one in the Old Testament, where God is referred to as *sheqed,* the Watcher. After our Lord's emphatic exhortation it was taken up heartily by the apostles and disciples, at times with such eagerness that one gets the idea that they really expected the end of the world to occur in their own day. Even though that did not happen it was a wise attitude regarding eternity and judgment. Hence what St. Paul says should be taken constantly to heart: "Be watchful, stand firm in your faith, be courageous, be strong. Let all that you do be done in love" (1 Cor. 16:13); "Continue steadfastly in prayer, being watchful in it with thanksgiving" (Col. 4:2); "Keep alert with all perseverance" (Eph. 6:18). Let me pray then: O Jesus, help me to live always with an eye out for eternity, ever anxious to do Your holy will....

Fire on Earth

"I came to cast fire upon the earth; and would that it were already kindled!" (Luke 12:49)

The Jerusalem Bible puts that last phrase thus: "How I wish it were blazing already!" Various interpretations of this passage have been given by commentators but let us here accept a favorite one that Jesus thereby referred to zeal, for this is something that should be characteristic of religious as apostles of Christ. St. Thomas Aquinas defines zeal as "an effort of love, love that has burst forth," while St. Francis de Sales says, "Zeal is love on fire, love which, not finding room in the heart, forces an outlet, bursts forth and pours itself out for the salvation of souls." St. Gregory Nazianzen puts it thus: "Add fire to piety and you have zeal. With zeal your faith is secure." The Greek word *zelos* means "to boil" or "to pulsate with heat," which fits in well with what all these saints have said. Zeal for souls, then, would mean a pulsing eager energy to save souls for Christ, but it can only be true zeal if it is merely the outward expression of the inward brightly burning flame of the love of God and neighbor intimately combined. Not all zeal is Christian and apostolic, but it is also true that the zeal of politicians and fanatics can sometimes put on a Christian or apostolic guise—worse still the travesty when found in a religious!

It is wise, then, to avoid mere semblances of zeal and ensure that I possess the genuine article. Can I truly say so of myself? What are my proofs? Are my motives really pure? How much "self" manages to sneak in? How can I avoid this in the future?

By the very fact that we religious are supposed to be striving in our own special committed way to be "other Christs," it is evident that we are also called to a special inward charity towards God and neighbor that shows itself outwardly also. Without this our zeal cannot be genuine. As a close follower of Christ I must be ready at all times to spend myself for the souls God commits to my care or allows me to contact. I cannot, therefore, measure out my services to them according to my own will or whim, checking off what I shall grudgingly or unctuously do and what I won't. No, the limit of my service must be the utmost limit of my ability such as obedience allows me. Hence, even with my very moderate equipment of talents and physical energy or that rather intangible thing called personality, Jesus can still use me to do wonders for Him and souls if my spirit of altruistic generosity can measure up to the point of boiling over in genuine zeal. It will be a wonderful compliment when Jesus can say of me that I am prudently zealous and zealously prudent.

But it must always be the deep and true love of God and souls that gives me the nerve to do things, that impels me ever onward to be more and more generous in giving of my time and talents, in giving myself as Christ wishes, viz., always within the bounds of holy obedience to those who represent Him. It is all this that counts rather than extraordinary talent, accomplishments, personality and charm. It is all this that can make even of me a positive tower of strength to Christ and in my community, a giant in apostolic initiative and a light of Christ to all with whom I deal. How close do I come to this picture of a truly zealous Christian and religious? If it makes me feel confused or ashamed, I must stop and find the reasons! Jesus, help me now....

Possibly that last question may have given me a rather hard jolt but it should not have stopped at that. What about resolution? I must find out for myself in my own life just how quickly I can either acquire or increase the virtue of zeal, how to persevere in it. It is not just a question of external works, for these should be merely the sign of deep love in action. If I have genuine love of God in my heart and I love souls truly for God's sake then my zeal will burst forth, ready to be guided lest it go astray through the filtering in of subtle self. "If only we could say of ourselves, 'Zeal for your house devours me'! (Ps. 119:139)

But here is the house of the Lord; here is the treasure of the Lord—souls! Let us do everything, therefore, for love of God, diligently, with exactness, with affection and with enthusiasm, even at the cost of sacrifice, and let us help one another to do good, always trying to find better ways" (Fr. Michael Rua, S.D.B.).

The heart of the whole question of zeal is love. If, then, through genuine love I am faithful to all my duties, trying to work untiringly (also with others) for souls, urged on only by that true love, then I shall pray much for souls, seek for souls (not wait for them to come), work hard for souls, consoled only by the thought that in this way I am living, laboring and loving as a Christlike apostle, looking for no human reward or praise but seeking always and in everything to please God alone. "Where there is love, there is no labor; but if there be labor, the labor itself is loved" (St. Augustine). Let me pray now to my Master for this great gift of zeal, asking Him also how to exercise it.

Bent...Straight

Now he was teaching in one of the synagogues on the sabbath. And there was a woman who had had a spirit of infirmity for eighteen years; she was bent over and could not fully straighten herself. And when Jesus saw her, he called her and said to her, "Woman, you are freed from your infirmity." And he laid his hands upon her, and immediately she was made straight, and she praised God (Luke 13:10-13).

As the evangelist continues the narrative we find the ruler of the synagogue and others criticizing Jesus for healing this woman and in His reply Jesus refers to her as "a daughter of Abraham whom Satan bound for eighteen years" (v. 16). "*As he said this, all his adversaries were put to shame; and all the people rejoiced at all the glorious things that were done by him*" (v. 17). Could they only have had the honesty to realize it, the enemies of Jesus were spiritually deformed in a far worse way than this poor woman's physical curvature. Judging from the general reaction at the end of the incident, the ordinary people were very much aware of this fact and had doubtless often been scandalized by the contradictions in the public lives of these men as contrasted with their more pious recommendations. We could here spend some time in backing up these statements by the known facts, delving into their psychological or even psychiatric reasons and then come away rejoicing at our own cleverness of "better-than-them-ness." Instead, let me avoid this pitfall and consider in this meditation how I too can all too easily develop a definite spiritual malformation through bad habits in thoughts, words and actions. And first of all, a downward curvature in thoughts. Shakespeare said: "There's nothing either good or bad but thinking makes it so" *(Hamlet)*. It has been said that we are what we think and that the brain is as strong as its weakest thing! Certainly, what a person thinks greatly determines what he becomes.

How much harm is done to individuals, groups and the whole world by wrong thinking! Am I really free from that danger myself? Have I no prejudices regarding politics, racism, nationalism, human, social and community relationships? These could indicate a very definite and harmful mental spine curvature that can be greatly or totally against Christian charity, maturity and upright thinking. The same danger might exist regarding bad thoughts in which I allow myself to indulge...nothing to reproach myself with? A preventative or reparatory prayer now?

Curvature in words? Quite possible—even in me! Pascal said that "kind words do not cost much." "If anyone thinks he is religious, and does not bridle his tongue but deceives his heart, this man's religion is vain.... Do not speak evil against one another, brethren" (Jas. 1:26; 4:11).

In his dining room as a bishop in North Africa, St. Augustine had these words publicly displayed: "Let whoever wants to slander the absent with his words know that this table is not for him." We are told that on a couple of occasions when this was forgotten or disregarded by no less than certain bishops, Augustine was most annoyed and told them firmly either to stop at once or else take down that notice and he would leave the room! Do I not slip up in this or similar ways in my words and conversations? Is there no danger of an uncharitable curve that has become rather fixed in my speech? If so I must pray for the necessary miracle of grace to cure it—which I shall never obtain until I make my own definite and persevering efforts to self-discipline myself. O Jesus,...

Deeds? Control of thoughts and words should lead inevitably to avoiding all uncharitable deeds also. St. Augustine says: "The force of words is in work. Speak by means of your works rather than with words." "Be kind in speaking and dealing not only with superiors but with all, especially with those who in the past have offended you or who at present look upon you with an unkindly eye" (St. John Bosco). In a mature person there should never be any such thing as spite or petty vindictiveness for what others have done or said against one: here indeed is the excellent opportunity of the Christlike turning the other cheek! St. Julie Billiart says in practical fashion: "Be well disposed towards all, show kindness to everyone; know how to keep for yourself the most difficult work in order to lessen the fatigue of others; deny yourself every sharp or stinging word; bear generously any annoyance that may be met with in daily intercourse; help one another, respect one another, love one another—this is what holy charity demands." Scripture tells us too that "God loves a cheerful giver."

So let me do all I can to conquer any tendency to uncharitable curvatures by my self-discipline also in being cheerful always, even under difficult circumstances. Every effort in this will be most appreciated, but above all by Christ my Master, to whom I shall now pray.

Prodigal Son

He said, "There was a man who had two sons; and the younger of them said to his father, 'Father, give me the share of property that falls to me.' And he divided his living between them. Not many days later, the younger son gathered all he had and took his journey into a far country, and there he squandered his property in loose living. And when he had spent everything, a great famine arose in that country, and he began to be in want. So he went and joined himself to one of the citizens of that country, who sent him into his fields to feed swine. And he would gladly have fed on the pods that the swine ate; and no one gave him anything" (Luke 15:11-16).

Just previous to this Jesus had narrated two other parables, the lost sheep and the lost coin, to illustrate the great mercy of God. Then He went on to this most famous parable of the prodigal son. The story is a very human one indeed which occurs over and over again in families, though not always with the same happy ending. It brings out effectively the spirit of ingratitude that too frequently marks the conduct of children, the human misery to which such behavior so often leads, the immense goodness of parents at times, but above all, the infinite loving mercy of God our Father.

Let us look at the general background of the parable. Deuteronomy laid down that a firstborn son had the right to two-thirds of his father's property when he died, a second son only a third and certain circumstances allowed one to demand this inheritance in advance. This right was advanced by the younger son in the parable and the father sadly conceded, unable to dissuade him from his decision to get away from parental control. How often one hears sad cases of similar indiscretions among many modern youths, of the riotous lives and habits they get into, the final degradation into which so many fall and from which only a very limited number are rescued. To the Jews of old, the final humiliation for the youth in the parable was to be reduced to looking after pigs (considered unclean by law) and even to sharing their cast-off scraps of food. Drugs and vice are the counterpart today even if the outward circumstances are not always those of direst poverty.

It would not be out of place here for me to pray for the souls of young people and to consider in what ways I can possibly help them, for they are so precious to Christ and His Church. But let me consider also, and perhaps with more practical profit here, the parallel conduct in my own past life at times, in my youth or later. God has so often given me gentle or firm warnings about the danger of sin and bad habits but He always respects my own free will, which too often perhaps I have abused in the past, squandering whatever spiritual riches I may have obtained from Him. How low was my lowest fall from grace? Looking back at it humbly now, surely I must recognize my own stupidity as I trace those awful descending steps. Please God, all that is past now and completely forgiven, completely made up for, and my Savior does not want me ever to be morbid about the past. However, prudence warns me never to forget the bitter lesson I have learned, for it is so easy for past sinful history to repeat itself. Please God, that will never happen to me, but let me at least now pray for my Savior's protection and help, invoking too the aid of His and my Mother Mary, the Help of Christians. O Jesus,... O Mary,...

But when he came to himself, he said, "How many of my father's hired servants have bread enough and to spare, but I perish here with hunger! I will arise and go to my father, and I will say to him, 'Father, I have sinned against heaven and before you; I am no longer worthy to be called your son; treat me as one of your hired servants.'" And he arose and came to his father. But while he was yet at a distance, his father saw him and had compassion, and ran and embraced him and kissed him. And the son said to him, "Father, I have sinned against heaven and before you; I am no longer

> *worthy to be called your son." But the father said to his servants, "Bring quickly the best robe, and put it on him; and put a ring on his hand, and shoes on his feet; and bring the fatted calf and kill it, and let us eat and make merry; for this my son was dead, and is alive again; he was lost, and is found." And they began to make merry (Luke 15:17-24).*

It is a positive grace when one who had made a serious mistake can reach the point of acknowledging it and being prepared to apologize humbly. It is amazing how many so-called strong characters fail on the last point! One could wish also that contemporary youth could more speedily recognize their errors and false philosophies, mature through acknowledgment and be sure not only of forgiveness but also of sympathetic understanding from their elders.

Am I myself still weak in this point of humility, of recognizing my mistakes and apologizing? It is a very good test of character strength. True, I am always certain of God's pardon when I apologize to Him but why should I consider it such a humiliation to apologize to one who is but a mere human being? Nor should rebuffs put off my duty of humility regarding this. Let me also be sure my apologies are sincere—to both God and man. I must be prepared for some form of reparation at times in human affairs, making up quite naturally for spiritual offenses. Turning from sin, I can always be positive of such a wonderful welcome from God my Father; hence never let me delay my return to Him by one second once I have come to myself like the parable's young man: "for this my son was dead, and is alive again" (from mortal sin) or "he was lost, and is found" (venial sin). Jesus,...

> *Now his elder son was in the field; and as he came and drew near to the house, he heard music and dancing. And he called one of the servants and asked what this meant... (Luke 15:25-26).*

The elder son grumbled, resentful of his errant brother's royal treatment on his return home. Full of self-righteousness about himself and his exemplary behavior, he cannot find it in his heart to be kind concerning his younger brother. Perhaps at times I too am that way. It is easy enough to be self-righteous but such people often get roundly condemned in the Old Testament, while Jesus blitzed them in the New. Am I hard in my attitude towards others, not easily forgiving them even when they show signs of repentance or pluck up courage to apologize? On what do I base my self-righteousness? Have I myself never made similar mistakes? Have I never sinned?! If such is my attitude towards the faults or even peccadilloes of others, have I any right to God's pardon for my own perhaps even greater faults, such as this very sin of uncharitableness and hardness of heart? If I honestly have nothing to reproach myself with on any of these scores, let me thank God and express my sincere gratitude for His multiple forgiveness and mercy, resolving to try and become more and more worthy of Him as my Father and Jesus as my elder, loving, understanding Brother. God, my loving Father....

Unfaithful Administrator

He also said to the disciples, "There was a rich man who had a steward, and charges were brought to him that this man was wasting his goods. And he called him and said to him, 'What is this that I hear about you? Turn in the account of your stewardship, for you can no longer be steward.' And the steward said to himself, 'What shall I do, since my master is taking the stewardship away from me? I am not strong enough to dig, and I am ashamed to beg. I have decided what to do, so that people may receive me into their houses when I am put out of the stewardship.' So, summoning his master's debtors one by one, he said to the first, 'How much do you owe my master?' He said, 'A hundred measures of oil.' And he said to him, 'Take your bill, and sit down quickly and write fifty.' Then he said to another, 'And how much do you owe?' He said, 'A hundred measures of wheat.' He said to him, 'Take your bill and write eighty.' The master commended the dishonest steward for his prudence; for the sons of this world are wiser in their own generation than the sons of light. And I tell you, make friends for yourselves by means of unrighteous mammon, so that when it fails they may receive you into the eternal habitations" (Luke 16:1-9).

Like most of Jesus' parables, this one was based on the ordinary social life and business of His times. In our modern business world perhaps that man's tricks would soon be cut short by an efficient accountant—provided he too was not bribed! Our Lord does not recommend him for his dishonesty, but merely points out that this man's human prudence should be a pointer to us to avoid his mistakes by practicing supernatural prudence and being always honest with God and all mankind. Whenever I am charged with any responsibilities I must never forget that I am not thereby given total independence, either from God or man. On every single point of my duty I must be ready at any time to give a sincere account to God of my stewardship, assuring Him of my willing, humble and joyful dependence on Him on all things: "Without me you can do nothing" but "I can do all things through him who strengthens me."

A great help towards acquiring this conscious attitude of willing dependence on God is the faithful daily repetition with great sincerity, of the Morning Offering as one of my very first prayers of the day. Better still when during the day I frequently recall the fact and renew the dedication of all I do to God's greater honor and glory. The more frequent the recalling of God's loving presence during the day, with even brief but sincere acts of love and offering, the more difficult it will be for sin to enter in and spoil whatever I am doing. It is when we forget God for substantial periods that sin sneaks in so subtly in one disguise or another. Through habits of spiritual dishonesty it can in time take over more and more of the administration of my life and eventually full control of the whole business, leading me by the nose into spiritual bankruptcy. The practice of frequently recalling God's presence should prevent this from ever happening in my case.

The last words of the great St. Thomas Aquinas were: "He who always walks in the presence of God will always be prepared to give Him an account of his actions and will never lose divine love by yielding to sin." I should be adept by now in this practice, but am I? How can I improve by some simple, easily-remembered ways of reminding myself? "When we love God, we find Him everywhere, we speak to Him everywhere" (Cassian).

With due recognition of my total dependence on God in all I do, let me be no less humble concerning whatever human responsibilities are entrusted to me. Even if my superiors allow me a certain amount of initiative let me be grateful to them for treating me as a mature adult. Let me never abuse their confidence in me by resorting to dishonesty or slyness in any form whatever, disguising the true facts, bluffing.... I can never hope to win God's blessing on my work in that way even if I do succeed in deceiving my superiors or others. In any case, as the very lowest motive, is it worth the risk?

Pride obviously is at the root of all such dishonesty that makes one feel so clever as to be able to pull the wool over everyone's eyes all the time. On the contrary, I should be most careful about such stupid pride and look upon whatever responsibility I am given as my own humble response to God's ability in using me as His unworthy but willing, grateful instrument. Regarding also those to whom I am ultimately responsible, let me not always wait to be called upon for an account of my stewardship but willingly go to them regularly for at least the sake of consultation and advice. In this way I can mature my personality and even improve my talents and abilities at a much faster rate, God happily measuring my spiritual and human growth by the responsibility I thus successfully shoulder. With one hand constantly in the practice of the presence of God and the other humbly placed in the spirit of obedience I shall never find the need for subterfuges but be happy to render an honest account of my stewardship, often volunteering it. How do I stand in this? Points to improve on? Prayer for help....

> *He who is faithful in a very little is faithful also in much; and he who is dishonest in a very little is dishonest also in much. No servant can serve two masters; for either he will hate the one and love the other, or he will be devoted to the one and despise the other. You cannot serve God and mammon (Luke 16:10, 13).*

Generally it is one's attitude or indifference to little things that spells success or failure when confronted with responsibility.

Have I a sensible attitude about so-called little things? "Negligence in little things in the practice of virtue is a great obstacle to perfection. In the service of God there is nothing really little or unimportant. An act, however insignificant it may be in itself, from the moment it becomes connected with the service of God through the rule or the command of the superior, is ennobled and is endowed with far greater importance and merit than the most important of worldly affairs. There can be no lawful excuse for neglecting to perform the little acts of virtue that duty imposes upon us. They are all easy and require but little effort or exertion on our part. If God were directly, or indirectly through obedience, to prescribe to us great and difficult things, we should perform them at any cost. How much more should we be willing to perform what is light and easy!" As Jesus Himself put it, "The man who can be trusted in little things can be trusted in great" (*Jerusalem Bible*). Jesus, what is Your opinion of me in this?...

Increase Our Faith

The apostles said to the Lord, "Increase our faith!" And the Lord said, "If you had faith as a grain of mustard seed, you could say to this sycamore tree, 'Be rooted up, and be planted in the sea,' and it would obey you" (Luke 17:5-6).

Modern times have witnessed a pathetically sad lowering of moral standards with a consequent diminishing also of religious belief, sometimes unfortunately even at an alarmingly high level. Pope Paul VI remarked very firmly on this sad phenomenon of those who, especially by their subversive, ill-founded criticisms of ecclesiastical discipline, seem to seek "an easier way of Christianity—a Christianity that would be deprived of the experience and development of its tradition, a Christianity conforming to the spirit of the opinions of others and to the ways of the world, a Christianity without obligations, non-dogmatic, non-clerical as they declare." The application of this in practice has been witnessed all about us and even at high levels in the Church itself. One can only fear that those responsible for it face a very severe judgment at death, for Jesus had said just before today's Gospel quotation: "Temptations to sin are sure to come; but woe to him by whom they come! It would be better for him if a millstone..." (Lk. 17:1ff.). Such crises of faith, however, do bring out the real qualities of Christians, separating the weak from the strong, the men from the boys.

Please God, I am still on the right side of Christ myself! If so, then I can be confident that even my own tiny beacon of faith, added to that of so many other generous souls, can still do a great amount of good in helping to light up the lives of those with whom I come into contact, either increasing their faith or else leading them to it. I have here a splendid opportunity for wonderful apostolate—a discreet but nevertheless powerful apostolate, for it is not a question of proselytizing but actually *living* the Faith in practice and in minutest detail. What is faith, then? The first of the three great theological virtues infused into the soul at holy baptism, planted there as a kind of seed that must grow and flourish and bear fruit. Faith is also our acceptance of the things said or declared by God, directly or indirectly. When we believe what God says, because He says it and we are convinced He is too good to deceive us because of His absolute trustworthiness, then our faith is indeed sublime. Jesus tells us faith is absolutely necessary for salvation and Romano Guardini describes it as "the obedience of the creature to the self-revealing God."

How strong is my own faith? Have I carelessly allowed it to weaken in any way? Lord, increase my faith!

We don't always understand what we are asked to believe, for the Bible itself says, "Who can know the mind of God?" We do, however, accept His word on the sole basis of His authority as truth itself. But how do we bring this intellectual commitment to revealed truth down to the practical level of our own daily lives? Sometimes God seems so far away! I believe He's there somewhere vaguely. I do want to contact Him and to do what He wishes, but it doesn't always work out so easily. In that case I can thank God at least that such a life-line still exists between us. Hopefully it's not just made of spider's filmy web that any gusty wind of trial or upset could blow away, making me give up everything. But even if it's only that at present, it can be strengthened bit by bit, until it becomes nylon thread, and that in turn a rope, then planks and steel girders, so that finally the bridge of faith between me and God is not only firm, strong and enduring, but well-used from both ends. It is faith alone that can put me onto God's wavelength, faith alone that will help me to look at the world and all about me with the eyes of God, seeing myself as God sees me, without any bluff or hypocrisy.

Faith helps me to see God in others, too, mindful of the many extraordinary disguises He can use at times to test my faith. Faith helps me to be ready not only to accept God's will when it comes, but to go a brave step further by searching for it always and everywhere in order to be able to recognize and embrace it even gratefully, even when it's not to my natural liking. This indeed should be the characteristic faith of a religious. Is it mine? If not, where are the weaknesses? Prayer.

Faith is not just something up in the air, a theological vagueness, a nebulous intellectual commitment to heaven-alone-knows-really-what! Faith is genuine contact, the bridge between us and God that brings us into meeting God in a very real and at times marvelous manner. It is by this that quite literally "the word became flesh and dwelt among us, full of grace and truth" (Jn. 1:11). It is this that can make us cry out with St. Peter's joy of deep realization, "You have the words of eternal life; and we have believed, and have come to know that you are the Holy One of God" (Jn. 6:68-69). Faith, then, for me (and this is quite fundamental) should become a personal commitment to God in the person of Christ: a commitment to everything He says, even if I find it hard to believe or understand or accept. Everything He has said in the Gospels must become personally meaningful to me, not just in an intellectual way but in actual practice: "The righteous shall live by his faith" (Hab. 2:4). There must be this living and conscious response of my mind and heart and body to Christ in the practical details of my daily life, so that I try to do *all* by faith for the simple reason that I believe each and everything and event comes from or is allowed by God's will. In this way I *live* the faith within me. Do I? Lord increase my faith deeply in all this, please!

In Our Very Midst

Being asked by the Pharisees when the kingdom of God was coming, he answered them, "The kingdom of God is not coming with the signs to be observed; nor will they say, 'Lo, here it is!' or 'There!' for behold, the kingdom of God is in the midst of you" (Luke 17:20-21).

If deep love goes hand in hand with strong faith then I should be ready at all times and in all things to surrender myself totally to Christ within me, with supreme generosity and confidence, so that He may do with me as He pleases in everything, nothing excluded. However, this act of holy abandonment is not something to be declared just once and for all: it is an act of faith and surrender that, like the seed, must cause the kingdom of Christ within me to grow daily, flourish and bear fruit. How? It may mean going back right down to that fundamental practice of more frequently recalling the loving presence of God within and about me, making it something real, vivid and vivifying in my daily life. Surely if I recall that it is a loving, active, interested, sympathetic and fatherly presence then I shall try to live and act *consciously* with that happy memory all day long, with frequent short prayers of union with God. If I have neglected all this, it may explain so many of my spiritual weaknesses, why I have or show so little faith and am still so far from the grade of holiness to which I should by now have attained. However, thanks be to God, if foundations sink or sag, it is still possible to prevent ruin by pumping in wholesome, strengthening concrete and this I can do also with the sinking foundations of my spiritual life by brave and persevering efforts to renew in myself the wholesome recalling of God's presence much more frequently each day, plus ejaculations. This in itself is already wonderful faith, a living faith which can at once grow and flourish.

The more I recall God's presence and kingdom, the more will my heart expand with true love and zeal, and from this in turn develops the firm desire to do even my smallest duties really well, with as much love as possible, for God alone. This is already the flowering of the tree of my faith, for by it I sublimate even the most ordinary, commonplace, perhaps even menial duties into something glorious. Those humble duties become like jewels blazing forth before the eyes of God because of the tremendous love I pour into them. How often do I allow God this pleasure as He gazes at the treasury in His kingdom? Jesus, my King, help me to....

St. Francis de Sales urged: "Do all things through love, nothing by constraint." This is faith sublime and yet eminently practicable in my ordinary, humdrum duties. There is a South African cactus which now and then suddenly bursts forth during the night into a glory of huge trumpet-like flowers called "Queen of the Night," but with the first heat of the sun they become limp and soggy and bear no single fruit. My tree of faith is not meant to be of the thorny cactus type, difficult to grasp, showing an occasional flashy flower but nothing permanent or worthwhile, for Jesus Himself says: "By their fruits you shall know them."

What should be my fruits? As simple as all this: every single duty well done, wholeheartedly, no matter what it may be, nothing slipshod or careless ("Oh that's good enough!"), nothing lazy, nothing shirked. A high standard? Too high for a religious? But surely the kingdom of God within me cannot be established on wishy-washy foundations! Surely Christ my King has the right to only the very best from me whom He loves and trusts so dearly, expecting me at least to aim high and to try my very best to do all this. Am I *really* trying to give Him of my very best at all times and in everything? O Jesus, my King,...

The psalmist exults: "Blessed is the nation whose God is the Lord, the people whom he has chosen as his heritage" (Ps. 33:12). Our Lord tells us that we are such, that God's kingdom is within us. All that Christ my King asks of me is to make that kingdom within me not just something vague or idealistic but actual, living, palpitating. All He asks of me is, out of sheer faith and love, to try to do everything well and thoroughly simply because I am grateful to Him who in turn loves me so tremendously and is deeply interested in all I think, say or do, for I am an important member of His kingdom. In this way He wishes to become the very King and center of my heart and life. Because of this anxiety of mine to serve Him perfectly He takes over the running of my life, showing me and helping me to drive out whatever is displeasing in me. His wounded hands reach down each time to help mine to lift and remove the big or small obstacles between me and God's love.

It is this spirit of dynamic practical faith, that can make my whole life really joyful and worth living. This is the challenge of faith Jesus offers me again today so that I may the more quickly become what He wants me to be. With this practical and persevering spirit of faith in my daily life, oh, what wonderful things Jesus can do with me—if only I would let Him, if only I would let Him! Jesus, help me to....

Rich Young Man

And behold, one came up to him, saying, "Teacher, what good deed must I do, to have eternal life?" And he said to him, "Why do you ask me about what is good? One there is who is good. If you would enter life, keep the commandments." He said to him, "Which?" And Jesus said to him, "You shall not kill, you shall not commit adultery, you shall not steal, you shall not bear false witness, honor your father and mother, and, you shall love your neighbor as yourself." The young man said to him, "All these I have observed; what do I still lack?" Jesus said to him, "If you would be perfect, go, sell what you possess and give to the poor, and you will have treasure in heaven; and come, follow me." When the young man heard this he went away sorrowful; for he had great possessions (Matthew 19:16-22).

By the grace of God I have responded to the initial call of Jesus to follow Him more closely by a special type of life that tries to go even beyond the duties of the ordinary Christian in loving and serving God. To the young man Jesus offered a very special challenge: "If you would be perfect...." The same challenge was offered me by Christ, not just once, at the beginning, for Jesus realizes I could not become perfect in a day. The main thing then was generously to accept the challenge, but the even more important point thereafter was to keep on striving after Christian perfection. Nor was it a one-sided proposition, for Jesus promised "You will have treasure in heaven." Nor is that the whole tale. It was never intended by Him to be a lonesome effort on my part, an unaided struggle against the obvious difficulties for a poor, weak human to become perfect.

Throughout the Old and New Testaments we get the oft-repeated assurance of God's constant desire to help souls, with predilection for those who are really trying their best to cooperate with His wonderful plans, e.g..

"The virtuous flourish like palm trees and grow as tall as the cedars of Lebanon. Planted in the house of God, they will flourish in the courts of our God, still bearing fruit in old age, still remaining fresh and green, to proclaim that God is righteous" (Ps. 92:11-15). Hence it is more than obvious that if Jesus has held out a very special challenge to me and I have accepted it, He is certainly not going to leave me in the lurch to make my own way as best I can. On the contrary, by the very fact of the special circumstances I can expect also particular helps and graces. In other words, it is not a question of one person but of two, Jesus and me, and if I keep my hand firmly in His – in spite of the hurt of the nails – then I can be sure of following Him exactly as He wants. My own experience has surely shown me, on frequent occasions not merely the usual list of special helps one gets by being a religious but also those specific graces meant just for me. How much indeed I have to be thankful for as a religious and as this very personal religious so dear to the heart of Christ! O Jesus,...

That virile soul, St. Teresa of Avila, used to challenge her nuns, saying, "You must be strong men!" That is the return that God expects for all He does and gives to religious: to be strong in our own love and life of giving. With God's ever-abundant grace constantly offered to me and my own efforts to cooperate and collaborate with Christ, my religious life can indeed be a most happy and consoling one in spite of its admitted difficulties, allowing me to say with the psalmist: "One thing have I asked of the Lord, that will I seek after; that I may dwell in the house of the Lord all the days of my life, to behold the beauty of the Lord, and to inquire in his temple. For he will hide me in his shelter in the day of trouble; he will conceal me under the cover of his tent, he will set me high upon a rock.... I will offer in his tent sacrifices with shouts of joy (Ps. 27:4-5, 6).

Trying to correspond faithfully with the enriching gifts of God's grace must eventually produce obvious effects in my internal and external life, in my thoughts, words and actions, in my whole personality and attitudes, grace building upon and perfecting my ordinary human nature and God-given talents.

I, too, in spite of all my weaknesses, can yet become lovable and holy by my persevering efforts to mature more and more in God's ways according to the example of Jesus, for "The steps of a man are from the Lord, and he establishes him in whose way he delights; though he fall, he shall not be cast headlong, for the Lord is the stay of his hand.... Depart from evil, and do good; so shall you abide for ever. For the Lord loves justice; he will not forsake his saints.... The mouths of the righteous utters wisdom, and his tongue speaks justice. The law of his God is in his heart; his steps do not slip.... Wait for the Lord, and keep to his way,...you will look on the destruction of the wicked.... The salvation of the righteous is from the Lord; he is their refuge in the time of trouble. The Lord helps them and delivers them; he delivers them from the wicked. and saves them, because they take refuge in him" (Ps. 37). O Jesus,...

In This Present Time

Then Peter said to him, "What about us? We left all we had to follow you." He said to them, "I tell you solemnly, there is no one who has left house, wife, brothers, parents or children for the sake of the kingdom of God who will not be given repayment many times over in this present time and, in the world to come, eternal life" (Luke 18:28-30).

God in His goodness certainly does repay "many times over" in this life those religious who not only have accepted the call of Christ to a special vocation but continually strive to live up to all that is implied in the close following of Jesus. Since the way of Christ is also the Way of the Cross it would be foolish for any religious to expect to go through life cross-less, but the grace of God is never lacking to those who are generous in spirit.

Naturally, one could find many things indeed to complain about in religious life: food, timetable, disappointments, misunderstandings, perhaps even mismanagement, lack of good organization.... It would be foolish and immature, though, to allow oneself to concentrate on such negative points when there is so much of the positive and even joyful side to be found in religious life. Think, for example, of the many consolations God sends us from time to time in our apostolate. The fact is that Jesus explicitly promised us not only eternal life hereafter (in itself a most wonderful buoy for all our hopes) but also a "repayment many times over in this present time." Possibly the best place to look for this fine reward is in our actual community life. As hinted, there is much of the negative side to be found there, but it seems safe enough to say that one can receive as much joy from community life as one puts into it. It is a question, then, of generosity of spirit, a question of giving oneself happily to one's brethren in whatever way possible. And the possible ways are so many! Think, for example, of the power of a smile. Someone has said: "A smile costs nothing, but creates much. It happens in a flash and the memory sometimes lasts forever. It cannot be bought, begged, borrowed or stolen, but it is something that is no earthly good to anyone until it is given away. So, if in your hurry or rush you meet someone who is too weary to give you a smile, leave one of yours—for no one needs a smile quite so much as he who has none to give."

Only a little thing perhaps but even smiling can have its part in the joy and the apostolate of community and religious life. Am I of this type?

Why is it that some religious find such real happiness in their community life and others little, if any? It depends, as we have said, on each one's individual spirit of generosity. A religious who has this spirit of giving of himself pleasantly can contribute so much to community happiness by his very presence and kindly, tactful ways. The sheer extroverts and naturally happy-go-lucky types have their own special blessings but must keep a constant eye on tact and consideration for the feelings and dispositions of others. The naturally timid and shy, the sensitive and suffering must also be ready to make efforts to make each their own positive contribution to the smooth running of life in common.

The general impression of community life should be that of a bubbling cheerfulness that signifies not only personal, individual happiness in one's vocation but the communal joy and consecration to Christ our Master. If the evidence of this were much more obvious it would surely make each community a magnetic pole that would soon arouse in many other generous spirits the desire to share in such a wonderful and apostolic life of dedication to Christ and souls. To give this witness could be, therefore, a matter of great responsibility for each community, for if it is missing it could be interpreted as a falsification of Jesus' words about the "repayment many times in this present time" and lead to an even further diminution of vocations. Do I play my own full share in this living witness Christ and the world expect of me? In what am I still lacking? How can I become more generous? Jesus, You have been so generous with me....

Since mortal beings make up a community, the human element in relationships cannot be totally eliminated. The variety of characters and temperaments is bound to cause awkwardness at times, perhaps even friction, but precisely because of the abundance of supernatural helps given, and the continual flow of God's grace into a community, it should become possible for all not to allow the mere human element to cause any prolonged upset or unhappiness. If each one, humbly conscious of his own defects and weaknesses, could force himself to be generous and brave in his spirit of kindly tolerance, compassion and helpfulness towards the others, for the sake of Christ's love, then how much more smoothly and happily things would go in spite of persisting deficiencies.

That spirit will make our "repayment many times over in this present time" more than obvious and "eternal life" all the more secure. "You are God's chosen race, his saints; he loves you, and you should be clothed in sincere compassion, in kindness and humility, gentleness and patience. Bear with one another; forgive each other as soon as a quarrel begins. The Lord has forgiven you; now you must do the same. May the peace of Christ reign in your hearts, because it is for this that you were called together as parts of one body. Always be thankful. Let the message of Christ, in all its richness, find a home with you. Teach each other, and advise each other in all wisdom" (Col. 3:12-16). Jesus, I do indeed thank You for....

Young and Old

For the kingdom of heaven is like a householder who went out early in the morning to hire laborers for his vineyard. After agreeing with the laborers for a denarius a day, he sent them into his vineyard. And going out about the third hour he saw others standing idle in the market place; and to them he said, "You go into the vineyard too, and whatever is right I will give you." So they went. Going out again about the sixth hour and the ninth hour, he did the same. And about the eleventh hour he went out and found others standing.... And when evening came, the owner of the vineyard said to his steward, "Call the laborers and pay them their wages...." And when those hired about the eleventh hour came, each of them received a denarius. Now when the first came, they thought they would receive more; but each of them also received a denarius. And on receiving it they grumbled at the householder, saying, "These last only worked one hour, and you have made them equal to us who have borne the burden of the day and the scorching heat." But he replied to one of them, "Friend, I am doing you no wrong; did you not agree with me for a denarius? Take what belongs to you and go; I choose to give to this last as I give to you. Am I not allowed to do what I choose with what belongs to me? Or do you begrudge my generosity?" So the last will be first, and the first last (Matthew 20:1-16).

It is recognized by exegetes that there is no need to try each time we read a parable of Jesus to interpret it perfectly. It is not always easy to find an exact parallel between allegory and truth and quite often in a parable there is much embroidery for the sake of interest. With regard to the particular parable in hand it is pointed out that the grumbling of the laborers probably belongs to this latter part, while the main emphasis is on God's free call to various people at the particular times that He in His wisdom chooses. This no doubt we all recognize without difficulty, and hence perhaps this meditation could profitably diverge a little from the point into matters of constant timeliness good to consider every now and then.

The subject of age groups need not be far at all from the lessons of the parable. In every community, practically, the problem of the age group occurs but one needs to recall that God's call is constantly there and that a great spirit of genuine charity is needed to bridge the gaps. Let us consider the three main age-groups: the young, the middle-aged, the old. It is good for each to study the other with love and sympathy. The young, of course, have always come under heavy weather in criticism: "Our youth today love luxury. They have bad manners, contempt for authority, disregard for older people. Children nowadays are tyrants. They contradict their elders, gobble their food and tyrannize their teachers." How often that is said today (even, partly, in religion) and yet the original was uttered in the fifth century B.C. by Socrates! Someone else said that from 4 to 14 they ask all the questions and from 14 to 24 they know all the answers! A wise schoolteacher remarked, "The trouble with the younger generation is that so many of us don't belong to it anymore!" What a lot of truth in that, and so there may be truth in this cynical statement also: "Growing up is the period spent in learning that bad manners are tolerated only in grown-ups!"

Youth, even in religious life, does indeed need much understanding, help and encouragement, and there should be a great spirit of cheerful give and take between younger and older; a certain tolerance of ways and behavior not manifestly wrong or sinful; never, on either side, a better-than-thou attitude that so easily embitters; a spirit of sincere kindliness in all dealings with one another, even when views are different. And especially in the latter case there should be much prayer for the other side and for ourselves, so that neither of us may miss the light of the Holy Spirit. In whatever age category I belong, what are my own personal efforts to preserve peace, harmony and even joy in the community? How can I improve?

Middle age should increase our urgency to mature in a Christlike manner. In middle age one has, or should have, far greater self-knowledge which one can shape more purposefully towards eternity. Middle age can, then, be a wonderful time and grace, something to respect, appreciate, enjoy and use well as Christ wishes. The middle-aged should also be the great bridge-builders in society, in congregations and in communities—almost a special vocation in itself, bringing great graces to both sides, and in the middle! O Jesus,...

There is also a special psychology of old age that should be studied by all three age groups as a real part of Christian and community charity. While the old should guard against pride and touchiness about respect, those who are younger should be the first to give it, sincerely. The psalmist says that "the righteous flourish like the palm tree, they flourish in the courts of our God. They still bring forth fruit in old age" (Ps. 92:12-14). Great comfort for the elderly lies in those other words of God through the prophet Isaiah: "Hearken to me, who have been borne by me from your birth, carried from the womb; even to your old age I am he, and to grey hairs I will carry you. I have made and I will bear; I will carry and will save" (Is. 46:3-4). Old age needs greater humility: "The greater you are, the more you must humble yourself; so you will find favor in the sight of the Lord" (Sir. 3:18). Instead of crankiness and over-sensitiveness, kindliness should be characteristic: "Make yourself beloved in the congregation; incline your ear and answer peaceably and gently" (Sir. 4:7-8); "A pleasant voice multiplies friends, and a gracious tongue multiplies courtesies. Let those that are at peace with you be many" (Sir. 6:5-6). A peaceful, even happy, preparing for the end: "Do not delay to turn to the Lord, nor postpone it from day to day" (Sir. 5:7); "In all you do, remember the end of your life, and then you will never sin" (Sir. 7:36). For all: "Do not disdain a man when he is old, for some of us are growing old.... Do not disregard the discourse of the aged, for they themselves learned from their fathers; because from them you will gain understanding" (Sir. 8:6, 9).

At whatever stage I was called to work in the Lord's vineyard, at whatever age I am now, let me try to be a kind, helpful, prayerful, understanding bridge of Christ. "The mark of a happy heart is a cheerful face.... Blessed is he whose heart does not condemn him and who has not given up his hope" (Sir. 13:26; 14:2). O Jesus,...

Christ's Sense of Humor

Do not look dismal (Matthew 6:16).

The philosopher Heine deduced that God must have a sense of humor from the very fact that He makes a kitten chase its tail! In fact there are many other things in nature which support the fact. Jesus Himself in His Sermon on the Mount said, "Do not look dismal" (Mt. 6:16), and He was perhaps familiar with the saying of the Jewish Torah: "A man who laughs is more to be cherished than one who weeps; a woman who sings than one who wails. And God is very close to the child who dances for reasons which he cannot explain." Laughter is such a natural part of man's nature, and a sense of humor finds appreciation amid the generality of mankind. Add these facts to the truth that Jesus came upon earth to be our model and example in all things but sin: how then can we exclude from His wonderfully human and beloved personality a good sense of humor? Let me think cheerfully about this!

How well appreciated a good sense of humor is in community life, where men are gathered together precisely in order to try to live a life that more closely resembles that of Christ in its fullest possible detail. Such a life naturally has its own peculiar difficulties for it is no easy thing for a number of people to live together in constant harmony in spite of the common aim. How easy for the human element to predominate, for pettiness to obscure the higher issues. But also how often, thanks be to God, it is the sense of humor of one or more that saves situations, prevents people from becoming wet blankets or losing their sense of balance. Surely on such occasions Jesus the smiling Master blesses those who restore equilibrium by some wisecrack or witty remark, some good joke or pleasant laughter. Let me thank God for such of my brethren and let me in turn make my sincere but tactful contribution when occasion offers, sure of the Master's blessings and His smile. O Jesus,...

One instance of the humor of Jesus is surely his narration of that funny image of the meticulous cleaning of the outside only of a dirty cup in Matthew 23:24-25. It is the mixture of sheer realism with absurdity that makes the irony and gives it its force. Did no one smile as the story was told? Did no one see the picture with his own mind's eye—no one grasp the humor and the irony with delight?

This is but one instance of very many which prove beyond doubt that Jesus had a good sense of humor which was sometimes very subtle but always very pleasant, even when chiding. I must watch out lest my wit be at times mere sarcasm, hurtful, unkind. Have I any such tendency? How can I avoid it? O Jesus, help me to be kind even in my sense of humor!

Little Zacchaeus

He entered Jericho and was passing through. And there was a man named Zacchaeus; he was a chief tax collector, and rich. And he sought to see who Jesus was, but could not, on account of the crowd, because he was small of stature. So he ran on ahead and climbed up into a sycamore tree to see him, for he was to pass that way. And when Jesus came to the place, he looked up and said to him. "Zacchaeus, make haste and come down; for I must stay at your house today." So he made haste and came down, and received him joyfully. And when they saw it they all murmured, "He has gone in to be the guest of a man who is a sinner." And Zacchaeus stood and said to the Lord, "Behold, Lord, the half of my goods I give to the poor; and if I have defrauded any one of anything, I restore it fourfold." And Jesus said to him, "Today salvation has come to this house, since he is also a son of Abraham. For the Son of man came to seek and to save the lost" (Luke 19:1-10).

Jericho was called "the town of palms" and King Herod had beautified it greatly with fine buildings, trees and gardens. It was an important town through which much traffic passed and a chief tax collector must have been quite well off. Zacchaeus apparently had heard of Jesus, His kindness, His miracles, His teachings, the way He treated publicans and other so-called public sinners. He became very anxious to see Him but there were two obstacles: a huge crowd pressed about Jesus, making access very difficult, and Zacchaeus was only a little man. In his official capacity, however, he had often to use his wits. Now he puts them to excellent service, by running ahead of the crowd and climbing a tree with horizontal branches, a sycamore, common in the Jordan Valley. On one of the lower branches he could be sure of a good view of Jesus and possibly also be able to hear at least some of His conversation. In Hebrew the name Zacchaeus means "pure" and it is obvious that there was some good in this man that made him so anxious to see and hear Jesus, unmindful of human respect concerning those who would scorn or laugh at a public official for actually climbing a tree like a curious boy. Interesting, too, the ever observant eye of Jesus that notices him up there. Both in the spiritual and in the material life whenever anything worthwhile is to be gained or is at stake, the old dictum serves good purpose: "Whatever is worth having is worth paying for." Zacchaeus certainly thought so and reaped far richer dividends thereby than ever he gained from his tax-collecting, rich man though he was.

It is a lesson worth learning or re-learning for me also, and especially in my spiritual endeavors. I have to be generously prepared to make the efforts necessary in order to acquire the various virtues, to overcome bad habits, to avoid sin. At times it may require a lot of self-discipline and control, going against human respect, restraining myself in multiple ways that will still cost me a lot. Often that is the only way, e.g. with a habit of uncharitableness, deliberately making acts of kindness for the one who is generally the object of my unkindness. This might be the thrust I need to run from my unkind self in order to climb up to where I can see the kind Jesus in my neighbor and hear the word of His approval. And I can be quite sure that the observant eye of Jesus is ever on me too, watching my conduct and reactions not merely with interest but even with anxiety. In what area can I now apply all this to myself?

Did Jesus' eyes light up with kind amusement to see little Zacchaeus in a tree? How ever did He know his name? The fact is that He read right into that despised little man's heart and saw a nugget of gold there. The words of Jesus in their intimacy ring with affection: "Zacchaeus, make haste and come down, for I must stay at your house today." Perhaps He even emphasized the word "must." How easy to imagine the astonishment of Zacchaeus when Jesus actually stops beneath the tree, his delight to hear his name called out by that manly voice, his joy to see the kindness that lit up those startling eyes and the almost unbelievable thrill that he was to be the chosen host of such a wonderful person! After that the words "so he made haste and came down" seem quite moderate: Zacchaeus probably leapt like a little monkey out of that tree and tore home on speeding feet to prepare a banquet.

Perhaps at times Jesus is amused at some of my antics too, my lack of common sense, my odd ideas and plans, my self-importance..., for I too am in many ways just an exaggerated little man. Please God, however, I hope that Jesus reads into my heart and sees that in spite of all these things there is still some good in me. Please God, there is still the desire to love Him better, to improve my ways, to take the necessary steps to do so, to become exactly what He wishes me to be. Yet I cannot afford to remain up in the branches of good desires! I've got to hurry down and fulfill them in action. After all, every single morning at my awakening Jesus is standing there saying: "Make haste.... I *must* stay at your house today." Surely I could never be so ungracious as to refuse Him entrance or let Him find the place in a mess or even only slightly untidy! O Jesus, please....

One is sorry to read in the Gospel that not merely the Pharisees but *all* murmured against Jesus for taking such special notice of a "public sinner" to the extent of even wishing to dine with him. Generalizations are always dangerous, especially when attaching labels onto people and situations; let me be on my guard not to be easily led by others here. Zacchaeus now joyfully receives Jesus into his home (fussy and excited? or like a little Napoleon among his own? It doesn't matter!) Was it at the end of dinner in a formal address that Zacchaeus spoke his famous words? Certainly his is a model speech as we read it, brief, a fine train of thought and the right terminal! It pleased Jesus immensely too, for He knew that Zacchaeus' words were not just airy nothings but sincere, resolute, generous, all based on a spirit of possibly new-found but nevertheless genuine humility. And what a lovely reward: "Today salvation has come to this house," for Jesus knew that the good example of Zacchaeus after his conversion would deeply influence his household also. Surely this incident is one of the most touching in the Gospels for all its humanity, simplicity, goodness, generosity, humility, kindness and firm resolve. How much influence do I exert in my own surroundings because of my good example, words, behavior? O Jesus....

Lazarus: Whom You Love

Now a certain man was ill, Lazarus of Bethany, the village of Mary and her sister Martha. It was Mary who anointed the Lord with ointment and wiped his feet with her hair, whose brother Lazarus was ill. So the sisters sent to him, saying, "Lord, he whom you love is ill" (John 11:1-3).

The raising of Lazarus from the dead constitutes one of the most remarkable miracles of Jesus, perhaps the greatest after His own resurrection which it foretold. The story is a long but interesting one, full of human angles and consolation. At this stage we find Jesus close again to Jerusalem, close to His passion. John the Evangelist records the whole event with charming simplicity, clearness and ease, with a richness of images and, we can say, with a psychologist's eye for significant detail. He mentions the family of Bethany as though they are surely well known to his readers as intimate friends of Jesus, and immediately we find the two sisters sending a message to Jesus which in its utter simplicity is a beautiful appeal to His friendship without directly asking anything: "He whom you love is ill." A telegram almost, such as sent in emergency to family members at a distance. Jesus, then, was looked upon as a member of the family, we can say. How greatly such a compliment is always appreciated and the Gospels certainly give us the impression that Jesus valued it highly. However, the two sisters show the usual refinement and delicacy that exists in such situations. They do not like in any way merely to "use" their friends, to take advantage of their friendship for their own gain. Here the case was different, for they knew how deeply Jesus loved and esteemed all three of them; they felt sure He would want to know and even come. As St. Augustine puts it: "They did not send a message saying: Come. A simple word was enough for one who loved; enough that He should know, for Jesus could not love and yet forsake those He loved." And so the distressed sisters draw up their simple little message, so pregnant with meaning for themselves and for its receiver. How lucky was that family to have merited the friendship of Jesus! In Him they found the fulfillment of Sirach's words in the Bible: "A faithful friend is a sturdy shelter: he that has found one has found a treasure. There is nothing so precious as a faithful friend, and no scales can measure his excellence. A faithful friend is an elixir of life, and those who fear the Lord will find him" (6:14-16).

Has my own friendship with Jesus reached such intimacy as enjoyed by the family at Bethany? The acquiring of this knowledge and intimacy is precisely the object of these meditations that try to help me bring Christ deeply into my life. Do I appreciate this? What real efforts do I make to translate them into action after formal meditation? O Jesus, he whom you love is....

In the delicate wording of their message to Jesus, Martha and Mary illustrated what St. Jerome would say later: "That is true and firmly-cemented Christian friendship which is brought about by no selfish interest, mere bodily presence, or deceitful coaxing flattery, but by the fear of God." Friendship forms one of the most charmingly expressed themes in the Bible, right from those earliest vignettes in the first chapter of Genesis: "So God created man in his own image...male and female he created them.... And God blessed them.... And they heard the sound of the Lord God walking in the garden in the cool of the day.... The Lord God called to the man and said to him, 'Where are you?' ...And the Lord God made for Adam and for his wife garments of skins, and clothed them." Later God chose Abraham as His special friend: "Abraham, my friend" (Is. 41:8). And Exodus tells us that "the Lord used to speak to Moses face to face, as a man speaks to his friend" (33:11). He blessed the very special bond between David and Jonathan whose words of beautiful friendship are so tenderly recorded in the Bible. The various sapiential books for holy Scripture say wise and wonderful things about true friendship. Jesus Himself came as the friend of mankind and demonstrated it in many ways. He loved the family at Bethany, He took an immediate liking to the young man who wanted to inherit eternal life ("And Jesus, looking upon him loved him"–Mk. 10:21); His friendship went out at once to Zacchaeus; His friendship with His apostles must have been something wonderful indeed ("I have called you friends"–Jn. 15:15); and there were other men and women besides who held the privileged title of friends of Jesus; at the agony in the Garden, as at the Transfiguration, three special friends alone were present.

In the centuries since, how many other special friendships have existed between Jesus and chosen souls. Am I one of them? I could be! Jesus, my friend....

The life of grace, to which all are called, really means to live in the intimacy and friendship of God. Calling mankind to follow Him, Jesus called me also to live in intimate friendship with Him. Let me see, then, how I measure up to these varied qualifications: "Friends have all things in common" (Pythagoras); "The only way to have a friend is to be one" (Emerson); "To love someone, you must have his happiness at heart, subordinate yourself to him, adapt and sacrifice yourself for his good" (Teine).

Am I anxious to have all things in common with Jesus? Am I prepared to suffer for His sake? In what ways do I prove my actual friendship with Him? Am I always anxious to please Him, to submit to His holy will, to adapt my own ideas to His, to sacrifice myself to fit in with His plans? O Jesus, help me to measure up to these standards of friendship with You not merely in sentiment but in living deeds.

Lazarus: Not Unto Death

But when Jesus heard it he said, "This illness is not unto death; it is for the glory of God, so that the Son of God may be glorified by means of it" (John 11:4-7).

At first one might get the surprising impression that Jesus was not really bothering much about His friend's illness. One might even have a lurking doubt as to whether, after all, Lazarus was really such a great friend of His. But then hastily we recall the omniscience of God: Jesus knew exactly what was going to happen. He knew that the Father willed Lazarus actually to die, so that Jesus might perform the mighty miracle of restoring him to life. Hence the sick man's coming death was only of a temporary nature: "not unto death; it is for the glory of God, so that the Son of God may be glorified by means of it." There is a purpose in everything that happens to us, and God's loving Providence sees to it that all things fit somehow into the divine plans, even when not directly willed by God but caused by the perversity or stupidity of men. The problem of suffering, however, is one of the shoals on which the confidence of those weak in faith so easily flounder.

The young Servant of God, Fr. Andrew Beltrami, S.D.B., who suffered much from illness, wrote: "The way of Calvary is the shortest cut to heaven, and suffering, borne for love of God can in a very short time raise one to the heights of perfection." It is well, however, to recall that a great deal of human suffering is caused by self-will and that in some cases God may send affliction in order to save men from the tragic consequences of their continued disobedience to His laws. Sometimes, too, sufferings follow automatically from our own wrong-doing; others too, cause us affliction. Whatever be the cause of my own past or present sufferings let me be happy now that at least they are no longer spiritually "unto death." Let me humble myself before God's all-embracing will and say with

St. Paul: "I consider that the sufferings of this present time are not worth comparing with the glory that is to be revealed to us" (Rom. 8:18). Jesus, you grieved over Lazarus; please...

The two combined statements, *"Now Jesus loved Martha and her sister and Lazarus,"* and *"So when He heard that he was ill, he stayed two days longer in the place where he was"* would indeed seem strange without the explanation we have already given. Again, too, it drives home further the previous point, for Paul assures us: "We know that in everything God works for good with those who love him" (Rom. 8:28). The intention of Jesus then, was to test the love and faith of the sufferers at Bethany in order to perfect them and then wonderfully to reward them by the miracle to follow. Even the very name "Lazarus" meant "God helps" and Jesus knew perfectly that the power of God was helping Lazarus not only to endure his grave illness but also to face the coldness of death and the tomb until His Son would come to raise him up again. Jesus must have known, too, that the faith of His friend would measure up. Does mine also when confronted with trials and sufferings? "Son, let not the labors which you have undertaken for my sake crush you; neither let tribulations, from whatever source, cast you down; but in every occurrence let my promise strengthen and console you" *(Imitation of Christ)*.

And so, as John of Avila says, "One act of thanksgiving when things go wrong with us is worth a thousand thanks when things are agreeable to our inclinations." Let me look back at my own past sufferings and try to re-evoke the spirit I brought to bear upon them. If I have cause for shame, let me now humbly apologize to the One who allowed or sent them for a purpose I unhappily missed. Jesus,...

Jesus even went so far as to wait a few days before setting out for Bethany thus trying the faith of those whom He loved. At times of suffering, Jesus may indeed seem so very far away, unheeding our cries for help, spiritual or physical, and then indeed faith is severely tried, together with hope and love. That may sound rather tough as the price of friendship but when it is a question of being a true friend of Christ the cost is small. That is why St. Paul could exclaim: "We rejoice in our sufferings, knowing that suffering produces endurance, and endurance produces character, and character produces hope, and hope does not disappoint us, because God's love has been poured into our hearts through the Holy Spirit who has been given to us" (Rom. 5:3-5).

Do I sufficiently value the friendship Jesus constantly offers me, asking for an ever greater intimacy? Am I convinced of the necessity of its high standards? Where do I fall short regarding them? How can I improve? Jesus, help me to....

Lazarus: Fallen Asleep

Then he said to them, "Our friend Lazarus has fallen asleep, but I go to wake him out of sleep." The disciples said to him, "Lord, if he has fallen asleep, he will recover." Now Jesus had spoken of his death, but they thought that he meant taking rest in sleep. Then Jesus told them plainly, "Lazarus is dead; and for your sake I am glad that I was not there, so that you may believe. But let us go to him" (John 11:11-15).

Continuing on His journey, at a certain stage, Jesus knew that His friend had died, but He tells the apostles, "Our friend Lazarus has fallen asleep." They take Him literally and their reply gives us to understand that they thought a good sleep would help Lazarus turn the point of crisis back towards health. This was common medical belief, but Jesus meant death, as He soon explains. I can pause here to make analogous reflections of help to myself. At times I fall asleep spiritually, I give in to weakening venial sins or small bad habits that make me temporarily forget Jesus while my poor suffering soul sleeps, my mind lulled by a false complacency and a not entirely balanced set of values. "After all," asks St. Eucherius, "can any sin be called light, since every sin involves some contempt of God?" Venial sins often committed are like the ever-growing tangleweed that can be a gardener's "despair." If not rooted out well and truly when first noticed it grows surprisingly fast; it can gradually throttle surrounding plants and flowers; it can take over a whole garden. So it is possible also for my little favorite bad habits to do the same in my soul, smothering flowers of virtue, strangling good habits, and becoming so dominant in my life that it becomes easy enough to reach the border between venial and mortal sin and to cross it smoothly.

How often in the past have I allowed myself to be lulled into this rather dangerous sleep of venial sin? And yet this kind of thing has a tendency to keep occurring. Why? Doesn't it point to a lack of generosity with Christ, a love that is by no means yet full? Let me now pinpoint my dangerous weaknesses and see what practical and firm steps I can take to overcome them courageously with God's grace. O Jesus, so often I fall spiritually asleep,...

How fortunate I have been indeed so far only to have fallen asleep in sin and not to have died! But how easily presumptuous one can get in this matter! We sin and repent, sin and repent, sin and repent—and take it too readily for granted that it will always be so—as the apostles put it, "he will recover"! Wouldn't it be rather terrible, though, if the pattern were some day to end not on the word "repent" but "sin"! Carelessness and callousness soon become closely allied in matters of sin, and sudden death during or immediately after serious sin is a frightening thought indeed. If only we could all have the same sense of sin that so many of the saints had, some of whom almost swooned at the thought. Unfortunately in our own days the sense of sin has diminished in such a frightening way that an eminent psychologist, Dr. Karl Menninger, could write a salutary book entitled *Whatever Happened to Sin?* How delicate is my own conscience about sin? Has it become numbed in certain areas, deliberately careless or uncaring about matters which I consider lightly as "merely venial sins" and therefore negligible? If I really love God with my whole heart, that can never be my attitude. The thought of even the slightest sin should disturb me greatly. Let me pray now to Jesus about this, asking His special help. Jesus, forgiving Savior, help me never to become careless....

When Jesus corrected the apostles, telling them that Lazarus was actually dead, the shock must have been quite great after their recent outburst of hope. Again an analogous reflection for myself: if venial sin is already so bad, a kind of sleep in which there is still hope of awakening and recovery, how terrible the death caused by mortal sin! But all this I know already surely! Have I become callous even about that? about hell and eternal punishment? How good Jesus has been to me when I have fallen into the death of sin in my past life and He has come to rescue me: "Let us go to him." Let me intensify my spirit of repentance and reparation, asking Him never to allow me to die to Him again through my foolishness. Jesus,...

Lazarus: Will Rise Again

Now when Jesus came, he found that Lazarus had already been in the tomb four days. Bethany was near Jerusalem, about two miles off, and many of the Jews had come to Martha and Mary to console them concerning their brother. When Martha heard that Jesus was coming, she went and met him, while Mary sat in the house. Martha said to Jesus, "Lord, if you had been here, my brother would not have died. And even now I know that whatever you ask from God, God will give you." Jesus said to her, "Your brother will rise again." Martha said to him, "I know that he will rise again in the resurrection at the last day." Jesus said to her, "I am the resurrection and the life; he who believes in me, though he die, yet shall he live, and whoever lives and believes in me shall never die. Do you believe this?" She said to him, "Yes, Lord; I believe that you are the Christ, the Son of God, he who is coming into this world" (John 11:17-27).

Bethany was only a small village set among fruit trees on the eastern foot of the Mount of Olives along the Jericho highway, but here Jesus always found a haven of rest among His intimate friends. This time, however, He returns to a house of sorrow. Lazarus was already four days buried by the time He arrived and, according to the ancient custom, the seven days of intense mourning, with frequent visits of sympathizers, were still in effect. Practical, efficient Martha received whatever visitors came, put them at their ease and then took them along to the room where her sister Mary would receive them more formally. In this case she even goes beyond the village to greet Jesus. One notices the healthy familiarity in the tone of Martha's preliminary conversation with Jesus; it sets in fact a fine ideal for my own conversations with Him in informal prayer. Martha repeats what she and Mary had probably said very sadly at the actual time of their brother's death: "Lord, if you had been here...." Almost a reproach and yet not quite, for she hastens to hint more than broadly at what she still hopes for, a miracle: "And even now I know that whatever you ask from God, God will give you." The exegetes point to a lack of faith there, saying she should have said "the Father" instead of "God." It may well have been that Martha indeed was not yet fully aware of the divinity of Jesus, but we do not find Him reproaching her for it and later she readily acknowledges Him as the Messiah. After all, not everyone can be an expert theologian! At any rate, Jesus accepts her as she is and is extremely gentle with her, for He knows that in spite of her efficient manner and sense of practicality she has a tender heart which has been deeply saddened by the loss of her brother. Jesus takes me too as I am, and therefore I should always be able to approach Him with the greatest possible naturalness in my thoughts and prayers (Why any distinction anyway!). He wants me to express my mind frankly, candidly pointing out the things I don't understand about His ways and plans, telling Him with all simplicity the desires in my heart and the reasons I have for still hoping He will grant them. All this can be a most beautiful prayer, even if extremely blunt. But the main thing is that it should be prompted by a deeply sincere love and appreciation of Him, and the will to conform to whatever He knows is best for me, cost what it may. Such prayer has made living saints. I could be one too through the same means! O Jesus, if You.... And even now I know that whatever....

Perhaps Jesus smiled kindly, as He said: "Your brother will rise again." And then in her simplicity she begins to argue, but lovingly! Sometimes Jesus may want that of me too, preferring such candor that wants to see things clearly or at least to be convinced to the point of resignation, rather than have me say, "Yes, yes, Lord," and continue to be rebellious interiorly. It can even be healthy to argue respectfully with my Lord, for He is also my Brother, and He would rather have my frankness and sincerity (above all in prayer) than have me resentful and kicking against the goad. For one thing, I can be perfectly sure that He has only my deepest interests at heart and will see that I, like Lazarus, rise again—to a better stage of maturity, progress, perfection, love. Like Martha I must fight hard for the faith within me, assuring Jesus that no matter what comes my way, I am determined always to cling to the faith within me, even to the last straw. What Jesus wants from me, then, is more bravery about my own personal difficulties of life and spirit, more confidence in Him, more candid confiding in Him. Yes, Lord, I know....

In the end Jesus gently corrects Martha's restricted view of His mission and power. He is indeed her very great friend to whom she may still speak in terms of boldest intimacy and candor, as He wishes, but He is even more than that, infinitely more than that: He is also her God! He tells her He is the resurrection and the life, using words that are quite forceful, so that her own simple act of faith at the end comes almost as an anti-climax, as though she said: "But I know all that already, Lord! I've always believed that! But don't forget, I'm just plain Martha!" How Jesus must have loved her for the reply she gave Him, for in all its simplicity it was indeed an absolutely splendid act of faith. So wholeheartedly does she accept His statement that she does not seek to probe into the hidden meaning of the words, nor does she any longer hint at her hope of a miracle. She just leaves it all to Jesus in a beautiful act of simple abandonment. How much indeed I too can learn from this frank and practical woman who loved Jesus so much. So often He asks me: "Do you believe this?" Do my actions always answer, "Yes! Lord, I believe that You are the Christ, the Son of God"? Let me really try harder to bring this Christ much more deeply into my life. O Jesus,...

Lazarus: Jesus Wept

When she had said this, she went and called her sister Mary, saying quietly, "The Teacher is here and is calling for you." And when she heard it, she rose quickly and went to him. Now Jesus had not yet come to the village, but was still in the place where Martha had met him. When the Jews who were with her in the house, consoling her, saw Mary rise quickly and go out, they followed her, supposing that she was going to the tomb to weep there. Then Mary, when she came where Jesus was and saw him, fell at his feet, saying to him, "Lord, if you had been here, my brother would not have died." When Jesus saw her weeping, and the Jews who came with her also weeping, he was deeply moved in spirit and troubled; and he said, "Where have you laid him?" They said to him, "Lord, come and see." Jesus wept. So the Jews said, "See how he loved him!" But some of them said, "Could not he who opened the eyes of the blind man have kept this man from dying?" (John 11:28-37)

It would seem that Mary was probably engaged with visitors, for Martha called her aside and told her quietly that Jesus was there and calling for her. Her response was typical of the Mary we already know from the Gospels. How often in my own life, in the midst of preoccupations or great activity, some messenger comes to me to tell me that the Master is present and is calling for my attention. How often I fail to recognize the messenger or the message. Our Lord wants to become part of even those preoccupations, of that activity, in order to help me bring to a successful issue all the things that concern me, for they concern Him too. Jesus has a tremendously personal interest in me as an individual, as His very dear friend, and therefore He will be so happy if I bring Him intimately into all my activities and concerns, consulting Him, letting Him help me, following His wise inspirations. In this way nothing whatsoever can really go wrong. Perhaps the groundwork for such a general attitude can be best worked out precisely here in my meditation periods, so that from here it can flow out into the details of my daily life. So much depends, therefore, on how much I actually put into meditation, doesn't it? With what state of mind do I come to meditation?

Notice how quickly Mary of Bethany got up to go to meet Jesus, to express her thoughts and feelings, to listen to His words. Especially at meditation Jesus waits to speak to me. I must rise quickly, waste no time in bringing Him straight away into the very heart of my thinking, giving Him opportunity also for inspiring my thoughts, guiding them, suggesting resolutions and, above all, chatting with Him familiarly and lovingly. What about some actual practice now? O Jesus,...

Mary said the same thing to Jesus as Martha had done, for in spite of their different temperaments, they were affectionate of each other and of Jesus and could both use the same approach and manner. Mary was weeping, however, and Jesus was deeply moved by her sorrow. At times in my candor I too may feel like showing my state of distress to Jesus and I should do so, for He wants me to express myself candidly in all situations, not just when I am calm and receptive. If I feel overcome by sorrow, greatly distressed by trials, rebellious against what is demanded of me, let me tell Him so, weeping my heart out if need be. All that He expects from me, knowing me for what I am.

But if, like Mary, I place myself at His feet in a spirit of humility and let Him know that I speak candidly only out of love, then my candor pays Him a most beautiful compliment which He will richly reward. What a comfort it becomes then to drop the tangles of life and its problems into the hands of Jesus and to leave them there confidently, knowing He will not only unravel them in His own good time and way but recreate out of them a much stronger bond between us. Have I always gone thus to Jesus with all my problems, doubts and sorrows? Have I kept aloof from Him on such occasions, rebellious, sulky, immature? O Jesus,...

Mary and those who mourned with her were anxious that Jesus should come and see where Lazarus was buried, for Jesus in fact had asked where. Perhaps the words that follow are among the most human, tender, and consoling in the whole Bible: "Jesus wept." What utter compassion He showed on that occasion, not so much for the death of His dear friend Lazarus (since He was just about to raise him) but for the sorrow of his sisters. Of this we can feel sure, even though the bystanders exclaimed, "See how he loved him!" referring to Lazarus.

And that is the way of Jesus with me too. I commit sins and faults and awful blunders but on such occasions Jesus grieves more for me than for those things. His heart goes out in tender compassion for the sinner, anxious at once to bring the straying or lost sheep back to the fold, to doctor its wounds, to forgive, console, reassure. The sin hurts Him but He grieves for me; He wants me to tell Him all about it, how it happened, why, to analyze the situation with Him so that I may learn from the sad experience how to avoid it in the future. Perhaps at times in my pride I may ask how it is that Jesus did not open my blind eyes in time so as to help me avoid the death of sin, but again it is question of my freewill which He respects. Let me not therefore blame my blindness on Him, nor my deafness to His many messages and warnings. O Jesus, how often I have caused You to weep, You who love me so deeply....

Lazarus: Come Out!

Then Jesus, deeply moved again, came to the tomb; it was a cave, and a stone lay upon it. Jesus said, "Take away the stone." Martha, the sister of the dead man, said to him, "Lord, by this time there will be an odor, for he has been dead four days." Jesus said to her, "Did I not tell you that if you would believe you would see the glory of God?" So they took away the stone. And Jesus lifted up his eyes and said, "Father, I thank thee that thou hast heard me. I knew that thou hearest me always, but I have said this on account of the people standing by, that they may believe that thou didst send me." When he had said this, he cried with a loud voice, "Lazarus, come out!" The dead man came out, his hands and feet bound with bandages, and his face wrapped with a cloth. Jesus said to them, "Unbind him, and let him go." Many of the Jews therefore, who had come with Mary and had seen what he did, believed in him (John 11:38-45).

When Jesus came to the tomb and was "deeply moved again," was it really for the death of His friend? After all, Lazarus was on the very verge of renewed life and perhaps this was the real reason for Jesus' emotion, a thrill of joy going through Him for the sake, above all, of His Father's glory at the miracle, but also for His dear friend Lazarus and his beloved sisters. How deeply human and lovable Jesus was—and is! Lazarus was buried in a cave whose entrance was blocked now by a huge stone, and when Jesus bade the men standing about (His apostles? They would have been the most natural ones to ask), "Take away the stone," perhaps His mind flashed joyfully ahead to that other speedily coming event which the resurrection of Lazarus was, in a sense, about to prefigure, the glory of the first Easter. This was, then, for Jesus a deeply moving moment as He stood before the tomb of His dear friend, knowing he was lying there inside, cold in death, his body wrapped in the long bandages which we now associate so easily with Egyptian mummies, the common custom. That, of course, is an easy image of sin, mortal sin that brings the utter coldness of death to grace, wraps the soul tightly with the cloyingly sweet aromatically scented bandages of false enjoyments, to prevent its escape, burying it away from the sight of God in the hope that His hatred of sin will cause Him to forget it so that it may rot in its own hell on earth and then in eternity. Nothing, however, is hidden or lost to the eye of Jesus. Even if the sinner has driven Him out, He will always come back tactfully, stand before the tomb and weep, hope forever welling up in that loving heart of His, awaiting the slightest movement of freewill back towards Him, even but one slight glance so that He may utter the powerful words: "Take away the stone," and put His enemies to flight who have thus held His dear friend in bondage. If only I could bring myself to a full realization of how sad Jesus becomes at sin in my soul, how utterly grief-stricken when it is in mortal sin, then surely I would make much better efforts rigorously to avoid it. If only I appreciated fully the strong but tactful efforts He makes to get back into contact with me when I have sinned, perhaps I would be quicker and more sincere in my repentance and conversion. O Jesus, how I have made You suffer in the past....

Martha, the ever practical Martha, cannot help but point out realistically to Jesus that dreadful smell! Knowing what was to happen, did Jesus smile gently at her then (Why not?) as He set about reminding her of the full implications of her very recent act of faith in Him? He wants me to be realistic too, in all things, even concerning the frightful smell of death attached to sin, and to draw more deeply at the well of faith within me in order to avoid sin and to believe in Him so fully that I shall follow Him faithfully in all things. Only then can I hope to see the glory of God within my soul, within my life; only then can I too look forward to total resurrection with Christ. If Jesus sees these dispositions within me, this sincerity and true love, then He with His own hands will remove so many of the stones that now stand between us as dangerous obstacles. O Jesus, I do believe....

The immediate prelude to the actual miracle is a prayer of loving thanks to the Father and of witness to His glory and power. Thanksgiving should be inseparably interwoven in all my prayers and meditations, for I indeed have an infinite number of things to thank God for. Nor should I wait only until a grace has been granted before saying prayers of thanksgiving: a good many grateful *Gloria Patri's* beforehand could even be a good bribe! Let me keep always in mind, too, the thought of God's glory in whatever I ask for, so that this thought may moderate my anxiety about getting what I myself want, regardless. Notice how Jesus calls out with a loud voice to Lazarus to come forth, snapping the bonds of death, restoring life and warmth to that body and soul, bringing utter joy and freshness once more to the previously cold and sunken face.

By trying to keep constantly aware of God's loving presence in my daily life and affairs, endeavoring to maintain frequent direct contact with Jesus in prayer throughout the day, I need never fear that Jesus will have to shout at me to bring me back to my senses. But even if mortal sin should subtly trap me, please God I shall hear His voice and acknowledge it humbly and gratefully so that He can say: "Unbind him, and let him go." O Jesus,...

Lazarus: At Supper

Six days before the Passover, Jesus came to Bethany, where Lazarus was, whom Jesus had raised from the dead. There they made him a supper; Martha served, and Lazarus was one of those at table with him (John 12:1-2).

After restoring Lazarus happy and alive to his rejoicing sisters, Jesus went off elsewhere for a while but returns now once again. We can imagine the even greater welcome He received this time in that well-loved home at Bethany. How thrilled and honored Lazarus must have felt to be once more at table with Him. It is by no means stretching spirituality too far to say that Jesus should be the Guest at all our meals also: that is precisely why we say grace before and after meals, to remind us not merely of God's Providence but also of His loving presence.

How easy it becomes for some people to grumble about food—indeed in this line there are some whom it is practically impossible ever to satisfy completely. If only we religious especially would bear in mind all the starvation cases throughout the world and the many desperately hungry people suffering at only a short distance from our own table perhaps, then we would be grateful for our food such as it is and not indulge in the luxury of throwing away merit when things do not come up to our expectations.

As the psalmist says: "I lack nothing.... You prepare a table before me...my cup brims over. Ah, how goodness and kindness pursue me every day of my life; my home the house of God as long as I live!" (Ps. 23); "Bless the Lord, O my soul, and forget not all His benefits, who satisfies you with good as long as you live; he does not deal with us according to our sins" (Ps. 103); "I give thanks to God with all my heart, he provides food for all those who fear him" (Ps. 111); "Give thanks to God, for he is good, his love is everlasting, he provides for all living creatures. Give thanks to the God of heaven, his love is everlasting" (Ps. 136).

If it should happen, then, that things are not abundant, not to my liking, poorly prepared or served, well then, hard as it naturally is, I have just to control myself exteriorly first of all, permitting myself no complaint, and then try to get the upper hand of my inner rebellion also, determined to be mature and sensible about this unexpected and therefore more valuable mortification allowed or offered me by Christ seated beside me at table. Have I anything to reproach myself with here? Any apologies to divine Providence?

Mary took a pound of costly ointment of pure nard and anointed the feet of Jesus and wiped his feet with her hair; and the house was filled with the fragrance of the ointment (John 12:3).

So thrilled was Mary to see her dear brother sitting beside Jesus again that she felt inspired to show some public act of gratitude. She goes and gets her precious alabaster vessel of rare aromatic balsam and proceeds to anoint the feet of Jesus lavishly with it so that the whole house was permeated with the exquisite odor. Then, in deep humility she uses her hair to wipe His feet dry. How Jesus must have loved her for the purity of her intention, her simplicity, humility, lack of human respect, and above all for her deep love.

Do I try to make my own life exude the perfume of the same virtues solely in order to please and thank the kind Master who has been so extremely good to me all through my life? What is the most precious ointment I can pour over His feet this day, sure that it will please Him?

But Judas Iscariot, one of his disciples (he who was to betray him), said, "Why was not this ointment sold for three hundred denarii and given to the poor?" This he said, not that he cared for the poor but because he was a thief, and as he had the money box he used to take what was put into it. Jesus said, "Let her alone, let her keep it for the day of my burial. The poor you always have with you, but you do not always have me" (John 12:4-8).

Judas objected to Mary's action, but on insincere grounds. He had not only been given an equal vocation with the other apostles, equal powers (he probably worked miracles like the rest when sent out) and equal friendship, but was even made bursar of the little congregation's meager funds—and he stole! It is very pathetic really, for from those petty dishonesties came forth eventually the final betrayal for the sake of more money than he could possibly hope to filch from the apostolic petty-cash box. Because of his present open insincerity, Jesus feels constrained now to rebuke him quietly but almost cuttingly: "Let her alone...." Was He reminding Judas too that He knew of his coming treachery ("Let her keep it for the day of my burial")? And when He said, "The poor you always have with you," did He not include with the materially needy also all those other poor cases that need our care and attention, the ignorant and awkward, the immature, the rebellious and the Judases? "You do not always have me": when there are wrong attitudes, insincerity, dishonesty, neglect, betrayal, then indeed we drive Jesus away, perhaps give the Judas-kiss and put Him to death in our souls. Let me never forget the warning example of betrayal that could take place even in the innermost circle of Christ's followers. My smallest faults, if nourished, can lead me also to become another Judas. O Jesus,...

And so we have come to the end of the public life and apostolate of Jesus, our God and Lord, our Model and Friend, to whom we owe so much, from whom we have learnt so much. Ahead lies His Passion, in which we also have an intimate part. Let me meditate with equal seriousness on that too, for St. Augustine says: "There is nothing more useful, nothing better calculated to promote our eternal salvation, than daily to consider the sufferings Jesus Christ underwent for our sake."

Daughters of St. Paul

IN MASSACHUSETTS
50 St. Paul's Avenue, Boston, Ma. 02130
172 Tremont Street, Boston, Ma. 02111
IN NEW YORK
78 Fort Place, Staten Island, N.Y. 10301
59 East 43rd Street, New York, N.Y. 10017
625 East 187th Street, Bronx, N.Y. 10458
525 Main Street, Buffalo, N.Y. 14203
IN NEW JERSEY
Hudson Mall — Route 440 and
Communipaw Avenue, Jersey City, N.J. 07304
IN CONNECTICUT
202 Fairfield Avenue, Bridgeport, Ct. 06604
IN OHIO
2105 Ontario St. (at Prospect Ave.), Cleveland,
Oh. 44115
25 E. Eighth Street, Cincinnati, Oh. 45202
IN PENNSYLVANIA
1719 Chestnut Street, Philadelphia, Pa. 19103
IN FLORIDA
2700 Biscayne Blvd., Miami, Fl. 33137
IN LOUISIANA
4403 Veterans Memorial Blvd., Metairie, La. 70002
1800 South Acadian Thruway, P.O. Box 2028,
Baton Rouge, La. 70802
IN MISSOURI
1001 Pine Street (at North 10th), St. Louis, Mo. 63101
IN TEXAS
114 East Main Plaza, San Antonio, Tx. 78205
IN CALIFORNIA
1570 Fifth Avenue, San Diego, Ca. 92101
46 Geary Street, San Francisco, Ca. 94108
IN HAWAII
1143 Bishop Street, Honolulu, Hi. 96813
IN ALASKA
750 West 5th Avenue, Anchorage, Ak. 99501
IN CANADA
3022 Dufferin Street, Toronto 395, Ontario, Canada
IN ENGLAND
57, Kensington Church Street, London W. 8, England
IN AUSTRALIA
58 Abbotsford Rd., Homebush, N.S.W., Sydney 2140,
Australia